Ernest Hemingway

Ernest Hemingway

The Writer in Context

Edited by
James Nagel

The University of Wisconsin Press

Published 1984

The University of Wisconsin Press
114 North Murray Street
Madison, Wisconsin 53715

The University of Wisconsin Press, Ltd.
1 Gower Street
London WC1E 6HA, England

First printing

Printed in the United States of America

Library of Congress Cataloging in Publication Data

Main entry under title:
Ernest Hemingway, the writer in context.
  Includes bibliographical references and index.
  1. Hemingway, Ernest, 1899–1961—Congresses.
2. Novelists, American—20th century—Biography—
Congresses. I. Nagel, James.
PS3515.E37Z58695   1984   813'.52   83-40268
ISBN 0-299-09740-4

For
Philip Young

Contents

Introduction

In 1973, at a conference at Oregon State University entitled "Hemingway in Our Time," Philip Young remarked on the phenomenal acceleration of scholarly interest in the life and works of Ernest Hemingway, a development Young observed with both awe and reservation.[1] Since he was, even then, firmly established as the honorary Dean of Hemingway studies, largely as a result of his deeply sensitive *Ernest Hemingway*, published in 1952, Young's comments were taken as wise counsel against undue concentration on ephemera and trivia. But what was not foreseen at the time, what perhaps could not have been known, is that rather than exhausting itself in the inconsequential, Hemingway scholarship was just beginning a new phase, a more mature critical application enriched by several decades of interpretive contemplation, additions to the Hemingway canon, the publication of the letters, and the availability of the manuscripts at the John F. Kennedy Library in Boston.

The manuscripts themselves provided the focus for a conference in July of 1980 entitled "Ernest Hemingway: The Papers of a Writer," an event that resulted, as did the earlier Oregon State symposium, in the publication of a book.[2] The 1980 conference, directed by Jo August Hills, curator of the Hemingway collection, was held on Thompson's Island in Boston harbor, and it resulted in several notable developments: the official opening of the Hemingway Room, the formation of the Ernest Hemingway Society, and the presentation of a dozen papers relating to revelations and clarifications in scholarship derived from manuscript materials. At this time the members of the Hemingway Society also decided to convene formally every two years to share discoveries and good fellowship. This decision led directly to the

1982 conference, "Ernest Hemingway: The Writer in Context," a program sponsored by Northeastern University in cooperation with the Hemingway Society and the John F. Kennedy Library.

This conference had as its central focus the encouragement of interpretations of Hemingway's works in the context of an ever-developing wealth of information about his personal life, his methods of composition and revision, his highly disciplined and yet elusive creative process, his relationships with other writers, and his attitudes toward enemies and friends, colleagues and rivals. The result was a varied but immensely rich three days (May 21–23, 1982) of concentration and controversy, of intense debate and joyous celebration begun on Friday evening with dinner at the Kennedy Library and comments by Patrick Hemingway and Tom Stoppard. The following two days were spent at Henderson House in Weston, the Northeastern University conference center, for the formal presentation of rather more "academic" papers ranging from Charles Scribner, Jr.'s recalling with affection and respect the courteous relationship Hemingway maintained with his publisher to other presentations on Hemingway's relationship with William Faulkner, Malcolm Cowley, Ezra Pound, and Henry James. These essays, along with others exploring specific themes and individual works, are published here as a commemorative record of three days of informed and engaging conversations about Ernest Hemingway.

The first section of papers, "Personal Comments and Reminiscences," presents three essays remarkable not only for what they contain but also for the unique access to information of the first two writers and singular stature of the third. As Edwin McDowell observed in his column "About Books and Authors" in the *New York Times Book Review* a few weeks after the conference, surely no one is more qualified to discuss "Publishing Hemingway" than Charles Scribner, Jr., chairman of the firm his great-grandfather founded in the nineteenth century.[3] In 1952 he began a period of contact and correspondence with Hemingway that lasted until the author's death in 1961. Since then he has been directly involved with the publication of *A Moveable Feast, Islands in the Stream, The Nick Adams Stories,* and other posthumous works, including *Ernest Hemingway: Selected Letters, 1917–1961,* edited by Carlos Baker. Mr. Scribner had earlier personally edited *The Enduring Hemingway* in 1974. But despite Hemingway's long association with Charles Scribner's Sons, no one in the company had ever recounted what it was like to work with its leading author, a lapse now corrected. In this reflective essay, which draws not only from memory but from unpublished letters to and from Hemingway, Mr. Scribner recalls the amiability and magnanimous spirit of the famous author as well as his kindness and loyalty in his dealings with the firm. It is a generous and sensitive remembrance, one that will serve to modify somewhat the public portrait of Hemingway's personality.

This section concludes with the transcription of two talks that began the conference, the after-dinner remarks of Patrick Hemingway and Tom Stoppard. They are presented here in an effort to preserve the informal comments of two remarkable personalities, but it should be said that these papers were not written prior to delivery and that neither aims at formal scholarly exegesis in the traditional sense. Nevertheless, the reminiscences of Patrick Hemingway on events portrayed in *Islands in the Stream* are noteworthy for what they reveal about Hemingway's creative use of real people and events for fictional purposes.[4] The reflections of the British dramatist Tom Stoppard on his extended fascination for the life and works of Hemingway also offer something unique and valuable to students of American literature. In attempting to explain the reason for this interest, Mr. Stoppard presents a series of fascinating readings of specific passages in Hemingway, comments valuable for their insight and critical acumen as well as for the fact that they come from one of the most important living writers in English.

The second grouping of essays, "The Craft of Composition," consists of two papers based on a detailed study of Hemingway's manuscripts, a mode of scholarship that has taken on new vitality since the Hemingway papers were made available at the John F. Kennedy Library. In "The Making of *Death in the Afternoon*" Robert W. Lewis offers a study of Hemingway's most extended piece of expository prose and one of the most intriguing essays on sport in English. Through careful consideration of letters and manuscript revisions, Professor Lewis is able to explore the background and genesis of this remarkable work as a means of assessing Hemingway's craftsmanship as well as the central thesis of *Death in the Afternoon*. Paul Smith's paper also involves previously unexplored manuscripts, those of the early story "Ten Indians." Smith's essay is valuable not only for its detailed examination of the composition and thematic structure of this neglected story but also for its demonstration of what a fully informed consideration of even a relatively minor work can reveal about Hemingway's creative process and methods of composition and revision. These two essays, both examples of the "New Scholarship" of textual analysis, point the way for future work on the manuscripts of Ernest Hemingway.

The next group of papers, "Interpretations Biographical and Critical," contains three essays that use new information and insights to revise the traditional understandings of various aspects of Hemingway's life and works. As Robert W. Lewis and Paul Smith drew on manuscript information to form new readings of important works, Max Westbrook's "Grace under Pressure: Hemingway and the Summer of 1920" uses new materials to form a reinterpretation of a central episode in Hemingway's youth, his eviction from the family cottage in 1920. Based on unpublished manuscripts and letters acquired from Hemingway's younger brother, Leicester, Professor Westbrook's essay explores the role of Hemingway's parents during this crucial period, casting their decision to forbid the family home to their eldest son in a much more sympathetic light than has hitherto been the case. In addition, he goes on to suggest that all of Hemingway's fiction is, to some extent, about his family.

Millicent Bell's paper relates to one of the most notable books in American literature in the last decade, Michael S. Reynolds's *Hemingway's First War*, a study that demonstrates with solid evidence that *A Farewell to Arms* was not the simple autobiographical novel that it was widely assumed to be.[5] Reynolds's book is thoroughly researched, fully documented, carefully reasoned, and a fine example of responsible scholarship. Despite the nearly definitive nature of Reynolds's book, Professor Bell, in "*A Farewell to Arms:* Pseudoautobiography and Personal Metaphor," is able to mount an original, deeply sensitive biographical reading of the novel. Basing her remarks on a study of the manuscript revisions, and drawing on her considerable experience as a biographer, she presents an interpretation of the novel as a correlative of Hemingway's state of mind at the time of composition. Following in the wake of Linda W. Wagner's "'Proud and Friendly and Gently': Women in Hemingway's Early Fiction," presented at the 1980 conference,[6] Carol H. Smith employs a similar women's studies approach to Hemingway's fiction. Arguing that Hemingway's novels reveal a fundamentally romantic vision, she explores the relationships between the lovers in *The Sun Also Rises, A Farewell to Arms, For Whom the Bell Tolls,* and *A Moveable Feast.* Professor Smith's insistence on the centrality of romantic love between complex personalities in these works represents an important modification of traditional feminist assumptions about Hemingway.

The final section of the book explores Hemingway's relationships with other writers. In "Exchange between Rivals: Faulkner's Influence on *The Old Man and the Sea,*" Peter L. Hays gives attention to Hemingway's relationship with William Faulkner, to the respect the two writers felt for each other, the similarities in their lives, the ways in which their works are intertwined, and the numerous thematic parallels in their fiction. Moving beyond these general considerations, Professor Hays explores the influence of Faulkner's most important story, "The Bear," on Hemingway's last novel, *The Old Man and the Sea.* Adeline R. Tintner, a leading authority on Henry James, documents the importance of James in Hemingway's work in "Ernest and Henry: Hemingway's Lover's Quarrel with James." Drawing from both letters and texts, she clearly demonstrates that Hemingway had read James's major novels, that he is mentioned throughout Hemingway's fiction, and that James was an important source and influence for Hemingway over the course of his career.

Jacqueline Tavernier-Courbin's paper, "Ernest Hemingway and Ezra Pound," makes use of new manuscripts, specifically three previously unknown letters from Pound to Hemingway that are here printed in their entirety. In essence her focus is to examine the complexity of the enduring friendship between the two writers, a relationship unique in Hemingway's life and directly counter to his well-known tendency to break with even his closest literary associates. Professor Tavernier-Courbin's discussion of this matter offers a new exploration of this friendship, drawing heavily on the newly discovered letters.[7]

"Invention from Knowledge: The Hemingway-Cowley Correspondence," by James D. Brasch, also draws on unpublished letters, the seventy-one exchanged between Hemingway and Malcolm Cowley, only two of which were included in *Selected Letters*.[8] In his exploration of this wide-ranging correspondence, which touches on literature and mutual friendships as well as an array of topics of the day, Professor Brasch focuses on creative "invention" as a dominant theme with a secondary interest in Hemingway's attitude toward literary biography. The candor of Hemingway's opinions on these topics makes these letters a valuable new resource for scholars of American literature.

As a group these essays offer both new information and original insights to the mounting body of scholarly thought about Ernest Hemingway, about his works, about their biographical context. Thus this volume takes its place among other significant studies published in recent months, a list that indicates something of the current vitality of Hemingway studies: *Ernest Hemingway: Selected Letters, 1917–1961*, edited by Carlos Baker; *Ernest Hemingway: A Study in Narrative Technique*, by P. G. Rama Rao;[9] *Hemingway: The Critical Heritage*, edited by Jeffrey Meyers;[10] *Hemingway's Reading, 1910–1940: An Inventory*, by Michael S. Reynolds;[11] *Hemingway's Library: A Composite Record*, by James D. Brasch and Joseph Sigman;[12] *The Tragic Art of Ernest Hemingway*, by Wirt Williams;[13] *Hemingway's Nick Adams*, by Joseph M. Flora;[14] *Hemingway and the Movies*, by Frank M. Laurence;[15] and the two-volume *Catalog of the Ernest Hemingway Collection at the John F. Kennedy Library*, edited by Jo August Hills.[16] To this selected list of books must be added scores of articles in scholarly journals each year along with the ongoing publication of the *Hemingway Review* and the *Hemingway Newsletter*. Current work in progress by Hemingway scholars also promises to make additional significant contributions, notably a biography of Hemingway's early life by Michael Reynolds, the full text of the Hemingway–Malcolm Cowley correspondence by James D. Brasch, and a manuscript study of the short stories by Paul Smith, to mention only three examples. And the plans now developing for a European conference on Hemingway to be held in 1984 promise to make the professional study of Ernest Hemingway truly a moveable feast.

Part of the joy and exhilaration of directing a literary conference is that such an event is by its very nature a collaborative effort requiring the efforts of scores of colleagues in order to succeed. I was fortunate, in directing "Ernest Hemingway: The Writer in Context," to be able to work with people who are not only professional in every sense but generous and considerate as well. Chief among these were Jo August Hills, Curator of the Hemingway Collection, and Paul Smith, President of the Hemingway Society, both of whom contributed directly to the planning and implementation of the conference, and to them I acknowledge my deep gratitude and admiration. Another debt is owed to Robert P. Weeks, Bruce R. Stark, Mark Spilka, Allen Josephs, Kinley Roby, Linda Wagner, Richard Astro, Daniel Golden, George Monteiro, Earl Harbert, Gerald Griffin, and Arthur Waldhorn, all of whom served as respondents to papers at the conference, and to Michael Reynolds and Robert E. Gajdusek, both of whom read papers at the conference that could not be published here. Carolyn Brown, my administrative assistant at the Center for the Humanities, Northeastern University, gave tirelessly of her time and energy to the arrangements for the conference, as have Gregory Zuch and Mary Gallenski to the publication of this book. As chairman of the Department of English, Kinley Roby made invaluable contributions to various aspects of the conference, especially in arranging for the appearance of Tom Stoppard. My colleague in the Center for the Humanities, Daniel Golden, was unflagging in his willingness to handle matters large and small, and I owe a great deal to his generosity of spirit. Dean Richard Astro, who had directed the 1973 conference at Oregon State, brought wisdom and kindness to his administrative counsel and "Ernest Hemingway: The Writer in Context" would not have been possible without his enlightened support. My oldest and most profound debt in Hemingway studies, however, is to Philip Young, whose *Ernest Hemingway* inspired me to enroll in the graduate program in English at Pennsylvania State University. As a student in his seminar on Hemingway, I came to know something of Professor Young's wealth of knowledge, the depth of his personal and scholarly sensitivity, and the respect and affection he has always inspired in students and colleagues alike, emotions that now find their expression in the dedication of this volume.

Northeastern University   JAMES NAGEL
August 1, 1982

Notes

1 See Philip Young, " Posthumous Hemingway, and Nicholas Adams," *Hemingway in Our Time,* ed. Richard Astro and Jackson J. Benson (Corvallis: Oregon State University Press, 1974), pp. 13–23.
2 *Ernest Hemingway: The Papers of a Writer,* ed. Bernard Oldsey (New York: Garland, 1981).
3 Edwin McDowell, "About Books and Authors," *New York Times Book Review,* July 11, 1982, p. 30.
4 See also Patrick Hemingway, "My Papa, Papa," *Playboy,* December 1968.
5 Michael S. Reynolds, *Hemingway's First War: The Making of "A Farewell to Arms"* (Princeton: Princeton University Press, 1976).
6 Linda W. Wagner, "'Proud and Friendly and Gently': Women in Hemingway's Early Fiction," in *Papers of a Writer,* pp. 63–71.
7 See also Jacqueline Tavernier-Courbin, "The Mystery of the Ritz Hotel Papers," in *Papers of a Writer,* pp. 117–31.
8 See *Ernest Hemingway: Selected Letters, 1917–1961,* ed. Carlos Baker (New York: Charles Scribner's Sons, 1981), pp. 603–5, 680–81.
9 P. G. Rama Rao, *Ernest Hemingway: A Study in Narrative Technique* (New Delhi: S. Chand, 1980).
10 *Hemingway: The Critical Heritage,* ed. Jeffrey Meyers (Boston: Routledge & Kegan Paul, 1982).
11 Michael S. Reynolds, *Hemingway's Reading, 1910–1940: An Inventory* (Princeton: Princeton University Press, 1981).

12 James D. Brasch and Joseph Sigman, *Hemingway's Library: A Composite Record* (New York: Garland, 1981).
13 Wirt Williams, *The Tragic Art of Ernest Hemingway* (Baton Rouge: Louisiana State University Press 1981).
14 Joseph M. Flora, *Hemingway's Nick Adams* (Baton Rouge: Louisiana State University Press, 1982).
15 Frank M. Laurence, *Hemingway and the Movies* (Jackson: University Press of Mississippi, 1981).
16 *Catalog of the Ernest Hemingway Collection at the John F. Kennedy Library*, ed. Jo August Hills, 2 vols. (Boston: G. K. Hall, 1982).

PART ONE

PERSONAL COMMENTS AND REMINISCENCES

1. Charles Scribner, Jr.

Publishing Hemingway

ERNEST HEMINGWAY'S long association with Scribners began in February of 1926 when he met with Maxwell Perkins—his future editor—in the publishing company's offices on Fifth Avenue in New York. The two men hit it off from the start, and their meeting resulted in Hemingway's accepting a contract covering both his novella *The Torrents of Spring* and the unfinished novel which would later be published under the title *The Sun Also Rises.*

For Perkins, that contract was the successful upshot of a long campaign to bring the talented young author onto the Scribner list. A year earlier, upon the strenuous urging of F. Scott Fitzgerald, he had written to Hemingway in Europe asking him to submit his work to Scribners. But by the time the Perkins letter reached Hemingway in Paris, the writer had already signed up with the firm of Boni and Liveright in New York. It was they who published Hemingway's first book-length collection of short stories under the title *In Our Time.* Hemingway's contract with Boni and Liveright gave them an option on his second book; and, if they accepted that, on his third. As it turned out they published neither, for they turned down *The Torrents of Spring* when he submitted it to them. It was too clearly a parody of their famous author Sherwood Anderson. This dilemma was a particularly painful one for Horace Liveright, who must have felt that he had earned the right to be Hemingway's publisher. He undoubtedly regarded *The Torrents of Spring* as a contract breaker. But what could he do? To Perkins, on the other hand, it was an unexpected reversal of fortune. He was now able to sign up a very promising writer at the cost of publishing a relatively minor work.

As it turned out, he was also taking on an extremely loyal author, for Hemingway remained on the Scribner list from the time of that first meeting until his death thirty-five years later. Today, when so many writers change publishers with as little hesitation as they might change accountants, Hemingway's loyalty seems all the more extraordinary.

In the course of Hemingway's association with Scribners, three generations of the family served as heads of the company. The succession began with my grandfather, who was a son of the founder. He was followed by my father in 1931. I became president a generation later when my father died in 1952. That is a great many Scribners for one author to put up with, but Hemingway took them as they came. There was also a succession of editors who worked with Hemingway during the same period. The relationship with Scribners covered virtually his entire career as a writer.

Many of the details of that relationship are likely to be familiar to students of Hemingway's life and work. Given all that has been published on the subject, it could hardly be otherwise. But I think that this may be the first time that a member of the Scribner family has testified on the experience of publishing Hemingway. For me it is an opportunity to pay a debt of gratitude to him that is long overdue. To the extent that my recollections may provide a sense of the kindness and loyalty of that extraordinary man, I shall have achieved my purpose.

During the first twenty years or so of Hemingway's association with Scribners, Max Perkins was his principal contact within the company. It was to Perkins that he wrote continually about his writing projects, his books, his travels, his ideas, his family, and his finances. Perkins was wholly devoted to Hemingway as a writer, and he was an entirely trustworthy friend and confidant as well. At the same time, he was able to maintain, when necessary, a degree of professional detachment which Hemingway preferred to a more effusive or solicitous approach. They were both shy men, although their shyness took on very different forms. In a situation where Hemingway might become boisterous and exuberant, Perkins would be more likely to withdraw into his shell. Of course, Perkins was also hard of hearing, an affliction that is not entirely a handicap for a book editor.

During the thirties and forties, Hemingway came to know other members of the Scribners' editorial team. After the death of Perkins, Wallace Meyer became his primary contact at Scribners. Hemingway got along well with his editors. On the other hand, he tended to distrust individuals belonging to the sales or business side of the company. He imagined that they did not understand or appreciate his writings and that they were not wholly committed to promoting his books. He later admitted to me that most writers seem to have eye defects when it comes to seeing advertisements for their books.

During the same period, a close friendship developed between Hemingway and my father. Their relationship was strengthened by occasional luncheons and dinner parties in New York and Paris and by visits of the Scribners to Cuba. It was during a visit to Finca Vigia that my father first had the chance to read in manuscript large portions of *For Whom the Bell Tolls*. Later, and with perhaps a trace of irony in his deference, Hemingway asked my father, who was an authority on horses, to check the passages about horses in the first part of the novel. It was important to him that all such details be technically accurate. Later, he wrote my father a letter filled with details of horse anatomy so minute that it would have astonished a veterinarian. He insisted on being the expert. From then on, he continually teased my father for being so wrapped up in horses. On one occasion, he tried to horrify him by filling a letter with the gory details of how he had run over a horse in an automobile. How much of that incident was horse feathers I shall leave to others to determine. It made a good story.

Although my father did not pretend to be a man of letters, Hemingway valued his naturally sound literary perceptions and his consistently active common sense. My father slipped easily into the role of Hemingway's closest friend at Scribners when Perkins died in 1947. Indeed, the two men entered almost at once into a voluminous correspondence in which they kidded and insulted each other in a way that bespoke a deep mutual affection. For example, my father would write, "I have just received your cheerful but rather vulgar letter," or would say to his famous author, "I had hoped you might have matured more over the years."

Because so many accounts of Hemingway's behavior depict him as churlish or capricious, I should like to comment on his amiability toward Max Perkins and my father. Before he admitted any individuals into the inner circle, he needed to trust them to an almost abnormal degree, and they had to adhere unswervingly to his image of them. Once he trusted someone, he would maintain a friendly informality and a boyish camaraderie. Throughout his life he enjoyed having his own gang. On the other hand, when Ernest dealt with individuals he was not sure of or who had an ax to grind, he was prone to truculence in self-protection. He did not like or dislike anyone half-heartedly.

I joined Scribners in 1946, the year in which it was celebrating its one-hundredth anniversary. Max Perkins was still editor-in-chief, and I was fortunate to have almost a year in which to see him in action before his death. Although I had been put in charge of publicity and advertising, my father and Max had a way of giving me other publishing chores which I was usually unqualified to handle. At that time, Scribners espoused the sink-or-swim method of instruction, and it was not always easy to stay afloat.

One of my special assignments was to supervise the production of an illustrated edition of *A Farewell to Arms*. It is still not entirely clear to me why that item was placed on my plate, but there were difficulties about the book, the greatest and simplest being that Hemingway did not care for the illustrations. Perhaps it was believed that this hot potato might do less damage to an innocent newcomer like myself, who was not responsible for its conception.

In any case, I set about proofreading the text and performing other routine tasks, little realizing that I was dealing with a potential *casus belli*. When the time came, I wrote to our famous author and gave him a deadline for the introduction he had agreed to write for the book. In due course he sent it to me. The introduction was written in an "o tempora, o mores" vein, denouncing war. As for the illustrations, he scarcely mentioned them at all except to describe the disappointment they caused him. He made no bones about that and spoke wistfully about how he would have preferred an artist like Winslow Homer or Renoir.[1]

In his accompanying letter to me, he brushed aside any worries I might have about publishing his introduction. I was not to worry about the feelings of the illustrator; illustrators have no right to have feelings. They rank little higher than photographers. I was also not to worry that what he wrote was politically subversive. His folks had been around a long time. They had all done their duty in time of war. Hemingway was not a pen name. He could take an oath that he had never been a member of the Communist party. He was not being snotty, he added, just kidding rough the way he did with my old man.[2] It was vintage Hemingway, a grand mixture of wild hyperbole and sweeping decrees. It was fun to read, and I also felt the implicit friendliness in Hemingway's writing to me in the same confiding vein that he used with my father.

I did not hear from Hemingway again until four years later when he wrote to me about my father's sudden death. I had been called back into the Navy and was stationed in Washington at the time. In his letter, Hemingway wanted me to know how bad he felt about having been away and out of touch when my father died. Since he had to die, at least he had gotten it over with. As for himself, I did not have to write him letters or have him on my mind.[3] I cannot imagine a kinder expression of condolence or a more delicate assurance of loyalty. And in the lovely phrase of Dickens, he was better than his word. For the next nine years of his life, he was as easy to work with as any author I have ever known.

When I was released from active duty in the Navy a month or so after my father's death, I returned to Scribners as president of the company. At that time, Wallace Meyer was still Hemingway's editor. All of us were looking forward to publishing *The Old Man and the Sea*. We had no doubt of its virtuosity. I was proceeding with a plan to bring all of Hemingway's books back onto the Scribner list. At that time, most of the titles had been licensed for hardcover reprints by the Modern Library or Grosset and Dunlap, or for paperback reprints by Bantam Books and others.

I had a master plan, and I wrote the following letter outlining it to Hemingway:

> I have asked for a complete report on the publishing status of all your titles because I wanted to be certain that nothing was sold on a reprint basis that might be sold by us on terms conceivably more remunerative to you.
>
> Frankly I am attempting to provide for the effects that the publication of the *The Old Man and the Sea* could have on all your earlier works. We anticipate a wonderful reception to this as would have to follow the publication of something so magnificent. Furthermore I feel that your books are, in any case, the foundation stones of our publishing reputation in this country. I believe that we must be continually self-critical with respect to operations on them.[4]

I do not think that my crystal ball is better than that of any other publisher, but I must admit that it was never so helpful as on that occasion. Hemingway endorsed my plan wholeheartedly even though it called for the cancellation of Modern Library editions for which he had strong sentimental feelings. Over the next few years we reissued all his books, at first in hardcover editions and then in paperback for school and college use. We redesigned the bindings, reset some of the older books, and redid almost all the jackets.

Hemingway was delighted by this deliberate revival of his books. He differed from our suggestions only once or twice, and then only in the most tactful manner. For example, he took exception to a drawing of a bullfighter for the jacket of *Death in the Afternoon* and wrote me as follows: "It has this against it, Charlie: the bullfighter is a Mexican, an Indian, and he looks almost as though he were suffering from leprosy in the peculiar swellings of his face."[5] We scrapped that jacket and afterward managed to have an Ektachrome photograph taken of the original of the Roberto Domingo poster at the Finca.

Another time one of our book designers thought it would be a good idea to print the interchapter pieces of *In Our Time* in red ink instead of in italics. Hemingway was very doubtful about that idea: "My mother at one time had some theory about transcribing music into color but I never subscribed to it."[6]

The correspondence between Hemingway and myself now belongs to Princeton and is on deposit in the Firestone Library. Before I reread those letters, I had the recollection that Hemingway had been very kind to me as a young man from the time of our first contacts over thirty years before. But that impression did not prepare me for the extraordinary warmth and kindness of his letters. I am much older now, and I have a better idea of the value of kindness.

The Hemingway that I dealt with professionally was as magnanimous as any man I have ever met. Most of my letters were written in a practical vein and involved business matters. I did not feel it would be appropriate for me to seek or to expect a personal friendship on the sort of easy footing that had existed between Hemingway and Perkins, or between Hemingway and my father. I think he understood that and was all the more gracious.

I suppose the greatest strain on our relation was in connection with an introduction I asked him to write for a paperback collection of his stories. This was in 1959, and Hemingway worked very conscientiously in Spain during May and June. When the introduction came in I was shocked by its contents and tone.[7] It would have been a disservice to his reputation to publish it for student use, and I saw no alternative but to bite the bullet and tell him so. I now suspect that there may have been an earth tremor in that part of Spain when my letter arrived. On July 3, I received a cable ordering me to stop work on the anthology and on all similar projects. It had been a big mistake that he would not make again.[8] Although the cable ended with "kind regards" I was terribly worried that I had ruined my relationship with Hemingway.

But a month later he wrote to me again, saying he was sorry about the school project's not coming off. He had really taken it seriously and tried to write something valid that would counteract the type of teaching children were getting on the short story. He was happy to have me try the alternative plan I had

outlined and went along with me completely as stated in my letter. With the confidence he had in me as a publisher, he said, that
was a very easy decision to make.[9]

During the years I corresponded with Hemingway, we did not
meet more than four or five times and all those meetings were in
New York City. The first was in June of 1953 when my wife,
Joan, and I went to the dock to see Ernest and Mary off on the
Flandre on the first leg of their trip to France, Spain, and Africa.

We waited for them rather self-consciously in their stateroom,
together with some other visitors whom we knew only by name.
Ominous bells and horns were sounding continually, and it
seemed likely that the ship would set sail with us on board and not
the Hemingways. We had almost given up hope when the cabin
door burst open and in plunged Hemingway with a large retinue
of men and women bringing up the rear. There was now no room
to turn around and the air turned blue with four-letter words and
Hemingwayisms.

Ernest's lawyer, Alfred Rice, had brought some important
documents that needed to be signed, but Hemingway pretended
to brush them off as trivialities. He was full of the wisecrack he
had heard that Hollywood was going to change the name of the
Spencer Tracy film from *The Old Man and the Sea* to *The Old
Jew and the Lake*. Spencer Tracy was also there, but that did not
faze Ernest. It seemed certain now that the last call for visitors to
go ashore had long since been given. But with all the loud talking
no one could have heard it.

In the midst of this confusion Hemingway even took time out to
inscribe for me a copy of the limited edition of his novella with
the slogan *Il faut d'abord durer*. Although we finally did disem-
bark in New York and not in Le Havre, our visit made me realize
the appropriateness of Hemingway's slogan. It was no small feat
to survive the strain of many such performances. Nothing in his
letters had given me an inkling of the frenzied pace of those parts
of his life.

I did not see Hemingway again until six years later, in
November of 1959. He had just returned to New York on the
Liberté and was staying for a few days in a borrowed apartment
on the East Side. His friend George Plimpton called me at my of-

fice and said, "Your famous author is in town and wants to see you." I hurried over. It was the briefest of meetings, mostly filled with small talk. I do not drink, and when I declined a highball, Ernest suggested a vermouth and soda water. It was virtually not drinking, he said, but it does light a little fire. I found that an appealing phrase, but I stuck to ginger ale.

One of the difficulties of visiting Hemingway in New York was that he was almost always accompanied by a number of well-wishers. Each of them appeared to believe that he or she had the special responsibility of protecting Ernest from all the others. As a result, a fair degree of tension was often generated. It was also difficult to conduct a serious conversation. Because our friendship had been created almost entirely through letters, it was probably natural that I at least had a stronger sense of meeting a stranger than I might have had upon meeting him for the first time with no preconceptions.

A few days later he had A. E. Hotchner deliver to me the first drafts of his "Paris Sketches," which we were to publish posthumously under the title *A Moveable Feast*. Naturally we read them at once and were so impressed by them that I called Ernest immediately to tell him so. I was astonished to hear him respond like a diffident young writer having a book accepted for the first time. He was obviously delighted. "I thought you'd be willing to lend me money on the strength of this," he said. Of course we would gladly have lent him all the money he wished, but he never borrowed any. That was just his way of expressing his pleasure.

The next meeting with him was in the apartment on Sixty-second Street that the Hemingways had rented. Our editor Harry Brague and I went over to see him and find out when he wished to publish the "Paris Sketches." Hemingway's health was very poor, and he agonized over the question in a way that made me feel sad. I wished that we had not raised the matter. He worried about the effect on his eyes from having to work on a book. How would he be able to shoot a gun if he couldn't see? Would he have to learn to shoot by ear?

At the end of that visit, he gave me a battered valise to take back to the office and hold for him under lock and key. He mentioned that it contained his will. "Don't lose it," he told me. I knew he had had some terrible experiences with lost suitcases in the past, so I reassured him as well as I could. Very early the next morning, Ernest appeared at Scribners. He wanted to look something up among the papers he had given me. I opened the locked filing cabinet outside my office and watched him rummaging around in the valise. Of course I realized that he had come only to make sure I had not lost it.

Then he came into my office full of cheer. To put me at my ease, he placed himself behind my desk. I stood there quite at a loss, not knowing where to sit and feeling wholly disoriented. Finally I offered him some coffee, and one of the secretaries brought in a cup with a great sense of mission.

"Would you like some cream?" I asked.

"Just enough to change the color," he replied with characteristic precision.

Although we exchanged letters afterward, that was the last time I ever saw Ernest. But I never forgot his instructions for pouring in the cream. Only Hemingway would have thought out a specific formula for performing such a routine task. In a way, it was an example of his whole approach to life.

Notes

1 Ernest Hemingway, *A Farewell to Arms*, illus. Daniel Rasmusson (New York: Charles Scribner's Sons, 1948), pp. vii–xi.
2 Ernest Hemingway, Letter to Charles Scribner, Jr., 29 June 1948. This and all other correspondence cited are in the Scribner Archives, Firestone Library, Princeton University, Princeton, New Jersey.
3 Ernest Hemingway, Letter to Charles Scribner, Jr., 25 February 1952.
4 Charles Scribner, Jr., Letter to Ernest Hemingway, 25 July 1952.
5 Ernest Hemingway, Letter to Charles Scribner, Jr., 1 February 1953.
6 Ernest Hemingway, Letter to Charles Scribner, Jr., 9 October 1954.
7 The introduction has since been published independently. See "The Art of the Short Story," *The Paris Review*, 79 (Spring 1981), 85–102.
8 Ernest Hemingway, Cable to Charles Scribner, Jr., 3 July 1959.
9 Ernest Hemingway, Letter to Charles Scribner, Jr., 27 August 1959.

2. Patrick Hemingway

Islands in the Stream:
A Son Remembers

I T is indeed an honor to be here. Apropos of the comment that my birth was one of the most famous births in literary history, I remember that once my father forgot my birthday after my mother and father were divorced. She promptly sent him a letter reminding him that he had forgotten. I remember his reply was that he remembered this more as an occasion for my mother than for me.

In the company of this very distinguished group of Hemingway scholars, I hesitate to voice any opinions on professional matters and would like to confine myself to the contrast between what I remember about the incidents on which his posthumous novel *Islands in the Stream* is based and the way they came out in the finished book. It was Napoleon, I think, who said all history is lies agreed upon. This probably applies to literary history as well. My version of what happened is not necessarily "the truth," but it does seem to me to differ in many instances from the way events are presented in that book. The novel, at least the initial part, is very much the story of an artist remembering his children, sort of coming to terms with them, under difficult circumstances. There are three boys, and all who have read Penguin editions of Hemingway know that Ernest Hemingway had three sons. I never could understand why that was one of the facts that was quoted in the brief biographical sketch. I've never seen his biography presented that way in any other edition of his work.

There are two incidents in the novel that interest me particularly: one is the catching of a fish, and the other is the shark attack. I think they are good stories, I enjoyed them when I read the book, but neither one of those incidents ever happened as far as I know. The middle son never had that fantastic experience of catching that fish, and no one was ever attacked by a shark. And I think this is a very good example of the pitfalls of taking things as being autobiographical unless there is some real evidence for it. There is a story called "A Day's Wait" that contains an incident about a little boy, my older brother Jack, who did not realize the difference between the Celsius and Fahrenheit scales. (And I think this story should be taught in school, now that we're converting to the metric system. It might create some good will for the conversion.) And that is truly autobiographical; it is absolutely reported as it happened, to the best of my knowledge. But in the case of *Islands in the Stream,* there seems to be a great deal of discrepancy between what actually happened and what is portrayed. The incident of the catching of the fish is really based on a true accomplishment of my younger brother, Greg. He was the runner-up in the pigeon-shooting championship of Cuba. This is a sport like trap or skeet shooting, except that in Cuba, it being a cruel Latin country, they shot real pigeons. They were released from a cage and then you had a very short time to shoot, and sometimes if they didn't fly you shot them on the ground. Greg's performance was an extraordinary accomplishment for a nine-year-old boy in the sense that there were outstanding shotgun experts from all over the world and he came in second and almost won. He just missed out at the very end. He was featured in the Cuban newspapers as *El Pequeno Rey de la Escopeta,* "The Little King of the Shotgun." And I think this is really the germinal idea for the catching of the fish, which, when you think about it, was probably easier for a small boy to do because catching one of those big fish, especially the way they were caught in those days, would have been physically impossible. So that episode owes a little bit to *Moby-Dick* and a little bit to Greg's involvement in that contest.

The shark incident is even more interesting. I think that episode is based on a story of Tolstoi's. I never heard about it before until just before I left Tanzania. There was quite a strong

Russian influence in the country in the sense that they were making available literary material and books on political science in the bookstores and one of them was a collection of Tolstoi's stories for children. One story concerned a visit of the Russian fleet to Djibouti on a goodwill visit: there was a connection between the Ethiopian church, the Coptic church, and the Russian Orthodox. So there were relationships between Russia and Ethiopia during Czarist times. The story Tolstoi tells is of a gunner in one of the naval ships anchored in Djibouti harbour whose son goes for a swim. He's attacked by a shark and the gunner loads his gun and blows the shark out of the water. I don't know that my father was even aware of that story, but it does considerably antedate *Islands in the Stream,* and there is a very close parallel.

Islands in the Stream is based to a large extent on a wonderfully exciting trip that my younger brother and I had the opportunity to make with our father, probably the last really great, good time we all had together. And it was just before he went away to World War II, which he was very reluctant to do. I think that was what really broke up his marriage with my stepmother Martha Gellhorn in that she felt he had been sitting around doing nothing in Cuba too long. He really wasn't very enthusiastic about going to the war in any capacity, but he finally did bow to major force and went. But before that he was doing a very valuable job in Cuba working with American intelligence. It was principally naval intelligence at the American embassy where they were intercepting agents sent by the Germans through Spain and Spanish boats who were being put ashore in Cuba and who then were supposed to help in providing information in the very successful war the German submarines were waging against American shipping, especially the oil that had to be shipped from Texas around the Florida peninsula to the East Coast. A reward for what was essentially almost a desk job (you know, he knew all about these people and their connections to the Spanish Civil War and so forth) was this Q-boat idea of using his fishing boat to capture or blow up German submarines. This was the operation we had a chance to participate in, and it was great fun. We all practiced: we had an unlimited supply of hand grenades and machine guns; we even had a marine radio operator who was attached to the boat; and we had all sorts of radios on the boat. I remember that there was an explanation for the Federal Communications Commission, the nickname for which on the *Pilar* was "Frankly Can't Communicate" because of all the difficulties of getting through. The radio man was a character: we had lots of time on our hands and there were books to read and one of them was *War and Peace.* I remember he read *War and Peace* from cover to cover and then he said, "You know, that was a very interesting book." He added, "Mr. Tolstoi really understands how to draw characters and really make them seem alive." And he said, "And it was especially interesting to me because I knew most of those people in Shanghai."

And then we also had a great friend of my father's along named Winston Guest. I remember my father one time when they were back on leave from these arduous operations and Mr. Guest was getting ready to go in town where he had a girlfriend. He came in all spruced up (because they'd been out for several days and this was the first time he'd had a bath and shaved) and my father looked at him and said, "Ah," he says, "Winston smells good, like a millionaire should." He got a lot of kidding. His nickname was "Wolfy." We also had another book called Renan's *Life of Christ* and Wolfy was reading it and he supposedly said to my father, "Papa, how does it come out?" But it was a nice atmosphere you know, everybody came in for a certain amount of kidding, and it was a great time. And I think that Winston Guest was the model for the early part of *Islands in the Stream* where the two men are on the island and it's a winter scene and they're burning the wood and so forth, that friendship between the two, and how low the artist feels when his friend goes away.

The great sport at that time was shooting flying fish with a .22 rifle. The water was sometimes incredibly smooth. In the summertime you get days when the trade winds die and it's very, very calm and you could just go through the water with a nice sort of wake and prow wave, and these flying fish would get up and just go along the surface of the water out at right angles. So you had twenty cartridges in the magazine and you could just shoot and you could see where the bullet landed and then you could correct it. I think you got about one flying fish for thirty or forty shots, but it was spectacular when you got one.

Another thing was the number of flamingos. Where we were operating on the great submarine hunt was the Cuban coast way down on the eastern end. There is a series of offshore islands and then an inward passage between those offshore islands and the coast. This is all described when they are hunting the submarine by people who have come off the submarine later on. Names that stick in my mind are Cayo Romano, Muevitas, Cayo Cruz; Cayo Cruz was manned by the Cuban army. They had a station there with a radio that sort of looked out for submarines. In that area there were lots of flamingos, and that was our principal source of meat. We lived on flamingos. And I was very surprised to find that the meat, as well as the feathers, was pink. You had this thing that looked like a cooked turkey and when you sliced it, it was bright pink. And Winston Guest had a pig that he kept on the island on Cayo Cruz. One day the pig decided he'd waited for death long enough and he swam out to the mainland and was never seen again. So we never did eat the pig; it was a big disappointment. A lot of turtles were done in because they were the ideal food. I hate to think this now when they're sort of an endangered species, but I think there were more of them in 1941. We would drop a hand grenade on the turtles (and of course this was justified by the need to learn how long it was between when you pulled out the pin and when it went off). The most vicious weapon we had was a .577 double elephant rifle, which everyone was convinced would shoot through the conning tower of a U-boat. I really don't think it could but we had brave men willing to try this if God called on them to do their duty. The really secret weapon was a fire extinguisher, a big red extinguisher which was filled with dynamite. And the idea was that the submarine would come up and moor alongside to rob us of our fresh fruit; we always carried a large supply of prominently displayed fruit; sort of like Carmen Miranda, you know. We had one ex-jai alai player who had to give up jai alai because he'd killed so many people with his strength. He was extremely strong and not very accurate with the ball. And so finally all the jai alai players in Havana had banded together and said this man can't be allowed to play anymore, and so that's when he joined our team. Anyway, if a submarine tied up next to the boat he was supposed to lob the canister of dynamite into the hatch. But I do want to stress that this operation, which was paid for by the American taxpayers, was completely justified because the serious work, the anti-espionage work, which was sort of John Le Carré-ish, was the real stuff. It was a very pitiful thing. I remember when one spy was caught and shot who was fond of canaries. I believe there was a big thing in the papers about how he was the "canary spy," sort of like the birdman of Alcatraz, an earlier version.

Isn't there a part in *Islands in the Stream* where he has this beautiful woman (sort of based on Marlene Dietrich) that comes to visit the protagonist of the story in Havana? I am sure that this was based on Marlene Dietrich. I remember later on when I was going to college, my father offered to send Marlene Dietrich up to visit me at my university accommodation. He was sure that that would enable me to launch a brilliant career with my classmates.

There is one other incident which is true and that is the one about how Thomas Hudson's sons are wiped out in an automobile accident with their mother. That is based on truth to a certain extent because just after the war when you could first get automobiles again, my mother got one of the very first of those black Fords that came out that looked just like the ones that they made before the war. We were going to take a trip all around Wyoming and Montana trout fishing, but we had to get there from Florida. My mother had never known how to drive when my mother and father were married, and he still remembered her when she didn't know how to drive. He was very apprehensive about her driving us out West. So he got my older brother, who had just gotten out of prison camp and really needed a rest and a nice summer, to come and drive us around, which he did and nobody was ever killed. But that must have made an impression on my father because he created that incident where they're all wiped out in an automobile accident.

But I do want to stress that sense of fun that appears in the earlier sections of *Islands in the Stream* when they go down to the bar and joke about the new boy and how he's a big drinker and all this sort of thing. I think this was very characteristic of that not-very-dangerous summer. It is my last real happy memory of childhood, and I'm very pleased that I was able to participate in it.

3. Tom Stoppard

Reflections on
Ernest Hemingway

WHEN Joseph Conrad died, Ernest Hemingway, by way of an obituary notice, wrote a little piece in the *Transatlantic Review*, in October 1924, and what he said was that if it could be shown that by grinding T. S. Eliot down to a fine powder, and by sprinkling the powder upon Conrad's grave, then Conrad would immediately jump out of his grave and commence to write, then he, Hemingway, would leave for London immediately with a sausage grinder in his luggage.

As a diversion we might consider nominating, from among contemporary novelists, candidates for the honor of being sprinkled upon Ernest Hemingway's grave. However, we should bear in mind that this year's list would undoubtedly differ from last year's; this decade's even more from last decade's. The further back we look, the stranger are the ups and downs of reputation. Is anybody safe? Edmund Wilson, who is very good on Hemingway, was saying in 1930 that it had become fashionable to disparage him. There were many people who would have cheerfully sacrificed Hemingway upon the graves of writers now long forgotten. (The vagaries of reputation can be seen across space as well as time: in France after the war, and for a long time after it, one of the most highly regarded English novelists was Charles Morgan, who was comparatively little read in his own country; while the French, I am told, were thoroughly bewildered by the way that the English gave Albert Camus a stature hardly lower than Sartre's.)

Hemingway, of course, had fame as well as reputation, a public fame which no doubt worked against his literary reputation even as it made his one of the best-known names on earth. In the smaller world of Hemingway's first American and British readers, the name H. L. Mencken must have seemed just as ineradicable in the twenties. In *The Sun Also Rises* there is a two-and-a-half-page passage, when Jake and Bill are fishing, in which affectionate fun is made of Mencken.[1] These two and a half pages must be baffling, and perhaps expendable, to many of Hemingway's present readers. If it crossed the author's mind that he was taking a bet on Mencken's posterity, it probably seemed a fairly safe bet at the time. I happen to like Mencken, but I don't know more than two or three people in England who have read him, let alone heard of him. I am dwelling on this ebb and flow between reputation and oblivion only to make a much-delayed point, that an entire conference on Ernest Hemingway, not to mention the existence of periodicals entirely devoted to him, in both senses, accords very well with my own opinion of his work and his lasting importance.

And this, apparently, requires some explanation. Several people, familiar with my own work, find it surprising that I should be a Hemingway enthusiast. Perhaps it is. I am not capable of confronting this puzzle head-on, but I ought to confess that this will be a somewhat egocentric talk; I will try to explain something of why I got bitten by Hemingway, and stayed bitten.

One gets badly bitten by writers perhaps only two or three times, between the ages of eight and eighteen. The first passion I remember was for a boys' stories writer, Arthur Ransome, when I was eight. I remember writing Runyon short stories in my teens, and a couple of Truman Capote short stories after I had left school, but I don't think I got thoroughly bitten again until I was about twenty, late for Hemingway. The general influence of Hemingway's style is, of course, much more pervasive than that of, say, Runyon or Capote. It seems much simpler to copy. Writers have been trying to copy it for over half a century now. The other day I looked up a short story published about twenty years ago, and the first of my texts is a quotation from this story:

It had taken me days to get that far, from Avignon where they dropped me off. I had a bad time to Narbonne and in

the square after the cafe closed it rained through the plane
trees and the lights of heavy lorries swung big and yellow
through the rain going south, but in the morning it was hot
walking over the bridge and down the long straight between
the vineyards, the country steaming brightly, and the first
lift was a good one to Barcelona and after that it was pleasant coming down the coast all the way round through Ma-
gala with the mountains arid-brown in the corner of your
eye.[2]

This is part of a story published in a book called *Introduction 2:
Stories by New Writers*. I was the new writer in question. So
what was the great attraction?

One of the frequent explanations of Hemingway's "fatal attraction" has to do with the glamorous interest of locale and subject
matter, the bullfighting, the fishing, the big-game hunting, and
the general flexing of muscles a long way from the coteries of New
York and London. Hemingway remembered a very funny conversation with James Joyce when Joyce expressed anxiety about the
"suburban" nature of his subject matter. Nora apparently
thought this was a good point. Jim ought to do a spot of that lion
hunting, she said. Joyce objected that he couldn't see well enough
to spot the lion, and Nora argued that Ernest could shoot the lion
and then lead Jim up to it so that Jim could touch it and smell it
and that is all Jim would need. In his marvelous Joyce biography,
Richard Ellman is sensitive to the same point: He refers to Bloom
as somebody whom it would be difficult to imagine catching a
marlin. But of course it doesn't matter one bit. The exotic locale
and action, and the cast of hunters, gangsters, boxers, soldiers
and so on, do not explain the attraction and the influence of the
prose.

A second favorite explanation is that Hemingway, with his
atomic prose, invented a new way of describing physical experience and the physical world. There is something in this. Hemingway certainly helped to bury the notion, if anyone seriously
held it, that the more you pile on the adjectives the closer you get
to describing the thing. Refinement works against the object. The
more adjectives one uses, the more precision is demanded of the
description, and the more the grail recedes. One might think that

this "law of refinement" would work in the opposite direction, so that the more spare the prose, the more successful the transfer of an idea or an image from writer to reader; but what it really demonstrates is that prose in itself does not describe at all. The words rely very much on what the reader brings to them. In fact, it is the associative power of words rather than their "meaning" that makes prose work on its ultimate level. It seems to me that Hemingway's achievement, whether calculated or instinctive, was to get his effects by making the reader do the work. This was not a completely original perception (as readers of *Huckleberry Finn* must know), but if one tries to write like Hemingway without understanding that, as I did twenty years ago, one ends up with merely a Hemingway gloss.

Somewhere in these comments is the root of what seems to me to be the inadequate truism that Hemingway is a writer who leaves things out. My own memory of reading Hemingway for the first time is of being often intrigued by what he had put in and left in. In "The Killers" when Nick tries to warn the boxer about the two gangsters who have come to the restaurant to kill him, he goes to what has been referred to as "Mrs. Hirsch's rooming house," and when he leaves the place he says to the woman who runs the house, "Well, good-night, Mrs. Hirsch," and she says "I'm not Mrs. Hirsch. . . . She owns the place. I just look after it for her. I'm Mrs. Bell." "Well, good-night, Mrs. Bell," says Nick.[3] Mrs. Bell says good night. What on earth is this about? It has nothing to do with the story. But it makes the boxer real and the gangsters real.

The mysterious nature of the power of prose to describe is best exemplified for me in the story "Big Two-Hearted River," because I have fished for trout since I was a small child and the power of the "association" as opposed to the "meaning" makes me one of the ideal readers of that story. At the same time, the way the words were put together disturbed me when I first read this story. Here is a paragraph from it:

As the shadow of the kingfisher moved up the stream, a big trout shot upstream in a long angle, only his shadow marking the angle, then lost his shadow as he came through the surface of the water, caught the sun, then, as he went back into the stream under the surface, his shadow seemed to float under the bridge where he tightened facing up into the current.[4]

This bothered me because as a journalist I was going to a lot of trouble trying to avoid repeating words, and the repetition of "stream," "upstream," "shadow," and "angle" at first jarred like music that had gone wrong. It was an education to me that there were different kinds of music and that prose could make a more interesting kind of noise in the brain.

But finding description persuasive and effective cannot depend upon its being checked against experience, and this brings me to the first three Hemingway quotations which made a great impact on me, and which in a slightly arbitrary way are going to be invoked now in order to help me to feel my way, by trying to explain the impact, toward some understanding of why I got bitten. The first quotation is from one of the vignettes in *In Our Time*, the death of the bullfighter Maera:

> There was a great shouting going on in the grandstand
> overhead. Maera felt everything getting larger and larger
> and then smaller and smaller. Then it got larger and larger
> and larger and then smaller and smaller. Then everything
> commenced to run faster and faster as when they speed up a
> cinematograph film. Then he was dead.[5]

I am in no hurry to check this one out but I thought then and I still think that this is extraordinarily brilliant and just as persuasive as the description of fishing for trout.

The second quotation is from *The Sun Also Rises*:

> The bull who killed Vicente Girones was named Bocanegra,
> was Number 118 of the bull-breeding establishment of San-
> chez Taberno, and was killed by Pedro Romero as the third
> bull of that same afternoon. His ear was cut by popular ac-
> clamation and given to Pedro Romero, who, in turn, gave it
> to Brett, who wrapped it in a handkerchief belonging to

myself, and left both ear and handkerchief, along with a
number of Muratti cigarette-stubs, shoved far back in the
drawer of the bed-table that stood beside her bed in the
Hotel Montoya, in Pamplona.[6]

When I read this paragraph I always think of some heavy object
bumping slowly down a flight of stairs, and in some way picking
up not moss as it rolls but bits and pieces, objects, debris, fragments of the whole novel, so that the life of the peasant who
didn't run fast enough in front of the bulls and the alien Americans with their romanticism and their self-indulgences are locked
up together and rubbed raw against each other in a paragraph
which is mostly concerned with small concrete objects, and
which, just to make the whole thing breathtaking, leaps forward
in time way beyond the point we have reached in the story. I
think that this is one of the greatest paragraphs ever written in
English, and if there is a better one perhaps it is this:

William Campbell had been in a pursuit race with a burlesque show ever since Pittsburgh. In a pursuit race, in bicycle racing, riders start at equal intervals to ride after one
another. They ride very fast because the race is usually
limited to a short distance and if they slow their riding
another rider who maintains his pace will make up the space
that separated them equally at the start. As soon as a rider is
caught and passed he is out of the race and must get down
from his bicycle and leave the track. If none of the riders are
caught the winner of the race is the one who has gained the
most distance. In most pursuit races, if there are only two
riders, one of the riders is caught inside of six miles. The
burlesque show caught William Campbell at Kansas City.[7]

This is a piece of writing that mimics its subject matter. It is a
paragraph in which a burlesque show is in a pursuit race with a
metaphor. And what happens is that the burlesque show catches
up on the metaphor and the metaphor has to get down from its bicycle and leave the page.

Looking back at my three quotations, and at my attempt to draw something from them, one wonders how subjective is my response, whether in fact I have succeeded in demonstrating anything at all, and one perhaps wonders, too, about the possibility of truly objective criticism and assessment. I have brought with me the first *Fitzgerald/Hemingway Annual* (1969), which contains an essay entitled "A Comparative Statistical Analysis of the Prose Styles of F. Scott Fitzgerald and Ernest Hemingway."[8] The first sentence is as follows: "Statistics supply the one asset in which literary criticism, especially stylistic criticism, has always been woefully deficient-proof." This is followed by a mild rebuke. "Numerical proof may never take the place of critical sensitivity, but by presenting good solid evidence, one can base his description and evaluation of an author's style on a good solid foundation that cannot be ignored by future critics who wish to escape into the never-never land of impressionistic criticism." At the end of the essay there are some statistical tables which reveal, among other things, that comparing "Big Two-Hearted River" with Fitzgerald's "The Rich Boy" the average sentence contains twelve and twenty-four words, respectively; that the percentage of simple sentences is 73 percent and 24 percent, respectively; that the percentage of substantives that are monosyllables is 72 percent and 61 percent; and so on, with other comparisons between each writer's early and late work.

The author of this essay is obviously a bright woman, easily bright enough to see that there is something dubious about the whole exercise. "It may be argued," she writes, "that differing subject matter and point of view affects reliability of comparative statistics." She mentions other limitations, and ends up more or less nullifying her first two sentences by conceding that "figures alone cannot describe or explain all of what makes a writer's style uniquely his own," and she adds that statistical analysis is useless to explain what makes a particular Fitzgerald sentence uniquely Fitzgeraldian.

This whole thing reminded me of a fight I once saw on television which was supposed to have been between Muhammad Ali and Rocky Marciano (who unfortunately had been dead for some years). The fight had been worked out by a computer. Muhammad Ali actually fought this person who looked like Mr. Marciano. I forgot who won, because, of course, the result was not memorable since it was not enlightening. In trying to explain the attraction of art, the more indisputable a fact the less useful it becomes. Consider the proposition that Virginia Woolf was the tallest woman writer in Bloomsbury in 1922. No doubt the computers are at work on her now and will prove a lot of things, including, if desired, her chances against Marciano.

I feel almost obliged to say something about *The Fifth Column,* which is "the Hemingway play." Here we have the Hemingway hero who affords ammunition to Hemingway critics. There is a beautiful woman who is mad about him, and he is very brave and much cleverer and wittier than the poor duffer who loved the woman before. Talking about *The Fifth Column,* someone once made what I thought was the perceptive comment that in this play Hemingway was going through the necessary process of separating from his involvement in a political cause and his closeness to events and getting rid of a crude version of a subject which he could approach later with an artist's detachment. However, Hemingway thought well enough of the play to have it published with his collected short stories, and this is the Hemingway who draws the fire of critics like Dwight Macdonald. When a professor of English remarked that Hemingway was essentially a philosophical writer, Macdonald thought it to be "a rather foolish statement, even for a professor of English." The feeling that loyalty and bravery were the cardinal virtues and that physical action was the basis of the good life didn't add up to a philosophy, said Macdonald. This does not seem to be an adequate comment. It is not simply physical action but the action of the physical world upon the individual that is important in Hemingway's work and in his thought, too, for it is also inadequate to think of "philosophy" as something quite so detached from the ordinary business of living and surviving. It is also surely part of Hemingway's philosophy, to use a word he probably wouldn't use, that an appreciation and celebration of the physical, sensual experience of life, which unites writers, philosophers, fisherman, bullfighters, and critics, are not to be despised by the ivory tower philosopher. The force of a code of behavior, of a personal morality, is that philosophy does not account for it but is accountable to it.

Notes

1 Ernest Hemingway, *The Sun Also Rises* (New York: Scribner's, 1926), pp. 122–25.
2 See *Introduction, 2: Stories by New Writers* (London: Faber and Faber, 1964).
3 Ernest Hemingway, "The Killers," *The Short Stories of Ernest Hemingway* (New York: Scribner's, 1938), p. 288.
4 Ernest Hemingway, "Big Two-Hearted River," *Short Stories*, p. 210.
5 Ernest Hemingway, "Chapter XIV," *Short Stories*, p. 207.
6 Hemingway, *The Sun Also Rises*, p. 199.
7 Ernest Hemingway, "A Pursuit Race," *Short Stories*, p. 350.
8 Elizabeth Wells, "A Comparative Statistical Analysis of the Prose Styles of F. Scott Fitzgerald and Ernest Hemingway," *Fitzgerald/Hemingway Annual* (1969), pp. 47–67.

PART TWO

THE CRAFT OF
COMPOSITION

4. Robert W. Lewis

The Making of
Death in the Afternoon

D*EATH IN THE AFTERNOON* is one of the most critically neglected of Ernest Hemingway's works in spite of Carlos Baker's remark that "for the student of Hemingway who is seriously interested in the developmental aspects of his fiction, a reading of *Death in the Afternoon* is indispensable."[1] Since its publication in 1932 it has received "mixed reviews" because of what seems to many readers a curious self-indulgence in a barbarous sport, particularly unattractive in the Depression years of America. Hemingway's attempt to explain the bullfight was hardly likely to find a wide and appreciative audience in America, any more than one might expect Egyptians to appreciate a book on baseball, no matter how good, particularly if the ballgame ended in the lynching of the losing pitcher. Hemingway's interest in bullfighting, of course, extended and enlarged the usual fanaticism. To him, and to many others, bullfighting should transcend mere spectacle or athletic engagement because, unlike all mere sports, it culminated in death and could, if properly conducted and executed, give one profound, even tragic, feelings.

Apparently Hemingway had conceived of such a book at least as early as April 15, 1925, when in his first letter to Maxwell Perkins he wrote about his hope to write "a large book full of wonderful pictures" on bullfighting.[2] Almost every summer Hemingway returned to Spain not only to see the fights but also to gather information and photographs relating to the history and

31

current state of bullfighting. When he was not in Spain, he read books and journals on the subject, and he began to write. It was a labor of love. At one point he wrote Max Perkins (1931) that his writing on the book "had never gone better than lately," and he described the nearly finished manuscript as "one hell of a fine book."[3] In 1930 he left Piggott, Arkansas, with the still-untitled manuscript, hoping to work on it in Montana and finish it by Christmas, but the plan was upset in the automobile accident on November 1, 1930, in which his companion John Dos Passos escaped injury but in which Hemingway suffered a badly broken right arm: "It was nearly done when I got hurt," he wrote Max Perkins on December 28, 1930.[4] It was not until another summer in Spain and six weeks of revision that "the manuscript was completed on January 13, 1932," and "at last published on the 26th of September,"[5] after much further revision, some of it suggested by Dos Passos.[6] For example, Hemingway wrote, "Am working hard. Cut a ton of crap a day out of the proofs and spread it around the alligator pear trees which are growing to be enormous."[7] By May 30, 1932, he could write Dos Passos that he had gone over the proofs seven times, and on June 28 he wrote Perkins that he was continuing to work on the proofs and the list of dates of bullfights, which, along with the other additions at the end of the book, he did not want labeled as appendices: the book was not the complete, exhaustive work he had conceived, and thus to call the additions "appendices" would be pretentious. In this letter he also asked Perkins to "bawl out" the "punk that slugged those galleys" each with "Hemingway's Death," as if to put a repeated curse on the superstitious author. Here too he revealed his intentions for the book and anticipated the mixed reception it would receive, in part because he had introduced material not on bullfighting: "If you try to sell it as a great classic goddamned book on bullfighting rather than some fucking miscellany you may be able to sell a few. Let the critics claim it has something additional."[8] This outburst was occasioned by a publicity release based on a version of the book that Hemingway had subsequently pruned of "philosophizing." The publicist Benjamin Hauser, like some later reviewers of the revised book, had ballyhooed what Hemingway thought was extraneous. With perhaps both modesty and apprehension, he wrote in the "Bibliographical Note" that the book "is not intended to be either historical or exhaustive. It is intended as an introduction to the modern Spanish bullfight and attempts to explain that spectacle both emotionally and practically."[9]

That others would read it for his comments on writing, art, love, and death bothered him; yet he did not excise all of the material impertinent to bullfighting, and six weeks later, on August 9, he wrote to Paul Romaine about his interest in bullfighting:

> For ten years or so—bull fighting was my recreation and amusement as whatever might be yours if you have any need to think about anything but your work. I wrote a book to clear them up and keep them—also something about Spain which I know a little about from having lived there.
>
> I have to live sometime and I have quite a few things to write and my mind is not occupied with lost generations and bulls.[10]

Clearly he felt defensive, and clearly he knew that the book went beyond a mere introduction to the bullfight. After the book was published with its lovely last chapter, a prose poem in which bullfighting is considerably reduced in importance, he wrote Arnold Gingrich of *Esquire:*

> Am glad you liked the last chapter. . . . It is what the book is about but nobody seems to notice that. They think it is just a catalogue of things that were omitted. . . .
>
> Am getting pretty well rid of a good lot of unsought popularity with this last book and hope to get out a pretty good one next time.[11]

He seemed unsurprised by negative reviews[12] but surprised and pleased by news of its good sales.[13]

A large part of the background to those feelings emerges from a study of the first manuscript of *Death in the Afternoon.* From the evidence cited in Carlos Baker's *Ernest Hemingway: A Life Story,* from Hemingway's letters, and also from suggestions in the manuscript itself, it is clear that the manuscript (303 pp.) purchased by the University of Texas (Austin) Library in 1958 is indeed, as it was advertised in the Parke-Bernet sales catalogue, "A Major Portion of the Original Manuscript of *Death in the Afternoon.*"[14] Further, it was that portion of the first draft Hemingway had completed before the auto accident of November 1, 1930, that resulted in the severely broken right arm and a long delay before he could resume work on it. Carlos Baker reports that at that time two chapters remained to be written, and the first draft (the Texas manuscript) ends after the very beginning of chapter 19.[15]

The Hemingways subsequently returned to their Key West home and to Piggott, Arkansas, and Kansas City, where a year after the accident Gregory Hemingway was born (still almost a year before the completion of the book). At some point, perhaps after the Texas manuscript was typed (all but nineteen typed pages are in Hemingway's hand), Hemingway gave this draft to Dr. Don Carlos Guffey, the Kansas City obstetrician who delivered both Patrick and Gregory Hemingway by caesarian sections. When in 1959 Hemingway learned that Dr. Guffey had sold "the stuff I gave him or signed for him," he bitterly wrote his editor, Harry Brague, that the "best investment I can make is writing manuscripts."[16] Indeed, by far the most valuable of the forty-one letters, editions, and manuscripts comprising the Guffey collection that was auctioned on October 14, 1958, was the draft of *Death in the Afternoon.*[17] It sold for $13,000; the other forty items, Hemingway's gifts, brought Guffey $6,784 more.

The Parke-Bernet Galleries sale catalogue further notes that

THIS IS APPARENTLY THE MOST EXTENDED AND IMPORTANT HEMINGWAY MANUSCRIPT EVER OFFERED FOR PUBLIC SALE IN THIS COUNTRY. ONLY 18 LEAVES ARE IN TYPESCRIPT AND THESE ARE HEAVILY CORRECTED AND EXTENDED IN THE AUTHOR'S HAND. THE REMAINING 285 LEAVES ARE ENTIRELY IN THE AUTHOR'S HAND, IN PEN AND IN PENCIL.

Although numbered up to 277, with a few leaves marked

"bis," the total is added to by a number of inserts, including
a group at the end.

The text, heavily corrected throughout, ends at p. 277,
with the first line of the last paragraph appearing on p. 235
of the first edition, at the third page of Chapter Nineteen (of
twenty). The captions for the pictures, the glossary and other
appendices are not present, nor does it contain the famous
insert, "A Natural History of the Dead."

THE EXTENSIVE CORRECTION AND GENERAL CONDITION OF THE
MANUSCRIPT IDENTIFY IT AS APPARENTLY AN EARLY WORKING
VERSION AND OF GREAT INTEREST TO THE SCHOLARSHIP OF
CREATIVE LITERATURE.[18]

Apart from miscounting the typed pages (there are nineteen
instead of eighteen), and apart from the fact that page 58 is now
missing, and apart from the inclusion of a laundry list in Spanish
and not in Hemingway's hand, the description is accurate and is
verified by the widow of the Hemingway bibliographer and book-
seller Capt. Louis Henry Cohn, who bought the manuscript on
behalf of the University of Texas.[19]

Some pages of the manuscript have been reproduced, notably
both the first page (largely typescript) and page 39 (entirely
holograph) in *Hemingway at Auction*, and these provide a fair
indication of the general appearance of the manuscript.[20] The size
of the handwriting varies greatly, but the number of lines on both
the regular and the legal-size sheets averages nineteen. The holograph lines invariably slant sharply downward to the right, as
illustrated on page 39.[21] Some sheets are so much mended and so
poorly written that only Hemingway himself could have edited
them accurately. At that time, Pauline Hemingway often typed
for him, and she or another typist could have consulted Hemingway for clarification. However that process of transformation
from one version to another was carried out, it was done with
accuracy for the most part, but mistakes were made.

Hemingway's holograph emendations are extensive, and different modes of mending (as in black ink, blue ink, and pencil) suggest at least several layers or stages of revision of the original

manuscript. Many minor changes, the addition of elaborations concerning bullfighting, and the insertion of "A Natural History of the Dead" in chapter 12 were made in subsequent typescripts and in the galleys (versions and fragments of which are in the John F. Kennedy Library). While Hemingway finally deleted some material he and others felt libelous or extraneous, in the first stage the changes were mainly additions. In length they vary from numerous word or phrase changes to extensive changes ranging from several paragraphs to several pages. In quality they include a few changes that seem not as good as the original version and many that are in the nature of improvements. These latter can be classified as developmental (clarifications, elaborations, and details); stylistic (tonal and rhythmic change and frequent additions of irony and humor); thematic (echoing or developing motifs used elsewhere, notably themes of sexuality-homosexuality, death-suicide, courage-cowardice, art, and luck or fate).

What emerges from a detailed physical examination of the manuscript is an awareness of the care with which he worked and revised. And even after these numerous changes, he planned others, sometimes, as in chapter 14, writing a marginal note to himself for yet another revision eventually to be made, presumably after he dug out more material on Ortega, the "newest white hope" for the revival of the classic bullfight. Five manuscript pages (9 bis, 63, 123, 189, and 238) have writing and/or arithmetic calculations on their reverse sides, the second possibly a calculation of his word count or progress; the third a false start ("The author—Worse Madame") in answer to the old lady's question "Are they affected with mumps?" (p. 94); and the fifth including a multiplication of 23 and 11 for which Hemingway's answer was 268.

On the reverse of Texas manuscript page 189 is (curiously) the beginning of "Mr. and Mrs. Elliot," the short story from *In Our Time* first published in the *Little Review* in its autumn-winter 1924–25 issue. The fragment is the first sentence and part of the second: "Mr. and Mrs. Elliot tried very hard to have a baby. They tried as often as Mrs. Elliot. . . ."[22] If it were not for the evidence of Hemingway's correspondence, one would be tempted to conclude that the writing of chapter 13 coincided with the 1925 publication. The original version of the short story was finished by May of 1924, but Hemingway rewrote and retitled the story by May of 1925, at the same time (April 25, 1925) he was first telling Max Perkins about his wanting to write a bullfighting book. If these compositions coincided, this part of the first draft would then have been written much before the presumed period of intensive writing on it in 1930–31. Another explanation would be that the virtually unused sheet was saved along with other sheets for later use, and Hemingway reportedly was a great paper saver.

It is interesting to see how much was subsequently added to the first draft but, except for chapter 20, most of the new material was elaboration and clarification of bullfighting technicalities. The lengths of the additions range from all of chapter 20 and most of chapter 19 (simply because that is where the draft breaks off, probably at the time of his November 1, 1930, car accident), to about sixteen of the thirty-eight pages of chapters 17 and 18, and shorter parts of the endings of other chapters, including some extensions of the author-old-lady dialogues. Other dialogue additions are in chapters 7 and 8; all of the dialogue in chapter 8 was added, indicating that Hemingway, liking the comic relief of the dialogue provided as a way to end chapters, seems to have backed up and added old-lady dialogue to conclude chapters 7 and 8. Three and a half pages were also added to the ending of chapter 2, but in general the more extensive additions were to the second half of the book, and generally they were soldered on the ends of the draft chapters. The earlier chapters are the least revised in this manner, although they have many short additions of a word or two that seem to have been meant to clarify or elaborate. Many of the additions were of matter that Hemingway probably gathered in Spain by direct witness and research in the summer of 1931. Some he presents as eyewitness account, some as historical information.

There are only a few phrases and clauses and four complete sentences added to chapter 1, which, with chapter 4, is the least extended of the chapters. Describing them illustrates the nature of this kind of revision. The first is the addition of the phrase "for myself" in this sentence: "So I went to Spain to see bullfights and to try to write about them for myself" (p. 3). The point made is that initially such writing was to be self-educative, unlike the book published nine years later that was written to instruct others. The next addition is the footnote on page 6, which is unusual for its candor, indicating that the author had (as many authors do but usually conceal if not deny) asked others to read his manuscript. Evan Shipman had updated the author's knowledge of the steeplechaser horse Uncas; and Hemingway reports that this late information is not received sentimentally or in any emotional way. The art of accuracy, not feeling, is important. The next addition in chapter 1 illustrates what might be judged an extraneous or at least questionable addition. After comparing a dead horse to a dead pelican, Hemingway also observes that "a live pelican is an interesting, amusing, and sympathetic bird"; then he added, "though if you handle him he will give you lice" (pp. 6–7). The point may be seen to illustrate further, and somewhat humorously, the need to be tough-minded.

In another comparison, of bullfighting and wine drinking, he again goes off on a tangent, self-indulgent but surely delightful and forgivable. That paragraph (pp. 10–11) is followed by the one beginning "This seems to have gotten away from bullfighting" and thus there is no question of the author's awareness of the digression. Yet the next paragraph insists on the comparison before finally returning to the topic of bullfighting. To the phrase "any other purely sensory thing" he added "which may be purchased" as an important qualification that also continues a motif of *value* in the book. At the end of the paragraph he added the last two sentences, the only complete sentences apart from the footnote that he added in this chapter. The sentences not only round off the paragraph but also tie in with the recurrent motifs of death and luck. The second of the two sentences states: "But there seems to be much luck in all these things and no man can avoid death by honest effort nor say what use any part of his body will bear until he tries it" (p. 11).

The other brief additions in this chapter are four subordinate

clauses, all of which seem appropriate clarifications or elaborations. One recognizes how both the matador and other artists are
separated from their audiences because most of the latter are
mere spectators and not aficionados. The others indicate the sub-
jectiveness of experience and the writer's difficulty in expressing
elusive facts. Since one of the values of this book is Hemingway's
often increasing comments on matters extraneous, strictly speaking, to *tauromaquia*, the additions are not unimportant.

Obviously, as he learned more about his primary subject, as he
updated his information about the current bullfighting in Spain,
and as he perceived the need for stylistic improvements, he revised, generally adding rather than subtracting. But many of the
additions go beyond the requirements of a well-written guide-
book to touch upon his attitudes and thoughts on topics like love,
art (and particularly writing), and suicide (and other forms of
death). That he added them and at the same time knew they were
increments a handbook could do without indicates his awareness
that the book was layered and really about *him*, his love affair
with Spain and all that passed between them, even though the
necessary focus would be on bullfighting.[23]

One other point bears mentioning in considering such changes.
In the heat of composition, much is written without conscious reflection; that is not to say "written automatically" but written
without the purposiveness one more likely has *after* a draft has
been written and when one can see what he has given birth to.
The process of adding and subtracting is done on a different
esthetic plane, and intentionality must ordinarily be more opera-
tive in the cooler process of revision than in the initial hard
groping toward ends of chapters and sentences. One small phrase,
"the dark of," was added to a sentence describing how to escape
the summer heat of Valencia but, unlike many of the other clarifications, it gives insight into Hemingway's integrity; one is being
taught to see with his painterly eyes. To escape the heat of Valencia one may swim at night in the sea, "lie in the barely cool
water and watch the lights and *the dark of* the boats and the rows
of eating shacks and swimming cabins" (p. 44). The point, for
getting "the real thing" (p. 2), for recreating that which will re-

create the emotion, is simply that at night one would not directly see silhouettes. It is a fine point of esthetic honesty as well as optics.

Hemingway revised in order to make *Death in the Afternoon* better, more complete, and more than a mere handbook. His book about art could be artful, so he wrote chapter 20 and added some parts not at all about bullfighting. The dialogues between him and the "old lady" were added and later expanded, even on the final typescript, like this addition about a restaurant in Madrid: "It is full of politicians who are becoming statesmen while one watches them" (p. 93). It is an enlarging and pleasing irony; it suggests Hemingway's skeptical *Weltanschauung*, and thus it belongs.

Another holograph addition to the final typescript was the sardonic conclusion "Like hell it would" (p. 99) of the paragraph comparing the transcience of the art of bullfighting to the permanency of painting: it *would* matter if Cézanne's canvases were lost. The history of art *would* suffer. Recorded art, such as paintings in museums and books in libraries, have a great advantage over the impermanent and unrecorded (except indirectly by photographs and verbal accounts) art of bullfighting. Thus, in T. S. Eliot's terms, there is a difference in this art in the balance of tradition and the individual talent. Additions of this sort were made on topics like suicide (p. 102) and revolution (p. 111), the latter a subject that he had covered in his journalism and now was beginning to think he would write another definitive "handbook" on, à la *Death in the Afternoon*.

A good example of a humorous addition about bullfighting, at the end of chapter 13, on the effect of the possible deaths of various matadors in the ring, illustrates Hemingway killing two birds with one stone: he furthers the handbook aspect and, for readers like the old lady, provides amusing ironic commentary on human nature. Killing the cowardly "El Gallo would be bad taste and prove the bullfight was wrong, not morally but aesthetically. . . . Do you know the sin it would be to ruffle the arrangement of the feathers on a hawk's neck if they could never be replaced as they were? Well, that would be the sin it would be to kill El Gallo" (p. 159).

In the conscious act of revision he could also direct his humor at himself, if not, perhaps, as bitingly as at others. In the dialogue at the end of chapter 15, after the bloody story of "A Natural History of the Dead" and countless buckets of bull and matador blood have been described, the old lady says, "I am a little tired of the dead."

> Ah, Madame, the dead are tired too.
> *Old lady:* No tireder than I am of hearing of them and I can speak my wishes (p. 179).

One final example of these additions illustrates two features: the writing was spread over such a long period of time that Hemingway acquired more information between first draft and publication and added and updated; and beyond the addition of more information about bullfighting there were also other important revisions. In 1927 Virginia Woolf had given Hemingway's *Men Without Women* a "mixed review" in the *New York Herald Tribune,* acknowledging his considerable skill but finding him "too self-consciously virile" and his talent contracting "instead of expanding."[24] At the time, Hemingway said the "review was damned irritating."[25] Thus, in explaining why cows behave differently from bulls in nonfatal amateur fights, Hemingway wrote that they were experienced, having been used but not killed in training. If trained, the bulls too would grow more intelligent through such experience. To the sentence denying "any innate superior intelligence in the female," he added, "as Virginia Woolf might suppose" (p. 106). The annals of cow fighting as well as bullfighting needed updating.

There is, however, material in the Texas manuscript that was never printed. In some cases, this material consists of cancellations by Hemingway in this draft. In other cases, the cancellations came later. This category also includes some accidental changes that were overlooked at various points between this draft and publication of the first edition. From the point of view of the author's intention, all but the last group of accidentals are relatively unimportant, but from the point of view of the creative process, they are of the greatest interest. They reveal first impressions and reactions, later modified by reason or taste, that give insights into Hemingway's mind. They must be approached with great caution, but taken in their totality in typed notes of over twenty pages, they can give a feel for the process of composition impossible to obtain in any other way. If they were omitted to avoid repetition, or to eliminate corny jokes, unsupported or unsupportable judgments, irrelevant or tangential material, to make the tone consistent, or to improve the draft in other stylistic ways, they are nonetheless the master's voice. And some of the uncovered tidbits, if not diamonds, may nevertheless delight the Hemingway aficionado.

Until someone undertakes a complete collation of the text and its earlier versions, there is little need to do more than illustrate the extensive changes. Thirteen manuscript pages comprise chapter 1, which runs to fifteen printed pages and which was lightly revised between this manuscript and the published version. Only four sentences and six phrases or clauses are in the published version that are not in the Texas manuscript. But, as one might expect in the groping and searching for tone and subject at the beginning of a book, chapter 1 is the most often mended in its first draft. Three of the thirteen pages were added as inserts or continuations, and there are over fifty instances in which material is either cancelled, added, or substituted. These changes range from a word or two up to a paragraph of fifteen lines and a section of thirty-three lines.

The book was not entitled until long after the first draft was written, but at some point Hemingway penciled the title at the beginning of chapter 1, itself originally entitled "The Poor Horses." Throughout the draft there is evidence that he seems not to have had a clear-cut structure by chapters in mind, at least early on. In two instances he made chapter divisions in the middle of what had been a longer section: chapter 3 was originally part of chapter 2; chapter 8 was part of chapter 7. Chapter 2 was the only one so labeled and thus unchanged in published form. Chapters 6, 7, 9, 10, 12, 13, and 14 were merely labeled "New Chapter," and chapters 4 and 5 had lists of topics such as "where to See [*sic*] fights, of the heat of Bilbao, advice to visit

Aranjuez on San Fernando day, of beauties and of Ronda and Somethg [*sic*] about Valencia and of the monument to Chaves" after the chapter number. The other seven chapters have titles; for example, chapter 1 is "The Poor Horses," chapter 11 "The Bulls," chapter 15 "The Cape."

Among the fifty-odd changes in chapter 1 most are simply idiomatic and stylistic, but he was also sweating over the opening lines. At one point he deleted the first three sentences and then restored them. Since morals are at issue, he inserted the word *modern* in the phrase "from a modern moral point of view" to be more precise, and four additions on page 13 underline his concern for art as a human activity: the words *integrity* (line 1), *technical* (line 12), *and esthetic vision* (line 15), and *commercial* (line 19). These additions in the description of the difference between the art and the mere mechanics of bullfighting serve to clarify the distinction between the commercial fighter and the true artist, a useful distinction that Hemingway insisted on in writing as well.

In this chapter there are the first of many references to fellow writers, about whom Hemingway was also revising his thoughts. It seemed as important to get the Gertrude Stein business straight as to be accurate about muletas and bulls, and so instead of giving Stein credit for introducing him to bullfighting, he cancelled the point and reduced her to a mere informant. Her stinging *Autobiography of Alice B. Toklas* was not to appear until 1933, but already the friendship had been strained, and perhaps he did not want to give her credit for anything important. Here he goes on to give the impression that he deliberately became an aficionado because, with the war over, bullfighting was "the only place where you could see life and death" anymore (p. 2). One other personal reference deleted from the draft concerns an anonymous American actress who spent a great deal of money combating the bullfight. The sardonic remarks, if kept, would have badly interrupted the comments about double bass players in symphonies (p. 10), and so he cancelled three sentences including, "She may have accepted the starving of bad actors as part of the casualties to be expected in the proffession [*sic*]." Indeed, the running battle with the Humanists and their animalarian associates begins in chapter

1, and he made several changes in that material. The first was the deletion of a crack against the Humanists who he anticipated would attack "a serious book on such an unmoral subject" (p. 4). He also cancelled a phrase about "Humanitarian feeling" in which he described disembowelings and two sentences again sniping at "right thinkers" and "animalarians."

Another chapter 1 cancellation of some length advances the central point about decadence in art somewhat clumsily and repetitiously (p. 8), and later he elaborates on the point anyhow. This draft chapter also contains an illustration of his occasional notes to himself for later writing. In the margin beside the description of the disembowelings of horses, he wrote a note calling for further description that he never added. (In other instances of these reminders, however, he later did add material.) Besides the change in the reference to Gertrude Stein in chapter 1, similar references to other living authors were mended and are of more than passing interest to the literary historian.

Throughout his life Hemingway seems to have had ambivalent feelings toward his greatest peer in modern American fiction, William Faulkner. Hemingway's observation about Faulkner suggests both great admiration and a sense of rivalry. At the end of chapters 14 and 15, the published version treats Faulkner with guarded and ironic admiration. Some readers thought Hemingway was attacking Faulkner here, but Hemingway did not think so.[26] In the original version of chapter 14 and what was omitted at the end of chapter 15, Hemingway alludes to Faulkner's first commercial success, *Sanctuary*, published the year before (1931), and in the original draft gives him praise unqualified by the phrase "for many years": "He writes the best of them of any writer I have ever read."[27] And Hemingway, badgered throughout his publishing days by censors, clearly had reason to be thankful to Faulkner for helping to liberalize editing. At the end of chapter 15, before telling the old lady the story of the homosexual encounter, Hemingway had promised to tell her a couple of stories: "I do not say they will equal those of Mr. Faulkner. But given such a story a good writer should be able to make something of them."[28] The passage was later cancelled, perhaps because he did not want to clutter the introduction, perhaps because he saw no need to give his admired contemporary any more praise.

The interesting digression on writing that ends chapter 16 was substantially changed from the first draft, which is less succinct but also contains some remarks of interest that are otherwise lost. One can guess that the original version is the sort of passage that Dos Passos suggested trimming as being irrelevant philosophizing, and it is more rambling than the published version but not much longer. The oft-cited analogy of good writing to an iceberg is in both passages as are attempts to justify his art. But beyond that the original is radically different. It contains nothing about Aldous Huxley, whose essay "Foreheads Villainous Low" was published in *Music at Night* in 1931 and which Hemingway probably read after the composition of the first draft. Huxley provided a well-known straw man against which to play off Hemingway's esthetic remarks in the final version.

In the process of streamlining, however, by focusing on a response to Huxley's criticism, remarks predicting civil war in Spain and ironic comments on the politicizing of literature in the 1930s were lost. "Do you not know," he has an imagined inquisitor asking him, "an artist or writer must have some economic viewpoint, that he must be for or against, that he must be a communist, a humanist, a Thomist, some sort of ist, for if he is none of these they will label him a defeatist, an anarchist, a symbolist or an art for arts-sake-ist." This inquisitor then asks why he has turned his back on America and the machine age, and Hemingway's persona replies that he, the reader, the customer, "is always right," but if the reader is a critic, he "can in the words of Mr. Joyce K.M.R.I.A. [kiss my royal Irish arse]." On the other hand, if the reader is a friend the author would explain that he wrote about bullfighting "because it is something that I know about and I have tried to write only about things that I know." As for America, he has not shunned it and "never had any desire to escape" it "but have only left for various periods for economic reasons, for pleasure, and to enable me to write better of it, until you all will have a bellyfull and will say we wish that bastard would go and write something about Spain again." Indeed, like his prediction of civil war in Spain, this prediction was to come true. His next novel, *To Have and Have Not*, was to be about America and the Depression, to make a pronounced political statement, to lead a number of customers to wish similarly for a novel about Spain, and eventually to be rewarded by *For Whom the Bell Tolls* (1940).

He returns to the topic of the "machine age" and avers that he is "a very poor mechanic," uses few machines (he alludes to preferring the pen to the typewriter), thinks human minds more interesting than machines and the human body capable of giving more pain and pleasure than machines can. (Having made two conscious predictions, he may have written this passage shortly before his severe automobile accident.)

Another excised literary comment explains the motif: he thought that the "temporarily discredited" Rudyard Kipling wrote "truly and bitterly of human beings" but "badly and romantically" of machines, as did any author who forgot that fiction was about people. Hemingway then goes on to the iceberg analogy and to "the deadly dangers of defeat" facing all writers, including joining organizations (he would again castigate such writers, "all angleworms in a bottle," in *Green Hills of Africa*),[29] writing patterned and easy material, or "acceptance of academic benediction." The original concluded the rambling apologia for writing about bullfighting more directly by citing three reasons: bullfighting is an institution like any other, including the Second Spanish Republic; its focus on death sets it apart from and elevates it above other "public amusements as football baseball and prizefighting"); and if it is not to survive posterity ought to have "a true contemporary account of it."[30]

Three other sections deserve mention. In chapter 4 Hemingway fondly remembers the town of Ronda with its "romantic background" and "modern comfort" (pp. 42–43). With ironic effect he had capitalized the phrases *Romantic Background* and *Romantic Scenery*,[31] then later made them lower case and inserted "in spite of all this" to make it clear that even though it seems stagey and overdone, it really is a wonderful town for an assignation or a honeymoon as well as good bullfights. After the paragraph that he kept, he had written and later cancelled a para-

graph of thirteen lines telling ways to get to Ronda, a hotel to stay
at, and sights to see ("fine old arab houses . . . and a wonderful
bridge"). Then he tells an anecdote that adds news of one other
injury to the many he suffered: he and some unidentified companions descend into the gulch below the town where "girls of the
town wash clothes," and one time joking with "some girls high up
above" who "were dropping pebbles," what "must have been
quite a big pebble, hit me on the top of head [*sic*] and that was all
I remembered for some time. There is no point to this except not
to joke with pebbles."[32] Later, reading his own conclusion about
the lack of a point, he cancelled the entire paragraph.

In chapter 5 he also originally included an extension of his
somewhat tangential description of Constantinople and a brief
account of fiesta days in Pamplona that he never wrote elsewhere. It too includes a semiserious reference to injury. After
writing how seeing the sunrise along the Bosphorus finished off a
night of carousing "with a healthy outdoor touch" (p. 48), he had
continued, "perhaps it was watching the sunrise along the Bos-
phorous [*sic*] that gave me athletes [*sic*] kidneys. I have never seen
the sun rise in Spain that I know of. I have never been able to last
through a whole night in Pamplona with the real drinkers." The
admission may seem surprising. He continues with an amusing
though possibly unconscious self-allusion after saying he never
awoke before 6:30 A.M.: "The sun probably rises while you are
getting breakfast."[33]

This chapter 5 concludes with his comments on Waldo Frank
and his book *Virgin Spain* (1926). Hemingway's definition of
estoque in the glossary also belittles Frank for his ignorance, no
doubt in part because Frank's book was published shortly after
his first visit to Spain, whereas Hemingway had been visiting
Spain for nine years and laboring on his book for seven. The first
draft is considerably different in wording but very similar in im-
port to the published version, which is more detailed except for
the discrete omission of a crack at the magazine *S4N*—"a now
happily dead little magazine."[34] Also missing is praise of Georgi-
ana King's *The Way of Saint James*, which Hemingway thought
was an informed if not popular book about Spain.

Another curiosity must relate to the extended composition of the book, both in time and place. In the manuscript, Hemingway does not quote from Waldo Frank's *S4N* article but, as in the published version, says he would quote from it but his copy is in Paris. No one, including Hemingway, seems to have noted the contradiction between first saying he cannot quote it and then following with direct quotes. The first draft is consistent, and apparently Hemingway revised it, including direct quotes, after he did in fact find a copy of the article. Like his biographer A. E. Hotchner, Hemingway layered his text.

The final group of differences reveals mistakes, oversights, or deliberate changes made in the editing and publishing process that result in a marred text different from Hemingway's intention.[35] He kept changing his manuscript in all stages, including the final typescript and the galleys. There are fortunately few mistakes, and they include inconsistent treatment of vulgar words. In the first draft, Hemingway himself was inconsistent, sometimes writing "f—k," sometimes spelling out the entire word. But in the *final* typescript at the end of chapter 8, he spelled out "fuck" and mended in his own hand "—ing" to "Fuckinging" [*sic*],[36] which ended up in the published version as "F—king" (p. 82). The Jonathan Cape and Penguin editions went even further and changed the obscenity variously to "blast," "damn," and "go and hang yourselves." Those British editions also omitted part of the graphic description of death by influenza containing "shits the bed full" (which was again modified when "A Natural History of the Dead" was published in *Winner Take Nothing*). But the most absurd change occurred in the British editions when, at the end of chapter 9, Hemingway's "horseshit" is changed to "nonsense" so that the exchange reads:

Author: Madame, . . . it may well be that we are talking nonsense.
Old lady: That is an odd term and one I did not encounter in my youth.
Author: Madame, we apply the term now to describe unsoundness in an abstract conversation or, indeed, any over-metaphysical tendency in speech.
Old lady: I must learn to use these terms correctly.[37]

Some other errors introduced by the publishing process include these:

Death in the Afternoon	Texas Manuscript
the harnessed mules for *handling* of dead bulls (p. 61)	the harnessed mules for *hauling* of dead bulls (p. 83)
as bullfighters, only the *bad* ones, the hardy tough ones (p. 70)	as bullfighters, only the *old* ones, the hardy tough ones (p. 98)
shortcomings *and* incompletely trained fighters (p. 92)	shortcomings *of* incompletely trained fighters (p. 121)
affected with mumps (p. 94)	*afflicted* with mumps (p. 123)
the marble a *sculpture* cuts (p. 99)	the marble a *sculptor* cuts (p. 128)[38]
punch drunkenness, *of* "walking on the heels" (p. 101)	punch drunkenness, *or* "walking on the heels" (p. 132)
get to table.—Within (p. 104)	get to table. Within (p. 137)
into the offensive (p. 211)	*onto* the offensive (p. 255)
the bulls carried terms in the hospital, *inevitable* (p. 222)	the bulls carried terms in the hospital, *inevitably* (p. 265)

Changes like these supported by manuscript evidence and not subsequently mended by Hemingway himself should clearly be made in the published version. Changes of mechanical matters are to be expected, but there should be a text approaching the author's verifiable intentions. That a book so concerned with art, focusing on bullfighting but seeing it as a metaphor for the beauty and accuracy of good writing, was marred in the production is an irony we can endure and even appreciate. Tracing this book's growth is tracing a part of Hemingway's esthetic process.[39]

Notes

1 Carlos Baker, *Hemingway: The Writer as Artist*, 4th ed. (Princeton: Princeton University Press, 1972), p. 149. Charles Scribner, Jr., noted that while Scribners is "reluctant to disclose" sales figures, to the best

of his knowledge *"Death in the Afternoon* has remained continuously
in print since its first publication in 1932" (Letter to Robert W. Lewis,
27 April 1982). Hemingway himself was pleasantly surprised by its
early brisk sales, given the Depression and an apparently pessimistic
Scribners: "My damned book *selling*—what do you think of that? I
thought of it as a book to end publishers—" *(Ernest Hemingway: Selected Letters, 1917–1961,* ed. Carlos Baker [New York: Scribner's,
1981], p. 376).

2 Hemingway, *Selected Letters,* pp. 156–57.
3 A. Scott Berg, *Max Perkins: Editor of Genius* (New York: Dutton,
1978), p. 194.
4 Hemingway, *Selected Letters,* p. 337.
5 Baker, *The Writer as Artist,* p. 146.
6 Hemingway, *Selected Letters,* pp. 355–56. On December 10, 1931, he
wrote that the book was finished except for "some hack work on the
appendix" *(Selected Letters,* p. 345). Over twenty years later he was
to recall the two years of hard work on the book: "It was a bastard to
do" *(Selected Letters,* p. 799).
7 Hemingway, *Selected Letters,* p. 356.
8 Hemingway, *Selected Letters,* pp. 361–62.
9 Ernest Hemingway, *Death in the Afternoon* (New York: Scribner's,
1932), p. 517. All further references to this work appear in the text.
10 Hemingway, *Selected Letters,* p. 360.
11 Hemingway, *Selected Letters,* p. 378.
12 Hemingway, *Selected Letters,* p. 374.
13 Hemingway, *Selected Letters,* p. 376.
14 Matthew J. Bruccoli and C. E. Frazer Clark, Jr., compilers, *Hemingway at Auction, 1930–1973* (Detroit: Gale Research Co., 1973), p. 34.
15 Baker, *The Writer as Artist,* p. 145. There is some evidence to suggest,
however, that some of the inserts to this version were written afterward, e.g., in references to events of 1931 like Faulkner's publication
of *Sanctuary* (p. 173).
16 Hemingway, *Selected Letters,* p. 894.
17 Bruccoli and Clark, *Hemingway at Auction,* pp. 33–49.
18 Bruccoli and Clark, *Hemingway at Auction,* p. 34.
19 Neither staff at the Humanities Research Center, University of Texas
(Austin), nor Marguerite A. (Mrs. Louis) Cohn could explain the missing page. Letter received from Mrs. Louis Henry Cohn, 14 June 1972.
20 Bruccoli and Clark, *Hemingway at Auction,* frontispiece and p. 35.
See another photo reproduction in Max Westbrook, "Necessary Per-

formance: The Hemingway Collection at Texas," *Library Chronicle of the University of Texas*, 7, No. 4 (Spring 1964), 26.
21 Bruccoli and Clark, *Hemingway at Auction*, p. 35.
22 Ernest Hemingway, *The Short Stories of Ernest Hemingway* (New York: Scribner's, 1938), p. 161.
23 See especially his Bibliographical Note, p. 517.
24 Carlos Baker, *Ernest Hemingway: A Life Story* (New York: Scribner's, 1969), p. 187.
25 Hemingway, *Selected Letters*, p. 264.
26 Hemingway, *Selected Letters*, p. 368.
27 Texas manuscript, p. 3 of "2nd insert to Bull fight book," following manuscript p. 210.
28 Texas manuscript, p. 2 of 3d insert, "New end of chapter insert—Bull fight book." Another hard-to-read marginal note at this point seems to identify the newsman who told him the story of the homosexuals as William Nash, a Paris acquaintance of the 1920s and a reporter for the *Chicago Daily News*.
29 *Green Hills of Africa* (New York: Scribner's, 1935), p. 21.
30 Texas manuscript, 6-page "Insert in bull fight book" between manuscript pp. 231 and 232.
31 Texas manuscript, p. 63.
32 Texas manuscript, p. 63.
33 Texas manuscript, p. 67.
34 Texas manuscript, p. 72.
35 I am familiar with the ongoing debate about whether or not we need new editions of Hemingway's work and if so what should the nature of new editions be. The extreme position that says Hemingway was a consummate craftsman and artist and thus whatever he published is sacrosanct, is pleasant and romantic loyalty to a nonexistent creature. He himself knew and said better, knew, for instance, that some of his early work was poor and ought to stay buried, knew that he kept writing because he kept wanting to "make it new," knew that he was a fallible editor and gave Maxwell Perkins permission to regularize such matters as punctuation.
36 Texas manuscript, p. 109.
37 Ernest Hemingway, *Death in the Afternoon* (Harmondsworth: Penguin Books in association with Jonathan Cape, 1966), p. 91.
38 Interestingly, the Penguin edition corrects this to *sculptor* (p. 94).
39 Marguerite Cohn, Mary Hemingway, Jo August Hills, and Charles Scribner, Jr., kindly responded to my queries. The staffs of the Hu-

manities Research Center at the University of Texas (Austin) and the Hemingway Collection in the John F. Kennedy Library (Boston) were always helpful and gracious. To them, my thanks, but special thanks to Max Westbrook of the University of Texas (Austin) whose energy and wisdom helped me to begin this project some years ago. To my colleagues on the Faculty Research Committee at the University of North Dakota, thanks for continued support.

5. Paul Smith

The Tenth Indian and the Thing Left Out

T HAT little attention has been given to Ernest Hemingway's title "Ten Indians" says something of the way we read the more innocent of those summer stories of Nick Adams's boyhood. Most readers simply add Nick's Indian girl to the nine drunken ones Joe Garner counts on the ride home from Petoskey on the Fourth of July, and they arrive at the sum of the childhood counting rhyme "Ten Little Injuns." Some may recall its first lines, "Ten little Injuns standin' in a line / One toddled home and then there were nine," but few can remember what happened to the last Indian. Yet imagine that T. S. Eliot, who so often alluded to popular songs and ballads, had fashioned a poem in 1927 following Hemingway's narrative and entitled "Ten Indians." The commentary on that title would have fixed in our memories every line of the song that is its source, even to the last couplet on the fate of the tenth Indian.[1]

Although the story, like its title, has rarely gone unnoticed in any critical review of Hemingway's short fiction, it has just as rarely been granted much importance, for it does not seem to strike the immediate, elemental, or enigmatic measures of such stories as "The Killers," "Indian Camp," or "A Clean Well-Lighted Place." Its dialogue has the accents of the cursory and occasional. Its ending—it ends with the solace of a sympathetic storm—may be marked as a classic literary fallacy. And its sentences have little of the obvious stylistic interest of those in "Big Two-Hearted River." So it is deceptively easy to read "Ten In-

53

dians" as the work of a writer whose prose is prosaic, not poetic; whose meanings are at hand, not distantly allusive; and whose tribal totem is, after all, the ox rather than the 'possum.

Or so it once was, for now with the renewed interest in Hemingway occasioned by the publication of his letters and studies of his reading, and especially by the new evidence of his manuscripts, it is apparent that his prose is poetic in more than the rhythmic or imagistic senses of that term, that his meanings resonate with complex and often literary allusions, and that if he assumed the role of the ox it was his way of playing 'possum.[2]

The published version of "Ten Indians" has an intricately symmetrical structure, and its effect is a doubled irony. An initial reading seems to establish the scene with the Garners as a standard for measuring what is diminished or missing in the scene at Nick's home; but a retrospective reading reverses the irony to suggest that his father's uncomfortable colloquy with his son offers a necessary sense of the world, or at least of that world of men without women. The structure opposes three dialogues during the ride home with the Garners against three dialogues between Nick and his father at their cottage. Each half of the story is introduced with a narrative paragraph, and the conversations in each section are marked off with narrative transitions.

I. NARRATIVE PARAGRAPH (331:1–8 "After one Fourth . . . on the wagon-box.")[3] Nick and the Garners return from the Fourth of July celebration.

  A. Dialogue: The Garners on the Indians
    Narrative Transition (331:25–332:3 "They drove along . . . the wagon again.") The trip home.

  B. Dialogue: The Garners on Nick and Prudence

II. NARRATIVE PARAGRAPH (334:11–19 "Nick walked barefoot . . . and went in.") Nick walks home.

  A. Dialogue: Nick's father questions him about his day.
    Narrative Transition (335:2–5 "His father sat . . . was huckleberry pie.") His father watches Nick.

  B. Dialogue: Nick questions his father about his day; the revelation.

Narrative Transition	*Narrative Transition*
(333:21–28 "They trotted	(335:36–336:2 "His father
down . . . on the wood.")	got . . . had been crying.")
Arrival at the Garners' home.	Nick's father leaves and
	returns.
C. Dialogue: Nick leaves the	C. Dialogue: Father's final
Garners.	offering; Nick's final
	question.

III. CONCLUSION (336:13–28 "Nick went into . . . his heart was broken.") Nick goes to bed, wakes in the night with the storm, wakes in the morning.

The first narrative paragraph (I) sets the scene as Nick remembers the occasion of the ninth Indian; the second (II) follows his walk from the Garners' to his own home. The dialogue that follows each introduction is a prologue to the succeeding dialogues. The first (I A) is restricted to the Garners' general conversation (all except Nick participate), with Joe Garner explaining the drunken Indians to his sons and his wife offering her moralistic expletive, "Them Indians." In the second (II A), Nick's father's dialogue is restricted to similarly general questions: from what sort of day it was, to whether his son is hungry, to where he left his shoes, to whether he has had enough to eat, and back again to the events of the day. Each section seems random and desultory and yet each is circular. The first begins and ends with Mrs. Garner's expletive, and the second is encircled by Nick's father's offhand questions about his son's relationship with the Indians.

The middle dialogues in each half of the story (I B and II B) focus on a set of questions about Nick's affair with Prudence; but, again, there is a crucial difference: in the first Nick is the respondent and in the second the questioner. Each begins with some apparently unrelated matter: in the first, Nick's seeing some skunks looking for dead fish on the lakeshore; in the second, his father's fishing for perch in the morning. The irony established by these two opposed dialogues rests in the fact that Nick's insistent denials that Prudence is his girl in the first prove to be true after his insistent questioning of his father in the second.

More important is the difference between the attitudes under-
lying the Garners' dialogue and the father-and-son colloquy. In
the first, the whole family participates, taking positions that provide the kind of familial equilibrium that is lacking in Nick's dialogue with his father. Once the issue of Nick's Indian girl is
raised by Carl Garner, his parents take opposite sides, each of
which differently reassures Nick. Mrs. Garner tells Carl to stop
talking; Mr. Garner laughs at Carl's quip about the Indians'
smell. Once Carl has been silenced by his mother with the remark
that he could not get an Indian girl, he is reassured by his father
with "You're all right, Carl." In this way the Garner parents incorporate the subject, playfully but with a serious if unspoken intent, into their own relationship. Joe contradicts his younger son,
Frank, when Frank says that his father would never have "a
squaw for a girl" and warns Nick that he had "better watch out to
keep Prudie," another unintentional prophecy of the revelation in
the second half of the story. The effect, however, is to invest
Nick's affair with maturity and seriousness as well as to align Mrs.
Garner more closely with Nick. Between Joe Garner's opening
and closing remarks on the condition of the road, Nick's experience is subsumed in the affectionate sexual banter of the
Garner parents. When Carl's taunting continues, Mrs. Garner si-
lences him with a rather harsh remark, as if to protect Nick as she
would her own son.

This family conversation contrasts with Nick's questions to his
father (II B). This dialogue comes close to a cross-examination. It
is as if Nick suspects that his father has seen and knows more than
he admits at first, a suspicion that may have been elicited by his
father's behavior and responses. The narrative transition introducing the dialogue states that "his father sat watching him."
This is repeated once, and, following the revelation, there is the
line "His father was not looking at him." The father's answers are
as leading as Nick's questions: he first tells his son what he did "in
the morning," begging a question about the afternoon. Once he
mentions that he saw Prudence up *by* the Indian camp, Nick asks
all but one of his questions twice: whom did he see, what were
they doing, how did he know it was they? The one question he

asks once—"Where were they?"—he returns to, hopelessly, in the final dialogue. What Nick is reluctant to pursue is not, at the end, with whom Prudence was making love but whether she was doing it in the place that, as "Fathers and Sons" tells us so precisely, was theirs.

The final dialogues (I C, II C) in each section again contrast the Garner family and Nick's. In the first, Mrs. Garner prepares a hot meal and invites Nick to join them. Nick declines with the remark "I *think* that Dad *probably* waited for me." Joe Garner repeats his wife's offer; Nick again declines and passes on the message that Carl's "mother wants him." It is as if the Garner family, having opened to hold him as one of their own, closes again as he leaves, mother and father and sons. In the last brief section of dialogue at home, the father returns, having given his son the chance to cry alone, and he twice offers him more cold pie, finally with an unfortunate and unintended pun, "You better have another piece." When Nick asks precisely where his father saw Prudence, and again looks at his plate, his father realizes the extent of his son's suffering and suggests that he go to bed.[4]

The four manuscripts of "Ten Indians" attempt three variant conclusions of the narrative: the Chartres version returns Prudence to Nick; the Madrid version (in two manuscripts) ends with the father's introspection; and the notebook version follows the broken-hearted son through the night.[5] However remarkable these differences among the three conclusions, it is just as remarkable that the rest of the larger structural elements of the narrative were there in Hemingway's original conception of the story. The Chartres version has some interesting variants on the story's first four pages, and there are some telling revisions between it and the Madrid version; but the three versions do not begin to differ crucially until the second dialogue between Nick and his father.[6]

The first of the "Ten Indians" manuscripts is dated Chartres, 27 September 1925. Hemingway had gone there alone a week or so after finishing the first draft of *The Sun Also Rises*, exhausted not only from the summer of steady writing but also from the alluring presence of Duff Twysden.[7] Carlos Baker's account of this period is entitled "Double-Crossings," and in the abundant evidence for that rubric he cites "Ten Indians." But the Chartres version does not deal with the "presumable betrayal of Nick Adams by his Indian girl, Prudence Mitchell," nor does it contain any reference to Prudence's "'threshing around' with Frank Washburn in the woods near Walloon Lake." Later Baker makes the point that the "sentimental midnight meeting between Nick and his Indian girl is lopped off."[8] It was; yet most of the narrative's structural elements remained, all but those in the last two crucial pages of the story.

This version approximates the published version up to the crucial dialogue in which the father tells Nick of his morning activities. Nothing in that narration or dialogue suggests that the father has anything to reveal to his son, and from then on the dialogue suggests a family situation as close and comforting as the Garners'. The father brings in some huckleberry pie he made while Nick was in town, and then Nick offers to cut him a piece. He tells his son that the Indians "came around with some blueberries" and suggests that they have them for breakfast. Nick agrees and promises to get the milk and make breakfast in the morning. They go into the livingroom, Nick makes a fire, and they settle down for an evening of reading. Then, as an afterthought, his father makes a remark:

> "Oh," he said. "There was a girl here to see you."
> "Who?"
> "Prudence Mitchell. She said you'd promised to go rowing with her."
> "Didn't she know it was the Fourth of July?"
> "I don't know. I guess so. She said that all her family were gone into Petoskey."[9]

Nick then thanks his father for waiting up for him, goes to bed, and says his prayers for "his father, his mother, and Prudence Mitchell." Later he is awakened by Prudence at the window. He dresses, walks quietly past the bedroom where his father is sleeping, and embraces her on the porch. They walk to the beach, he tries to kiss her, she refuses, and the version ends:

"What's the matter?"

"I won't ever kiss anybody again."

"Kiss me."

"All right."

Prudence got into the stern of the boat and Nick shoved it off and stepped in.

"I'm still asleep," Nick said.

"I had to come," Prudence said, "They all came back drunk from town."

This is less an ineffective ending than it is a new beginning. It seems to serve two purposes: first, it offers an affirmative scene between the father and son to balance the positive relationships in the Garner family; then, perhaps with the original introduction in mind, it introduces Prudence not only as Nick's girl but also as another child in a third and more difficult family situation: "They all came back drunk from Petoskey." Hemingway might have meant to imply something of Prudence's sense of shame or guilt in her resolve never to "kiss anybody again." And if he meant to associate this shame with her remark about her family's coming back drunk from Petoskey, he could have been alluding to a situation close to incest. In any case, he had started more than he could finish by introducing the tearful Prudence. This ending may strike some readers as a "sentimental midnight meeting," and insofar as it points to a reunion of the two lovers, it may well be. However, if it is directed toward some revelation of her sense of shame at having kissed or been kissed by someone close to or within her family, then the ending centering on this stricken tenth and only sober Indian is a far more serious matter.

The second and third manuscripts of the story were written in Madrid some time during or soon after the marathon of composition on 16 May 1926 that Hemingway described in his interview with George Plimpton:

The stories you mention I wrote in one day in Madrid on May sixteenth when it snowed out the San Isidro bullfights. First I wrote "The Killers," which I'd tried to write before and failed. Then after lunch I got in bed to keep warm and wrote "Today is Friday." I had so much juice I thought maybe I was going crazy and I had about six other stories to write. So I got dressed and walked to Fornos, the old bullfighters' cafe, and drank coffee and then came back and wrote "Ten Indians." This made me very sad and I drank some brandy and went to sleep.[10]

Hemingway's recollection of that day in May is a curious, but perhaps typical, interweaving of candor and reticence. He admits to having failed with the earlier manuscript of "The Killers" but is silent on the first version of "Ten Indians." Perhaps something in the revision of the Chartres manuscript, something that made him "very sad," was enough to create the "memory" of beginning the story for the first time. In any case, there is good reason to trust his memory of the cold and lonely bedroom. The sexual metaphor, implying that sexual deprivation is conducive to fictional creation, was by this time common in his writing. By May of 1926 Hemingway was well into one of the blackest years he had known. His marriage to Hadley was irreparably broken; she was at Cap d'Antibes with Bumby, who was quarantined with whooping cough; and Pauline was traveling in Italy. In his cold room in Madrid, he would have associated the end of the affair with Prudence with whatever he knew or imagined of his father's marriage and what he knew very well of his own.

Since there are two "Madrid versions," it is probable that Hemingway's memory in 1958 conflated his work on two manuscripts of the story. The first, entitled "Ten Indians," is the more heavily revised of the two; most of those revisions are incorporated in the second; and the conclusion of the first reads like an immediate sketch for that of the second—all of which suggests that the latter version, bearing the title "A Broken Heart," was written on or near the date of the former in May of 1926.

Each of these Madrid manuscripts again approximates the final version to the point at which Nick's father reveals Prudence's faithlessness. With minor differences between the two manuscripts, this revelation is followed by a discussion of how rotten people are.

"I'm sorry, Nickie," his father said, looking at Nick, "But that's the way people are."

"They don't have to all be rotten," Nick said. His voice hurt him to talk.

"Just about," his father said. "It's a fairly rotten place, Nick."

"I guess it's so," Nick said. He choked.

"No, it's not so," his father said. "Everybody's not rotten."

"Oh, it's so all right," Nick said. "You said it. You can't take it back now."

"I was just bitter when I said it, Nick," his father said. "You know how I talk when I'm bitter. I just shoot my mouth off. People aren't all really rotten."

"They are. They're all rotten to hell."

As Nick goes off to bed, the narrative point of view shifts to the father and his remorse at having told his son so much; then he turns in. He has told his son how things are in the world, tried to console him, seen him into bed, apologized twice, and been, for the moment, pardoned. Then—

His father blew out the lamp and went into his own room. He undressed and knelt down beside the bed. "Dear God, for Christ's sake keep me from ever telling things to a kid," he prayed. "For Christ's sake keep me from ever telling a kid how things are."

Then he got into bed. He lays crossways in the big double bed to take up as much room as he could. He was a very lonely man.

He lay in the bed a long time but could not sleep. He got up out of bed and in the dark walked in his bare feet across the living room to the door of Nick's room. The door was open and he listened and heard Nick breathing regularly. Nick was asleep. Nick's father crossed the room to the table, felt in the dark for matches, lit the lamp and carried it into his own room. He would read for a while and perhaps it would put him to sleep.[11]

This version turns the story away from Nick's sorrow to his father's anger at himself for so abruptly disillusioning his son, and from there to his father's own lonely predicament. Both he and his son are men without women, and the title, "A Broken Heart," refers as much to the father as to the son.

With this ending, Hemingway risked an obvious inconsistency in narrative point of view: to this point the narration has been restricted to what Nick experienced or thought or felt. That Hemingway took that risk, although not a serious one, attests to his new sense of the structural implications of the story. The ending transfers only one element from the Chartres version: there Nick prayed for his father, his mother, and Prudence; here his father prays that he will never again reveal to his son " how things are." What he is thinking of is, obviously, how things are for men without women, his son without Prudence and himself without Nick's mother. The earlier hints of Prudence's story are dropped to draw some explicit contrasts between the Garner family and Nick's own and to add other dimensions to the contrast between the story's two fathers. The emotional equilibrium between the Garner parents is set against the imbalance between Nick's, one man crossways on a double bed. But Nick's father's role goes beyond Joe Garner's. He tells him exactly why (in Garner's words) "he better watch out to keep Prudie." He gives him hard facts, as a witness; and he will not—because he cannot—pretend to compete for Nick's girl to tease his wife. He tells him exactly how things are, however much he regrets it later, not only because he knows about Prudence but because he sees the similarity between his son's recent and his own long-standing loneliness. That moment of recognition comes when he first generalizes from Nick's experience: in response to Nick's remark "They don't have to all be rotten," he replies, "Just about. . . . It's a fairly rotten place." Then, possibly realizing that Nick may see a similarity in their situations, he retreats from his position, both for his son's and his own sake: "No, it's not so. . . . Everybody's not rotten." By then, however, it is too late; he, as well as Nick, realizes that he cannot take back what he said. Hemingway, having gone this far into the father's experience, seems compelled by his narrative both to

punish and to pardon the father's act through his self-condemn-
ing prayer and the pathos of his loneliness.

The last of the "Ten Indians" manuscripts comprises six heavily
revised pages in a notebook including a draft of a descriptive
paragraph for "Che Ti Dice la Patria" and a list of ten titles of the
fourteen stories published in *Men Without Women* (1927).[12] A
letter to Maxwell Perkins of 4 May 1927 dates this version of the
story's conclusion and momentarily gives it yet another title:
"Within three weeks at the latest I plan to send you two more
stories—Italy 1927 ["Che Ti Dice la Patria"] and After the
Fourth—these I am rewriting now."[13] These pages are more a
worksheet revision of the second Madrid version than a final
draft. With only a few deletions or additions, it follows the dialogue in II B from Nick's question "What were they doing?" to
the narrative conclusion at which Nick goes to his room. Hemingway had the general features of his conclusion in mind: a paragraph describing Nick's solitary reaction to the loss of Prudence as
he drifts off to sleep, wakes once in the night, and then again the
next morning.

What he apparently did not have in mind was the arrangement
of those elements. Hemingway's attempts to construct the final
paragraph take up three manuscripts pages of the notebook version. The first (cancelled page 10) is little more than an outline of
the elements he will develop in the final version (Hemingway's
deletions are bracketed):

[After a while] [He was sure that his heart was broken] He
heard his father blow out the lamp and go into his own
room. He heard a [cool] wind come up in the trees outside
and felt it come in cool through the screen. Nick lay for a
long time with his face in the pillow and [finally] after a
while he went to sleep. It had been a long day.

The second page 10 begins with a reconsideration of the
cancelled line "He was sure that his heart was broken" and recasts
it as: " 'My heart's broken,' he thought. 'If I feel this way my heart
must be broken.'" With its distinction between the way he feels

and the sentimental cliché, this line prefigures the last line of the story. From there to the last two sentences the paragraph is identical to the final version. But at that point Hemingway wavered. Three variants of the last sentence on the cancelled page 10 are written and cancelled again. First: "It had been a very long day." With its echo of a sentimental parent's concern, "Ah, little lad, you've had a long day," it was clearly inappropriate. The other two sentences, with their references to a "cool night good for sleeping," would be incorporated later.

The final page of the manuscript includes the revisions of page 10 up to the last two sentences of the final version. When he came to revise them, Hemingway had two related questions facing him: how to develop Nick's last thought, that if he feels this way then his heart must be broken; and how and when to introduce the reference to the building storm. He resolved these issues by taking the cancelled reference to the high wind with its implication of "a good night for sleeping" and introducing it in the penultimate sentence of the final version:

> When he woke in the night he heard the wind in the
> hemlock trees outside the cottage and the waves of the lake
> coming in on the shore. . . .

He then tried three versions of Nick's memory or response to the loss of Prudence:
1. "He was happy and went back to sleep."
2. "He did not remember what he had felt badly about."
3. "He did not think about anything . . . and he went back to sleep."

All these were rejected in the final version; it is a good night for sleeping and a better night for sleeping than for thinking well or ill or at all about the past. Then Hemingway began the last sentence, inserted another reference to the storm, and concluded with a reference to the thought that introduced the paragraph:

> In the morning there was a big wind blowing and the waves
> were running high up on the beach and he was awake a long
> time before he remembered that his heart was broken.

The story's final paragraph has attracted a variety of comments, and most of them rest on a reading of the metaphor of a broken heart. It is introduced with Nick's thought "My heart's broken. . . . If I feel this way my heart must be broken." As he lies awake he hears his father as he blows out the lamp and goes "into his own room" and, later, the cool wind coming up in the trees. With those two sounds he forgets "to think about Prudence" and goes to sleep. In the morning, with the wind still blowing, "he was awake a long time before he remembered that his heart was broken."

That image of a broken heart first appeared in the title of the second Madrid version, in which Hemingway felt certain enough about his ending to rewrite all of the first Madrid version and turn it to an evocation of the father's solitary life. In the laborious revision of the ending in the notebook version of 1927, he reconsidered Nick's sense of the relationship between the rather sentimental statement "My heart is broken" and the way he feels. He portrayed an adolescent boy trying, not all that successfully, to fit his immediate and private emotions into a conventional phrase, a pathetic nostrum of ordinary life. Nick momentarily conjoins and explains, even explains away, his feeling with the phrase a "broken heart." Then, hearing his father going to bed alone and the wind in the hemlocks clears his mind of the memory of Prudence, and for a time in the morning he forgets that his heart was broken.

The distance between the statement "My heart is broken" and the sense that "I feel this way" is a metaphor for the distance between the two families: the Garners at the family farm on a high meadow, wet with dew, and Nick's in the cottage in the dry beech woods with its two solitary occupants. The image of a broken heart is a commonplace, and so offers the comfort of a shared and universal experience. It is of a kind with the deleted line "It had been a long day," the sort of remark that one might finally expect from Mrs. Garner. "If I feel this way" rises out of the immediate experience of his father's telling him the way things are with Nick and, silently, with himself.

That Nick would have recognized the similarity between his own and his father's situation would have been a natural conse-

quence of maturation. If a boy's first sexual experience calls forth
questions about his father's sexual life, then his first disappointment in love might as naturally summon up a darker analogy between their experiences. This is the thing left out but still implied
in "Ten Indians"; it is there in the story's final narrative structure
and is confirmed by the manuscripts.

"Ten Indians" offers an exemplary instance of the writer's
practice of the theory of omission and might well settle some of
the unresolved critical issues that theory has raised. The theory
appeared first in *Death in the Afternoon* (1932) and was adum-
brated on several occasions in the late 1950s. In its first form it
read: "If a writer of prose knows enough about what he is writing
about he may omit things that he knows and the reader, if the
writer is writing truly enough, will have a feeling of those things
as strongly as though the writer had stated them."[14] Since then
the theory has been invoked to account for a legion of "things left
out." It has been cited with no distinction among those things
that have been *omitted* (like Nick's war experiences in "Big Two
Hearted River"); those that have been *deleted* (like the beginning
episode, "Three Shots," in "Indian Camp"); and those that have
been *replaced* (like the Madrid conclusion in "Ten Indians").
These differences are important, and critical discussion of the
theory will be confused until we distinguish between acts of *omission*, which occur prior to writing and often rest on Hemingway's
own comments on his fiction, and acts of *deletion* or *replacement*,
which occur in the process of revision and are demonstrable with
the evidence of the manuscripts. Moreover, most of the critical
commentary on the theory has given little notice to Hemingway's
clear understanding that the only elements that could be left out
were those that would, in a sense, still be "there" by virtue of the
implications of those that had been left in.

The usual strategy for discovering the thing left out is to draw
upon analogies among the narrative and thematic elements of
several related stories in order to infer some veiled experience in
Hemingway's life.[15] Most of the details of setting and character in
"Ten Indians" have been traced to their originals in Hemingway's

boyhood in Michigan. Constance Montgomery has traveled the route along the Washout Road from Petoskey, turning at the schoolhouse on Resort Pike, then continuing up the hill where the lights of Petoskey and Harbor Springs can be seen, and down to the Bacon farm; then later, across the meadow, the ravine, and through the beech woods to the Hemingway cottage at Walloon Lake. Her speculation, from interviews with Joseph Bacon, that the Garner family of the story was based on the Bacon family of Hemingway's youth, is substantiated by the earliest manuscript which, like so many others, uses the names of then-living persons. The Joseph Bacons had six children. None was named Frank, but there was a Carl who, during the summers of 1915 and 1916, had that familiar and competitive friendship with Hemingway that informs the dialogue between Carl Garner and Nick Adams.[16] Prudence Mitchell figures in two other stories, as Trudy Gilby in "Fathers and Sons" (1933) and in the manuscripts of "The Last Good Country." Her original was Prudence Boulton, the daughter of Dick Boulton, named in "The Doctor and the Doctor's Wife." Three years younger than Hemingway, she helped in his mother's kitchen at the cottage. She was an attractive girl, especially to Hemingway at about that time when he went through the rite of passage to long pants.[17] He never forgot her: she appears in his fiction of the 1930s and 1950s; and in 1944 he identified her (to Mary Welsh) as the first woman he "pleasured."[18] Whether the sylvan sex of "Fathers and Sons" is a matter of fact or fantasy may be argued, but if it did not happen, it might as well have for the lasting impression it left.

With that much known of Prudence's original in life it is curious that nothing in the fiction, the biography, or the letters acknowledges her death, much less the way she died. So with this negative evidence one might argue that what has been omitted of the experience from which the story originated is any reference to the death of Prudence Boulton. She was sixteen in February of 1918, when, according to one report, she committed suicide with her lover, whom she intended to marry and whose child she was carrying.[19] Whether Hemingway ever knew that, and so could deliberately omit it, is a matter of conjecture. He never indicated any awareness of her death, even in "Fathers and Sons," where the memory might have been appropriate, if somewhat melodramatic. Nevertheless, it is difficult to imagine that he did not hear of her death, given his lasting memory of her part in his life. After her death in February 1918, her body was kept in a vault until the spring thaw that would permit her burial. Hemingway returned to Michigan in late April and early May of that year for his last fishing trip before being called to service in the American Red Cross. In the following year, after his wound and recuperation, he returned three times (to Horton Bay, the Pine Barrens, and the Upper Peninsula) between early June and late August, and from late October to December of 1919 he was living in Petoskey.[20] If neither his close friend, Dutch Pailthorpe, nor the newspaper accounts revealed her death, it was perhaps an unusual stroke of luck. But by 1932, when he began "Fathers and Sons," he knew more of her story than he allowed in the published version. In an early pencil manuscript of that story, Nicholas Adams mentions her fictional character when his son asks him about the Indians:

> "There was an Indian named Prudy Gilbey that I was very
> fond of. We were very good friends."
> "What happened to her?"
> "She [had a baby] went away to become a hooker."

Two questions remain: If Hemingway knew that much, how much more did he know of the fate of *that* tenth Indian? And what is to be made of the similarity between Nick's response to his son's question and what he recalls of *his* father's response when he asked the same question? In that early manuscript of "Fathers and Sons" Nick evades the question and then reflects: "And so I wonder what my father knew beside the nonsense that he told me and how things were with him because when I asked him what the Indians were like when he was a boy he said that he had very good friends among them, that he was very fond of them."[21]

In its various versions, "Ten Indians" drew upon memories of Hemingway's adolescence and the lives and characters of those close to him: his boyhood friends, their parents and his own, and his first girl. Those recollections must have been evoked by his own difficult experience between the time he first went to Chartres in the fall of 1925 to reconsider his first novel and his first marriage, and the spring of 1927 when he began his second marriage and his second novel. In the last few months of that period, the memory of his first disappointment in love might well have been called forth by the writing of "Che Ti Dice la Patria," which draws on his discontent on the trip through Italy, the preceding winter, with those high winds, the Italian whores, his remorse over the loss of Hadley, and his tears and prayers at roadside shrines.[22] A little later, when he turned his narrative of "Ten Indians" away from the Madrid version's account of the lonely father sleeping crossways on the big double bed, he might have counted on our recollection of the last of the ten little Indians:

One little Injun livin' all alone,
He got married and then there were none.

Appendix

The Chartres version begins with one and a half paragraphs describing the drunken Indians in Petoskey on the Fourth of July and leads into the introduction as it appears in the final version. This section is slightly revised in the first Madrid version (728) and deleted in the second (729). The other variants in this version all suggest that Hemingway thought of Nick as somewhat younger than in the later version:

(In I A 331:12) The inside of his shirt was full of firecrackers he had saved up [for future use.] He had two pockets full of unexploded firecrackers he had salvaged in the streets and on the Fair Grounds. They had no fuses but he would make squibs of them. He was wishing he had saved some punk and was looking. . . .

(In I B 332:7) He felt the firecrackers inside his shirt and was happy.

(In II; Narrative Paragraph 334:11) Nick was barefoot, he had taken his shoes off in the wagon coming out from Petoskey. In town was the first time he had worn shoes all summer. They hurt his feet. Now he walked carefully along the path.

The remaining variant occurs in I C (334:6) after Nick says goodnight to Mr. Garner.

> "Where's Carl?" Nick asked. Carl opened the door of the stable.
> "Who wants me?" he asked.
> "Your Ma wants you."
> "All right," said Carl. He stood in the stable door holding the lantern. He was short but heavy and thick-necked. He never wore a hat and he was brown, almost as brown as an Indian.
> "Going home?" he asked.
> "Yeah."
> "Aren't you going to eat with us?"
> "No, I better get back to Dad."
> "Well, so long."
> "So long, Carl."

There are two probable explanations for the deletion of these passages in the Madrid version. Nick's boyish delight in the firecrackers would trivialize his feeling of loss and would compete with his feeling "hollow and happy inside himself to be teased about Prudence Mitchell." Transferring the parting remarks from Carl to Joe Garner also reinforces the parallel with Nick's father's later invitation to eat, and the reference to Carl's Indian-like complexion might well have been a false lead to the tenth Indian.

There are two crucial points in the early versions of the story at which Hemingway directs his narrative toward different conclusions. The first is in the Chartres version; it follows the final narrative up to the early part of the dialogue in II B; its narrative transition introduces the dialogue with the sentence "His father sat watching him eat." But at this point it is as if Hemingway had decided not to reveal why Nick's father was watching him. The dialogue continues:

> "What did you do, Dad?"
>   "I went fishing."
>   [Note: He does not add, "in the morning."]
>   "Get anything?"
>   "Just some perch."
> His father brought in the pie.
>   [Note: There is no second reference to his father's watching him.]

The second crux occurs in the Madrid versions. The first of these moves beyond the discussion of the father's morning to his activities during the afternoon. Here his father is watching him and the dialogue reads:

"What did you do?"
"I went for a walk."
"Where did you go?"
"Up back of the Indian camp."
[Note: Not up *by* the Indian camp, thus locating the spot more precisely for Nick.]
"Did you see anything?"
[Note: Not anybody.]
"[Well] I saw something I didn't like."
[There is an insert in the MSS. "Something in Nick stopped. He did not know why."]

Here the second of the Madrid versions more closely approximates the final one; the two dialogues continue:

MS 728	MS 729
"What was it?"	"I saw your [girl] friend, Prudie."
["The Indians were all in town and the young] The young Mitchell girl was in the woods with Frank Murphy from Dungan's. . . ."	"Where was she?" "She was in the woods with Frank Washburn. I ran into them. They were having quite a time."

The Chartres version begins its variant of the conclusion at II B (335:10) in the scheme I have used; the two Madrid manuscripts advance the final form of the dialogue only fifteen lines (to 335:25) and then develop two similar variants of the second conclusion. In the writing of those fifteen lines of dialogue Hemingway made the decision to include Nick's father's experience and awareness of his son's feeling for Prudence as well as the significance of their meeting place, up *back* of the Indian camp.

Notes

1 The song, written by Septimus Winter "for the American minstrel shows of the 1860s," is reprinted in *The Annotated Mother Goose*, ed.

72

72

72 *Paul Smith*

William S. Baring-Gould and Ceil Baring-Gould (New York: Bramhall House, 1962), pp. 304–5.

2 See *Ernest Hemingway: Selected Letters, 1917–1961*, ed. Carlos Baker (New York: Scribner's, 1981); James D. Brasch and Joseph Sigman, *Hemingway's Library: A Composite Record* (New York: Garland, 1981); Michael S. Reynolds, *Hemingway's Reading, 1910–1940: An Inventory* (Princeton: Princeton University Press, 1981).

3 Page and line numbers refer to Ernest Hemingway, "Ten Indians," *The Short Stories of Ernest Hemingway* (New York: Scribner's, 1938).

4 That last question, answer, and reaction may inform some of the previous dialogue. Once the father says that he was up at the Indian camp, Nick asks whether he saw anybody. His father's reply, "The Indians were all in town getting drunk," might well strike Nick as an evasion; since he has been to Petoskey and has not seen Prudence, he knows that not all the Indians were in town. Thus his further question, "Didn't you see anybody *at all?*" suggests that Nick suspects his father is withholding something. His father, then, knowing what Nick suspects, tells him what he saw.

5 The manuscripts in the Hemingway Collection of the John F. Kennedy Library are items 202-C, 727–730. These are considered here in their sequence of composition and referred to as:

1. *The Chartres Version* (Item 202-C): Notebook dated "Ernest Hemingway/Chartres/September 27, 1925." It includes an ink manuscript of "Ten Indians" beginning, "The Indians came into Petoskey on the fourth . . . ," with pencil corrections, untitled. 16 pp.

2. *The Madrid Version* (Item 728): EH typescript, with pencil corrections, titled in pencil. EH has penciled "Madrid" on first page. 8 pp.
    (Item 729) EH typescript. Titled "A Broken Heart" in pencil, with ink and some pencil corrections. 8 pp.

3. *The Notebook Version* (Item 727): Manuscript fragments. Untitled pencil manuscript. Small notebook of graph paper.
    Item 730 is an uncorrected, untitled typescript. 6 pp.

6 See Appendix to this essay.

7 Carlos Baker, *Ernest Hemingway: A Life Story* (New York: Scribner's, 1969), p. 155. The notebook that contains this version also includes a rejected foreword to "The Lost Generation: A Novel"—an early title for *The Sun Also Rises*. It was revised some thirty years later

for *A Moveable Feast*, his elegy on his Parisian years and his apologia to Hadley.

8 Baker, *Life Story*, pp. 157, 169.

9 Item 202-C. Passages from the Chartres and Madrid versions which are cited for their narrative interest incorporate Hemingway's revisions and include my own minor corrections.

10 *Writers at Work: The Paris Review Interviews*, 2d Series, ed. George Plimpton (New York: Penguin, 1977), p. 232.

11 Item 729.

12 The pagination indicates that it is a continuation and revision from page 6 of the Madrid version.

The paragraph describes a heavy wind blowing the smoke off the tops of the stacks of ships moored in a river, and the sand from the cracks between paving stones, features of the landscape and weather during his stay at Spezia with Guy Hickock in January, 1927.

The four *Men Without Women* titles not on the notebook list are "A Banal Story," written in the summer of 1926 and probably included as an afterthought, and the three stories then in progress: "Che Ti Dice la Patria," "Hills like White Elephants," and "Ten Indians."

The "final" typescript (730) is close to the published version. It was typed from either 729, pp. 1–6, and a lost typescript of the notebook conclusion or a conflation of the two; no typist could have made sense of the notebook version.

13 Hemingway, *Selected Letters*, p. 250.

14 Ernest Hemingway, *Death in the Afternoon* (New York: Scribner's, 1932), p. 132. In "Hemingway's Early Manuscripts: The Theory and Practice of Omission," *Journal of Modern Literature*, 2 (1983), 268–88, I have considered the theory in its various forms from a letter to F. Scott Fitzgerald of December 1925 to "The Art of the Short Story," an introduction to an unpublished collection of stories of 1959. The contexts and occasions of the theory's several expressions suggest the different meanings it had, and purposes it served, for Hemingway.

15 Julian Smith, "Hemingway and the Thing Left Out," *Journal of Modern Literature*, No. 2 (1970–71), 169–82.

16 Constance Montgomery, *Hemingway in Michigan* (Waitsfield: Vermont Crossroads Press, 1977), pp. 96–101.

17 Baker, *Life Story*, pp. 13–29.

18 Mary Welsh Hemingway, *How It Was* (New York: Knopf, 1976), p. 102.

19 I learned of the circumstances of Prudence's death first from a letter from Donald St. John (15 August 1976). Since then Jack Mol, Chief of

Police in Charlevoix, MI, has confirmed that the following item in the *Petoskey Evening News*, 15 February 1918, p. 3. records the suicide of Prudence Boulton:

CHARLEVOIX MAN AND WOMAN COMMIT SUICIDE THERE FRIDAY MORNING

Richard Castle, of Charlevoix, and a young Indian girl with whom he had been living, committed suicide this morning about seven o'clock at the home of Castle's father at Charlevoix. They took strychnine. . . .

20 Baker, *Life Story*, pp. 39–47.
21 Item 382.
22 Baker, *Life Story*, pp. 182–84.

PART THREE

INTERPRETATIONS BIOGRAPHICAL AND CRITICAL

6. Max Westbrook

Grace under Pressure: Hemingway and the Summer of 1920

G RACE HEMINGWAY has been portrayed as a frustrated opera singer and failed mother. Supposedly, she unmanned her husband and, in the summer of 1920, tricked him into supporting her cruel decision to evict Ernest from the family home.[1]

A reading of the Hemingway family letters suggests that this characterization is inaccurate and unfair.[2] A corrective essay on behalf of Mrs. Hemingway might seem, at first, a gratuitous and dubious courtesy. Surviving friends and relatives do not need second hand judgments; and, normally, family disputes should be left to family privacy. Five members of the Hemingway family, however, have written books which include their versions of one dispute or another; and Ernest himself, though insistent on his right to privacy, frequently indulged in public or unguarded criticism of his parents.[3]

More important is the fact that our understanding of Hemingway's parents influences and often controls our interpretations of stories featuring Dr. and Mrs. Henry Adams. The Adams-Hemingway association is so established, so automatic, that it is almost impossible to read the words *the doctor's wife* and not see in our imagination Grace Hemingway as Destroyer, rather than Grace as she actually was or Mrs. Adams, the literary character. Indeed, according to the approach commonly identified as psy-

chological or Freudian, Hemingway's fiction should be inter-
preted in the context of family quarrels and on the assumption
that Grace was a destructive person.[4] The thesis of this approach
is that Ernest Hemingway never matured as a person or as an artist, his growth being stunted by adolescent resentment of his
mother's tyranny. The result, so the argument goes, is a fiction
limited to heroes who are either macho or emasculated and to
heroines who are either predators or mere sex objects. Hemingway was immature and dehumanized, and thus his fiction is
immature and dehumanized.

The Hemingway family letters do not suggest that Grace has
been totally misrepresented by the Freudian critics or by Hemingway's biographers. Rather, the evidence, which is mixed, has
been selected and presented with a bias for Ernest and against his
mother. What is needed is a judicious characterization of Grace
Hemingway, not the replacement of one extreme with another.
In brief, we read Hemingway's fictive mothers with glasses made
by a flawed prescription. The lenses need adjusting.

Grace Hemingway was a strong and dogmatic person. The
children did get on her nerves at times, and she did prefer the fine
arts to domestic chores. But she tried to understand and to support her husband and her children and be a loving and devoted
mother. The housework she is accused of neglecting was done by
domestic help paid with money she earned by giving singing lessons. To a considerable extent, Grace was a liberated woman
born too soon, and the much-loved Dr. Clarence was the family's
best nominee for the role of cloying Victorian "mother." The
family's problems, that is, were complex. There were no villains
and no angels, just some unusually talented and energetic human
beings, all of them fallible, all of them admirable. And if the
eventual disillusionment was more painful than with most families, the cause, in part, was that the good times had been, for at
least a dozen years, both extraordinarily fine and doomed.

The tensions and paradoxes characteristic of literature were
present, and the Freudian critics are right in saying that Ernest
kept on writing, more or less, about his family. It is also true that,
even late in life, he made unkind remarks about his parents, espe-

cially his mother.[5] Perhaps such indiscretions can be attributed to alcohol, perhaps not. Certainly the extent to which he achieved a sympathetic understanding of Grace and Clarence is subject to debate. My contention is that Hemingway *as artist* grew beyond the advertised hang-up with his parents and achieved a vision that is mature, realistic, varied, often bitter, and yet affirmative.[6] Hemingway's use of Grace as the model for Mrs. Adams does not constitute a license for biographical criticism. The mother in "The Doctor and the Doctor's Wife" is fundamentally different from Grace Hemingway, and the mother in "Soldier's Home" is quite different from both Mrs. Hemingway and Mrs. Adams.

Grace and fictive versions of Grace have been merged because what we know about her has come primarily from two biased reporters, her sons. Whether innocent or guilty, Ernest was profoundly hurt when his parents "kicked" him out, the climax of conflicts which had begun earlier and which were soon to be heightened when Dr. and Mrs. Hemingway rejected his early publications. Under such circumstances, Ernest could not be a judicious and reliable source. Leicester, whose selected presentation of the family letters has been the major available source for others, charmingly confesses to hero worship of his big brother.[7] Granted the difference in age and the magnetic personality of the accomplished and successful Ernest, who could blame him? Grace's side in the family quarrels has been presented by her oldest daughter, Marcelline; but Marcelline was not present at Windemere in the climactic summer of 1920. She and Ernest were estranged, and her brief defense of Mrs. Hemingway— though fair and accurate so far as I know—has carried no weight.[8]

What happened in the summer of 1920, according to the story told by Ernest and Leicester, is that Clarence was innocently busy with his medical practice in Chicago while Ernest was vacationing with the family at Windemere and working to develop his writing skills. Grace supposedly became angry with Ernest because of an irreconcilable difference in temperament, because she did not believe that writing was work, and because Ernest had bravely opposed her self-indulgence in building a separate cabin for herself with money that should have been used to send the younger daughters to college. After winning Clarence's support with false information against Ernest, Grace is then said to have distorted a midnight picnic into a crime justifying Ernest's expulsion forever from the family home.

Ironically, there is enough information in Leicester's book to refute this standard version of what happened. The two most important pieces of previously available but consistently ignored information are that Clarence was at Windemere long enough to make his own decision—without depending on reports from Grace—and that he wrote two "kick out" letters *before* Grace finally spoke up in a way that could not be ignored.

The calendar of events needs to be established. On July 1, 1920, Clarence wrote Grace from Chicago about his plans to come up to the cabin.[9] After a two-week vacation at Windemere, Clarence returned to Chicago and promptly—on July 18—wrote to Grace at Windemere: "I have written Ernest. . . . I have advised him to go with Ted down Traverse City way and work at good wages and at least cut down his living expenses."[10] Writing to Grace on July 22, Clarence referred again to his first letter of dismissal to Ernest: "I have written to him that I wanted him to get busy and be more self supporting and respectful and leave the Bay and go to work down Traverse City way." In that same letter of July 22, we learn that Clarence has written a second "kick-out" letter to Ernest: "I will write to him and enclose herewith for you to read and hand to him."[11]

On July 25, Clarence wrote to Grace saying he had "received" her "big envelope letter with the letter of Thursday evening, after Ernest's birthday supper."[12] Leicester took this to mean that Grace prepared "a ceremonial dinner . . . while getting ready to slip the guest of honor a letter asking him to kindly leave the family premises."[13] The evidence, however, from passages Leicester chose for quotation, is that Grace did not provide a birthday feast topped off with an ill-timed letter of dismissal. Clarence's two remarks—"You surely gave him and his friends a good time"[14] and "the wonderful 21st supper you wrote about"[15]—do not suggest an ugly scene. Clarence's July 25 letter, furthermore, reaffirms his understanding of what was going on: "I hope he went back to the Bay with Bill and that you read and have mailed him the letter I wrote to him to stay away from Windemere until he was again invited."[16] Thus it is clear that Clarence considered his letters to be decisions requiring Ernest to leave and that he expected Ernest to be gone by the time his second and confirming letter of dismissal had arrived. The conclusion must be that Clarence took the lead or was at least a full partner in the decision.

Grace's testimony, completely omitted by Leicester, also indicates that her actions followed Clarence's. On July 27, Grace wrote to Clarence: "I called Ernest and Beumice into the livingroom & told them to pack up all their things and leave this morning, that I did not wish to see them again this summer."[17] A copy of Grace's letter of dismissal begins with a formal notation: "Copy of letter handed to E.M.H. Tues, July 27th 1920."[18] The ink is different from that used in making the copy, suggesting that the notation was made after the letter had been copied; but the handwriting is clearly Grace's, and a variant appears on the envelope: "Copy of letter handed to Ernest Miller Hemingway July 27th 1920 at Windemere."[19]

On July 28, Clarence wrote Grace that he had "received a very definite letter of denial from Ernest."[20] Ernest, that is, was responding to a decision made by Clarence and not to the letter Grace handed her son on the twenty-seventh. This reading of the sequence is confirmed by a July 30 letter from Clarence to Grace—"Ernest's last letter to me after reading the one I sent you to hand him, does not require an answer"[21]—and by a July 28 letter from Grace to Clarence: "Your letter I handed to Ernest on Monday Morning [July 26]."[22]

What is supposed to have happened is that Grace conceived and initiated the whole affair, unjustly and on her own, deceiving the innocent Clarence, who was practicing medicine in Chicago and thus ignorant of the true story. What actually happened is that Clarence spent the first two weeks of July at Windemere, then returned to Chicago and promptly wrote Ernest two letters telling him to leave and go to work. Grace handed Ernest her letter of dismissal the day after Ernest received Clarence's second letter of dismissal.

The lightly dismissed midnight picnic also needs reconsideration. On the morning of the twenty-sixth, Grace handed Ernest his father's second letter of dismissal. "After reading it," Grace writes, "he chopped a few pieces of wood, enough for 2 days, about, then he tried to fix the pier, and *did* after a fashion though it is very wobbly."[23] On July 27, Grace wrote to Clarence explaining what happened next:

> Of course Ernest called me every name he could think of, and said everything vile about me; but I kept my tongue and did not get hysterical. The immediate cause was the pounding on my front door of Miss Loomis & Mrs. Loomis at 3 o'clock this morning with a lamp in hand—wanted to know of their 13 year old girls—Elizabeth Loomis and her little friend and what those men wanted with them. I made them come in while I investigated for I felt sure our children were all asleep. They had gone to bed quite ostentatiously—I ran up in my nightgown . . . and found Ernest & Beummie's, Ursula's & Sunny's beds empty and unslept in.
>
> Mrs. Loomis was in a towering rage, and said she would pack up & take her whole family back to Oak Park, unless we could do something to get rid of those grown men loafing around. . . .
>
> Oh! but he is a cruel son. I got supper for him when he came home at 9 o'clock, last night, and sat down with him, for I had had none, and he insulted me every minute; said "all I read was moron literature," that Dr. Frank Crane who writes such glorious helpful articles in the *American* was the "Moron's Maeterlinck" and asked me if I read the *Atlantic Monthly* just so some one would see me doing it.
>
> I did not explain to you that the escapade last night was a plan of the Loomis boys and girls to have midnight eats, and fire, up the lake, not wicked; except in the deceit practiced, and the general lawlessness that Ernest instills into all young boys and girls.
>
> He is distinctly a menace to youth.
>
> I think our girls have had a very good lesson but its most killed their mother.[24]

The feelings of someone named Mrs. Loomis may seem unimportant when reading Ernest Hemingway in the 1980s, but she awoke to find her thirteen-year-old daughter missing, along with her daughter's thirteen-year-old playmate, for whom she was responsible. It was 3:00 A.M., and they were in a sparsely populated country of lake and wilderness. Mrs. Loomis and Mrs. Hemingway could not chuckle and go back to bed. They could not say, "It's all right. Give him time, and he'll write *The Sun Also Rises.*" Their rage, to any responsible parent, is understandable.

From the viewpoint of Ernest and the midnight revelers, the episode was innocent, and Grace recognizes this in telling Clarence that the outing was "not wicked." What has been omitted from previous accounts, however, is, first, Grace's version and, second, the fact that three things happened on the same day. On Monday morning, July 26, Ernest received the second letter of dismissal from his father. That same evening, at a nine o'clock supper, he insulted his mother gratuitously; and, at some unknown time during that day, he agreed to accompany a party of youngsters who wanted to slip out of bed after midnight and go for a picnic. Even if we sympathize with Ernest and not with his mother, the timing does not suggest that Grace Hemingway was the villain. One could even argue that in responding to his father's dismissal by insulting his mother and leading a midnight escapade Ernest was insisting on his own eviction.

Clearly, the midnight picnic was not an isolated event which Grace, because of self-serving headaches, expanded into a pseudocrisis. She had been under considerable pressure for a very long time, and her efforts to act positively—rather than submit to pain—were often met with resistance. Her separate cabin, said to be another example of her selfishness, is also a different story when told from her viewpoint.[25]

The story, as told by Grace, begins with the draft of a letter to Clarence. There is no first page, no date, and the draft begins in midsentence. The year would be 1919, possibly in May:

. . . until the agony in my spinal nerves forced me to lie
down and then up again and at it, day in and day out. Too

exhausted to swim or go anywhere when the opportunity offered. These have been my summers for many years until the
very sight of Windemere brings the tears to my eyes and a
sob to my throat.

This year, hope, that springs eternal in the human breast,
bade me rejoice, for I said to my husband, when he was not
in a contentious mood, "Would it not be lovely to have a little 'haven of refuge' on our hill, a little shack where we
could sleep, and be alone, for a while or have just the little
children with us"—and he said "go ahead, look into it and
see what can be done."[26]

Grace then describes herself "happily" drawing up plans, only to
find that the cost, "almost $2,000," was too high. Working with a
different builder, Grace then revised the plans to get the cost
down to "approximately $1,100" and later to a proposed ceiling
of $1,000.

Grace was an artist trying to take care of six children. She
wanted the cabin as relief from pressures, paid for it with money
she had earned, and handled the details herself in order to spare
her husband. Drafts of letters to Mr. Morford, the builder, make
this clear. "Now as Dr. has many things to take care of," Grace
writes, "I want to say to you that I am assuming the entire Ex-
pense of this building with my own Earnings."[27] In another draft,
Grace draws a neat sketch of the cabin for Mr. Morford and asks,
"Would this be less expensive and more artistic?"[28] Another
stresses her willingness to change the materials to keep the expenses down. On May 15, 1919, Grace drafted a letter to Mr.
Morford which suggests that she has been driven to appealing
outside the family for sympathy:

> Now, with these changes I wonder whether you could keep
> it within our limit of $1,000? I want so much to have this lit-
> tle house that I cannot bear to give it up for the present,
> though everybody is saying "What a foolish time to think of
> building."
> What do you think about it?[29]

Mr. Morford must have approved, or at least Grace was pleased with his work, but Clarence was adamantly opposed. On May 26, 1919, Clarence drafted a letter to the builder. The draft is unfinished and may or may not have been completed and mailed, but Clarence's thinking is clear:

> I have learned my dear wife Grace Hall-Hemingway is expecting to build a cottage on top of a hill known as "Red Top Mountain" on Lot 1., Section 10. Bay Township across the lake from our Windemere Bacon side of Walloon Lake. This [I] want you to know, that she assumes herself without my advice and agrees to pay for herself with her own money. She holds the title to the land. I own no land in my name. All was placed in her name. I am unable to understand the necessity.[30]

On the same day, Clarence wrote to Grace stating his opposition. He called her plan impractical, made it clear that she would have to pay all expenses from her own money, and added that he would write Mr. Morford and deny any responsibility for paying. This is rather strange, since Clarence had given his initial approval and since Grace had made it clear from the start that she would pay for the cabin with her own money. Clarence acts as if he is being badgered and tricked, implying that he must take steps to keep Grace from obligating him financially and against his expressed wishes.

Nonetheless, Grace responded as if she had to have Clarence's approval to spend her own money, drafting a long, carefully marshalled series of arguments. The draft, undated, is partially in outline form. "I have studied all your objections," she writes, "and will classify them under three heads." The first is "Those referring to the investment." Grace then quotes and answers each of her husband's objections. "Improvement does not appeal to average purchaser therefore could not sell," for example, is answered with the assertion that she wants "to live in it," not sell it. The second category, "Those referring to the site," is concerned with argument and counter-argument about prevailing wind directions, drinking water, wash water, wood supply, refuse disposal, soil conditions, and accessibility. The third category, "Those referring to me and my needs," is the longest, turning finally from the outline format into the following poignant statement:

> It has been my purpose for 14 years ever since I purchased the farm in the face of strong opposition *and much abusive language* to build a little cottage on this very hill. It appealed to me so that I bought the farm to carry out this plan. That it has been steadily thwarted up to the present time not only piled up disappointment—as each year against my advice & desires the farm was leased to thieving tenants who stole from the place wood and crops, fruit and the very seed sent to them to plant. When finally they left having robbed the place to their utmost I renewed my pleas to build even the farm house which would be a stepping stone to my long looked forward to little nest on the hill top and which would appeal to even a farmer's sense of values in property. This was thwarted. I have gone faithfully 21 summers to the same place. Windemere which was very pleasant and adequate for 8 or 9 years but after my father's death & two subsequent attacks of typhoid fever which undermined [the last two words are inserted, fragmented] to say nothing of other causes the place became hateful to me, so much so that I had a nervous break down summer after summer when ever I was forced to spend a summer there, shut in by the hills & lake, no view, no where to go, acting the part of the family drudge, standing at sink & cook stove.[31]

So Grace felt that she had been appointed the family drudge, though she was accused of neglecting the duties of a housewife. Ernest, for his part, thought he was doing too much work for the family, while his parents thought he was doing too little. Who could adjudicate such disputes? One thing we can learn from the family letters is that the breakup did not start in 1920 or in 1919. However implacable Grace seemed to Ernest, she was and had been for a long time an individualist who was nonetheless

devoted to traditional values. Returning from a visit to her
brother Leicester, Grace received on January 4, 1904, a letter
concerning some undescribed quarrel. Leicester asks forgiveness
for his "brutal plainness in criticizing" Grace, asserts that he
spoke out of love, and warns his sister that they "have both been
handicapped by a careless bringing up." It is obvious that Grace
has been found guilty of some breach of etiquette, for Leicester
assures her that "true refinement of manners are absolutely essen-
tial." She must not "handicap" her "children by neglecting their
training along these lines."[32]

As we learn from Marcelline, there were many other breaches
of decorum by Grace, plus a lifelong habit of variations from the
norm. She shocked the neighborhood by riding a bicycle, showed
off to her children by kicking up to a lamp over her head and
turning it off with her toes, took saw and hammer and made fur-
niture for Grace Cottage, published original songs, wrote verse,
gave lectures on classical literature, learned how to paint and
made money doing it, and late in life took seriously to a Christian
version of spiritualism. Above all, she was a genuinely talented
singer with a phenomenal memory for music.[33] Comparisons with
Ernest are inescapable, though his variations from the norm were
more shocking, his walking on broken glass, for example. Ernest
held spiritualism in contempt, but he carried good luck charms
and respected the power of both good and bad omens. His memory, like his mother's, was said to be remarkable.[34] Grace's problems, in a general sense, were comparable to her son's problems.
Both wanted to create and thus needed solitude, both wanted a
home and family yet found domestic and family responsibilities
an interference, and both tried to compromise between the two.
As with F. Scott Fitzgerald and others, Hemingway quarreled
with his mother, at least in part, because she practiced what he
considered a contemptible version of values embarrassingly close
to his own. The contrast between Pilar reading Robert Jordan's
palm and a Christian seance is instructive. Pilar sees death. Grace
saw Christian beatitudes confirmed.[35]

Clarence's problems also had a long birthing and also need to
be understood as those of an individualist who was nonetheless
dedicated to traditional values and thus inclined to dichotomize

reality. Clarence was an unusually good person, a dedicated and innovative physician, and a man who suffered, early on, from serious problems. It was his habit to write daily, when he and Grace were parted, and to write in a tone that was often martyred, cloying, perhaps obsessive. As early as 1904, he apologizes for missing a day. This was to become a major characteristic of Clarence's letters, the apology being followed by the explanation that he failed because he performed some other duty for some other person.

On October 18, 1908, Grace wrote to Clarence at the New York Lying-In Hospital, where he had gone to study obstetrics. She encourages him not to read *Oak Leaves* and "get into the old train of thought" but to rest and relax.[36] In a letter dated October 17, concerning Clarence's plans to vacation before coming home, Grace asks, "Do you want me to let the local press know about this vacation? Don't you think it perhaps wiser to let them keep the 1st idea in their minds that you are taking 'post grad' work in N.Y.?"[37] Grace does not say what the "old train of thought" is or why it might be invoked by a reading of the Oak Park newspaper; and the quotation marks around the words *post grad* may have been intended to indicate merely an abbreviation. It is clear, however, that Grace thought her husband's problems so serious that his vacation cure should be kept secret.

The letters of both Clarence and Grace, in fact, are characterized by a troubled determination to do what is right and by references to serious problems within. On September 5, 1914, Grace wrote Clarence from Nantucket about her own vacation cure: "I am in hopes of coming home rested and benefited, so I can be of help and not a hindrance to each of you."[38] On May 5, 1917, Clarence makes a comparable statement. Writing to Grace from Oak Park, he states that he will have a hernia operation on the seventh, expects "without any fear or sentiment" that he will do fine, and concludes, "I shall hope to return to my home duties the twenty second of May a better and stronger father and more able to carry on my life responsibilities."[39] Both shared their son's stoicism but unfortunately expressed it in a rhetoric opposite to the uncomplaining manner that Jake Barnes begins to learn and Thomas Hudson has mastered.[40] Grace responded to Clarence's letter about his operation, for example, by saying that even though broken herself she still has the bravery to think of her husband, that she is more concerned with his not feeling guilty than with her own suffering: "Don't think for a moment that your going to the hospital for a necessary operation has made me ill. I have been breaking down steadily since a year ago."[41]

Such protestations of concern for others may have, of course, their own integrity. Dr. and Mrs. Hemingway, I think, were two fine human beings. Still, the repeated claim of a devotion to duty when combined with confessions of intense suffering is a rhetorical trap, an invitation to self-pity, and may explain why Ernest became so contemptuous of people who agonized in public.[42] One striking example—a letter from Clarence to Grace, dated August 12, 1917—is further evidence that the family breakup had a long beginning and cannot be blamed on Grace alone. Ernest, Clarence writes,

is just as headstrong and abusive and threatening as ever. I am sure if he can *work* & *board* at Dilmuths & pay his board it would be *good* for him. I am about to my limit with the *Six* alone. I try to make them happy and the more I do for them, the more they take advantage of me. No word whatever from Uncle Leicester. Erniest [*sic*] had not written him up to yesterday. He is so pessimistic, says it wouldn't do any good. Brother Tyler told him, he could get Ernest a job on the *Kansas City Star*, & Ernest could live at his house until he was well started. . . .
Would appreciate very much if you would put your mind on Some of these problems and offer suggestions. . . . I made all very happy making three extra fine *blue berry pies* between 10:30 a.m. [and] 11:15 a.m.—"Just like Mother used to *eat*."[43]

Thus protestations of love and duty are undercut with bitterness, the word *eat* being underlined to make certain Grace does not miss the dig.

During the first two months of the summer of 1920, the tone of Clarence's letters to Grace and the children became even more

plaintive, long-suffering, possessive. Featuring repeated asser-
tions of his eagerness to do everything he can to make his family
happy and including an astounding attention to details, the letters are replete with martyred protestations of his devotion and
their negligence. He is working late hours, the weather is cruelly
hot, but he will do all he is physically able to do for his family.
When he does not hear from Windemere, he writes to ask if something is wrong. When a letter from Grace does not mention Carol
and Leicester, Clarence writes to ask if they are sick. There is
even something poignant, under the circumstances, about the
fact that Clarence numbers his daily letters, as if he wanted
Grace to see the count, the quantitative record of his devotion to
family duty.

Clarence's "mothering" tone is especially clear in a letter of
June 27. There has been a terrible train wreck and a difficult
delivery in which the baby died, but Clarence is writing to "dear
Gracie and all at Windemere" even though his arms are "nearly
numb from the extra strain last night" and he can "hardly hold
the place on the typewriter." This is not to appeal for sympathy,
he explains, but merely to apologize for any "mistakes" he might
make. Then, proving his devotion under any circumstances,
Clarence mentions a church bulletin, enclosed, which he is certain will give them pleasure. Finally, he is also sending them a
copy of today's *Oak Leaves*.[44]

Clarence's letter of June 28 is quoted extensively in *My Brother,
Ernest Hemingway*, but Leicester omits the close: "We must
believe that all things work together for good for those who love
the Lord. Pray for me my darlings, as I need your help to keep
you all having the good vacation."[45] This is, I think, the keynote
of Clarence's letters: he is working to the point of exhaustion; the
weather is extraordinarily hot in Chicago; he is happy that his
family is having such a wonderful vacation up on the cool lake; he
is delighted to take care of any minor detail that might give them
the slightest pleasure; and, though longing to be on the lake with
his family, he is happy to be able to work hard and suffer so much
to provide so well for his family.

Frequently, Clarence's description of his own dedication is

contrasted with the negligence of others. Marcelline's trunk arrives, on June 29, and "Daddy was here to attend to it, so again she is in luck. No word from her." Clarence then states it overtly: "I am planning all the time for you darlings, as unselfishly as I can, so there will be something to go on with next Fall and Winter."[46] On July 1, just before leaving for his own vacation at Windemere, Clarence makes a characteristic apology: "I was so overworked from early to late yesterday that I did not get time to qrite [sic] you."[47] After returning to Chicago, Clarence wrote on July 16 that he was "so glad to be here to help in many ways."[48]

Courteously omitted by Leicester are his father's letters indicating that the summer's "insurrection" included the Hemingway daughters. On September 1, 1920, with Grace continuing her vacation, Clarence wrote her about the impending return to Chicago of their daughters:

> I will have their rooms all clean and spick and span, and
> they are to keep them so, or in some way suffer the penalties
> of "Insurrection." There will be no "Sob-stuff" from me.
> They will get into the game and do right or they will wish
> they had. Tell them to do right and there will be no trouble
> whatever. I am to help them get an education, if they will
> accept it. If not they will have to go to "Work" and pay
> their own freight. See? I am sorry for you my darling. It is
> too bad that the daughters who have had so many priveleges
> should pester you so by their great lack of appreciation of
> their mother's love. Keep up Courage, that is my pass word,
> one day at a time, always try and do our best.[49]

Once the girls returned to Chicago, Clarence may have pushed with excessive rigor. On September 13, he wrote to Grace:

> Marcelline does not see why I should be so anxious about
> the girls, and they are as you know some rebellious at times.
> I am firm and gentle and it would surprise you to see Sunny
> see it as I do while Ursula is going *off*! She cools off after a
> whoile [sic], but I can see in her Ernest's teachings.
> No need to worry.[50]

Just two days later, Clarence seems to have changed his mind:

> Get thoroughly rested and at peace with the world before
> you return. I want so much for you to regain the love and
> affection of all your daughters, and it will only be possible
> when all are rested and in reasonable frames of mind. I am
> doing the unselfish thing to stay here to protect and guide
> the girls and so far have succeeded and see no reason why
> they should not continue to improve all the time.[51]

The implication is that the girls have criticized their mother for
her role in the quarrels at Windemere and that Clarence, at least
to some extent, has been persuaded.[52]

Leicester's presentation of this September 15 letter has left us
with a quite different impression. First, Leicester introduces his
selected quotation with a sentence implying that Clarence's trust
in Grace was collapsing before the evidence of her perfidy:
"Another letter came from Ernest later and Father wavered even
more in his belief that all had been as represented to him."
Second, Leicester selects a single sentence on the subject of the
Hemingway daughters, one suggesting that all is well: "The girls
are all doing very well in school." Third, having set the context,
Leicester then quotes a passage that could be taken only as damaging to Grace: "If you falsely accused him [Ernest], be sure to
beg his pardon, even if he had made many mistakes. For false ac-
cusations grow more sore all the time and separate dear friends
and relatives."[53]

And thus have we come to believe that Grace falsely accused
Ernest to gain the support of an innocent Clarence in her plans to
evict her son from the family home. It is far more likely that
Clarence, who was much braver in correspondence than in direct
confrontation, was wavering because of his own lack of strength.
His September 18 letter to Ernest, certainly, is revisionist history,
a distortion of complex events he had witnessed and a flat denial
of the decision he had made himself: "In as much as there were a
few misunderstandings between you and your mother this summer I am sure if you will make this effort [that is, close up Winde-

mere for the winter], you may right the matters and I will continue to pray that you will love one another as you should."[54] As
Clarence had to have known, the family problems were not
merely "a few misunderstandings," were not simply a matter of
the relations between Grace and Ernest, and would not be re-
paired by Ernest's willingness to do a simple chore for the family.
Ernest had to have known, too; and it may well be that some of
his harsh feelings toward his mother were caused by the fact that
the father he loved but could not respect was unmanned not by
Grace but by himself.[55] Grace, it is clear from the family letters,
worked hard to bolster her husband, but she was guilty of having
the strength that Clarence lacked.

Perhaps the climax of the Hemingways' "dangerous summer" is
a letter from Clarence to Grace dated October 2, 1920, and written apparently from Windemere, where Clarence had gone to secure the cabin (Ernest must have rejected his father's simplistic
proposal for a solution).[56] The spelling and punctuation are probably an indication of Clarence's emotional state:

> My darling I love you,—
> Herewith check for One Thousand Dollars, in Case of
> some onforseen accident I should not return, also Keys,—Are
> Vault Box #686—Therein Liberty Bonds & Emergency
> funds.—Ford Keys & Spark Coils in little basket & gas
> turned off with Stilson wrench/.—I hope to be home by Oct
> 11. 1920
> Much love—
> Clarence[57]

Without belaboring the implications of a possible suicide, we can
assert that what seems to have happened in the summer of 1920—
a son's adolescent rebellion against a Victorian and tyrannical
mother—was but the manifest expression of far more complex
problems. Essentially, Clarence and Grace were paradoxical
combinations of determination and insecurity. Both were talented, energetic, loving, moral, and independent; yet both suffered from within and suffered severely. Life was full of wonders,

but the center seemed in constant jeopardy. Challenges were to be met head on and duties performed without fail, but the capacity to do so needed constant reinforcement.

We cannot know the extact intentions behind Ernest's dismissal of his complicated parents, one with reluctance, the other with bitterness. When he called his mother "a bitch,"[58] was he telling the truth as he saw it, indulging in dramatics, simply defending himself, rewriting the past? A letter in the John F. Kennedy Library raises another possibility. On December 22, 1920, Ernest wrote to Grace saying he was obeying her wishes, behaving well, and working hard.[59] The letter is chatty and affectionate, making one think the eviction of 1920 may have been less damaging than the parents' rejection of Ernest's early publications.[60] Perhaps all of these conjectures have their element of accuracy. What can be said with confidence is that Ernest purged himself of his parents' Victorian taboos and then wrote about a world in which the good and honest life is jeopardized by the possiblity that values may be illusions, by betrayal and weakness and sentimentality from within, and by indifferent powers and circumstances and authorities from without.

It is well known that Ernest adopted his father's love of fishing and hunting and good foods and shared his father's remarkable capacity for attending to details. In the Hemingway family letters, we find that the words Ernest used in testing fidelity within the family—*loyalty, betrayal*—are the same words used by his parents. The money analogy used by Grace in her "kick-out" letter has seemed absurd, but, as critics have shown, Ernest wrote effectively and carefully about the relation between money and ethical duty.[61] In generously hosting guests and insisting on taking care of every detail—at Key West, for example—Ernest repeated his parents' performance at Windemere, his good-humored graciousness turning, at times without warning, to resentment. With hindsight, we can see that there was something threatening the good times at Windemere: Grace's desperately needing an escape cottage, Clarence's shocking letter of October 2, implying possible suicide, Ernest's responding to his father's second letter of dismissal by bawling out his mother and lending his adult approval to the midnight picnic. And there is something threatening the good times of Jake's little family at Pamplona, the peacefulness of Frederic and Catherine in Switzerland, and—in a different sense—Thomas Hudson's sense of fulfillment at the beginning of *Islands in the Stream*.[62]

Living in what seemed to them an either/or world (we do it right, or else it is all wrong), Clarence and Grace fell into a rhetoric of absolutes. Their talented son's rhetoric to describe a realistic and far more complex version of right and wrong became, virtually, a new dialect of the English language. Basic to Hemingway's fiction, perhaps a rhetorical version of his iceberg theory, is the unsaid, the unvocalized lower layer. In its simplest form, one character sees realities another character does not see and—because of youth, a bad will, or illusions that have become internalized—need not be told.

"The Doctor and the Doctor's Wife," for example, is a story about what Dr. Adams discovers within himself and cannot possibly explain to his wife or to Nick or, indeed, scarcely accommodate within his own consciousness. In reading the story, we have slighted the unsaid and focused on Mrs. Adams as the Devouring Mother because we assume that Ernest was accurate in his comments on Grace and that Mrs. Adams is a portrait of Mrs. Hemingway.[63]

Certainly the model for Mrs. Adams is Grace Hemingway; but as Hemingway said himself, fictional characters based on actual people are *re*-created in the author's imagination and take on their own integrity.[64] Grace avoided bright lights because she had suffered from scarlet fever as a child, had been blind for a time, and, upon suddenly regaining her sight, found thereafter that bright lights were excruciatingly painful.[65] With Mrs. Adams, hiding from sunlight is obviously a comment on her character. She prefers her closeted world of eternal and total goodness. Her husband's suggestion that Boulton may have acted with a bad will is dismissed immediately and without need for evidence. Grace, by contrast, was fully aware of evil, could recognize it, and—as shown when she gave the game wardens a good dressing down for aggressive rudeness and for abuse of their badges—could be stouthearted in standing up to it.[66] Mrs. Adams does not, as so often claimed, dominate her males.[67] She asks the Doctor what he is going to do next, he tells her, and there is no evidence suggesting he needs her approval. Nick's supposed defiance of his mother is actually a very casual putting off of an indefinite request: "*If* you see Nick, dear, will you tell him his mother wants to see him?"[68] And the screen door the Doctor is usually said to slam because of his humble apology is a trap for critics. The Doctor does not slam the door. "The screen door slammed behind him" (p. 102) means it slammed of its own accord, the spring snapping it shut because the Doctor's mind is elsewhere. His minimal apology, his not arguing with his wife about Boulton's intentions, the separate bedrooms, and, especially, his not telling her what he is really thinking are all signs of their relationship: the Doctor protects his wife from reality because she is constitutionally unable to face reality. Surrounded by defenses, Mrs. Adams is so totally committed to illusions that enlightening her is not even mentioned as a possibility.

Mrs. Adams thus adds one more turn of the screw to the story, for if the Doctor's idea about Boulton's intentions is immediately dismissed, how could he possibly share with her the much more shocking discovery he has made about himself? The story, then, is about the unsaid. Frustrated by Boulton's cool insolence, Dr. Adams breaks out, from some unacknowledged lower layer, and makes a tough-guy assertion: "If you call me Doc once again, I'll knock your eye teeth down your throat" (p. 101). The act itself, knocking a man's teeth down his throat, is violent enough. The specific detail, "eye teeth," is an appropriate threat for tough guys capable of selecting with precision the physical parts to be damaged. When the battle-wise Boulton says, "Oh, no, you won't, Doc" (p. 101), he speaks as one who knows his man. Of course Dr. Adams will not do any such thing. He is not that kind of person. He is not even the kind of person who voices such boasts. Physical cowardice and humiliation are subliminal tones in the story. They contribute to density, realism. But the story beneath the visible events is that the moral, controlled, and determinedly responsible good Doctor finds a part of himself he is shocked to find.

Thus the drama of "The Doctor and the Doctor's Wife" lies in discoveries that cannot be voiced or shared. If Mrs. Adams cannot

believe that Boulton would intentionally start a fuss to get out of
work, how could she possibly believe that her civilized husband
has found himself capable of wanting to knock Boulton's eye teeth
down his throat? Dr. Adams's distance from his own inner self is
played off the distance—the separate rooms, the Christian Scien-
tist married to a medical doctor—between the husband and wife.
The Doctor is unable to handle something deep within, and the
unopened medical journals—something else unhandled—are thus
an irritating aside.

Following a paratactical contrast of her religious tracts with his
shotgun, Hemingway creates an even more unnerving act of discovery by describing an apparently irrelevant action. Frustrated
with Boulton, his wife, and with himself, Dr. Adams sits "on his
bed now, cleaning a shotgun. He pushed the magazine full of the
heavy yellow shells and pumped them out again. They were scat-
tered on the bed" (p. 102). Talking to his wife, alone and unseen,
he wipes "his gun carefully with a rag. He pushed the shells back
in against the spring of the magazine. He sat with the gun on his
knees. He was very fond of it" (p. 102).

Why does Dr. Adams load the shotgun, unload it, and load it
again? Obviously, he would like to do a good deal more to Boulton than simply hit him. He is not going to shoot anyone, of
course, any more than he is going to become an efficient brawler.
He is merely toying with the dark desire he had discovered, and,
ironically, it is Mrs. Adams who accidentally ends the game:

> "No. I can't really believe that any one would do a thing
> of that sort intentionally."
> The doctor stood up and put the shotgun in the corner
> behind the dresser. (p. 102)

The word "intentionally" is immediately followed by the action
of putting the gun aside. Of course he cannot do it. Why play
games with impossible intentions? But the dark desire is
nonetheless real, and the gun is apparently set aside—contrary to
the practice of good hunters—still loaded.

Dr. Adams has come to a place he does not want to be, and the
chain of events began with his own choice, his *choosing* to believe

that logs adrift on his beach would not be retrieved by their owners, his probably racist or class-conscious resentment of Boulton's lack of respect. He does not know what to do, where to go. The dock is a place he had to walk away from, aching with fury and frustration. The conversation with his unrealistic wife is certainly no relief. So he thinks of going for a walk, finds Nick wanting to go "where there's black squirrels," and says, "All right. . . . Let's go there" (p. 103).

"Soldier's Home" also illustrates the need for critics to see that Hemingway's literary mothers should not be equated with characterizations of Grace, biased and unbiased. When Hemingway found the germ for a story in his family life, the artist would take over and—as with actual people made into literary characters—rewrite the actual into something created and quite different from the original.[69] Mrs. Krebs is a stereotypical mother of her time and place. She is quite different from the Grace Hemingway who sang opera and painted pictures, who struggled throughout her life to assert her own individual self apart from the role assigned by society.

"Soldier's Home" is in part the story of a young man who wants to reject the life his parents have chosen for him. Thus it describes a situation that Mrs. Hemingway, Mrs. Krebs, and millions of other similar and dissimilar parents have found themselves in. What sets it apart from other tellings of this archetypal story is signaled by its most famous exchange:

> "Don't you love your mother, dear boy?"
> "No," Krebs said. (p. 152)

The pathetic and innocent-sounding "Don't you love your mother" is a sentimental tyranny, a mother's demand for the loyalty oath. It is a rhetorical trap common to life and to literature, and it is a characteristic strategy in Hemingway's art, most notably in *A Farewell to Arms* when the battle police ask retreating officers why they have betrayed their country.[70]

The verbal mechanism of the trap is the blurring together of two quite different subjects. With Mrs. Krebs, *don't you want to settle down and live the life we want you to live* is blurred with *don't you love your mother.* Krebs, for his part, has been to war and found that—*contra* Nick Adams—he liked it and now wants to talk about it, though society assumes he will have been horrified by combat and unwilling to discuss it. Krebs will try to love his mother, or at least avoid hurting her, but he knows he cannot become a Charlie Simmons and marry the girl next door and clerk in a store.

In urging her son to settle down, Mrs. Krebs is playing Joe Mc-Carthy on behalf of community values. She pretends that obeying mother is the same as loving mother, and yet Hemingway draws her portrait without viciousness. Mrs. Krebs is herself a victim of the indoctrination she is now trying to pass on to her son. Krebs's "No" is a defense against the rhetorical trap, a rejection of love which claims obedience as the price of continued love. Mrs. Krebs speaks as a representative of community values, and Krebs answers her accordingly. But in cheapening himself to make a clichéd apology and in going through the motions of prayer when he cannot pray honestly, Krebs is caught in the trap after all, at least for the moment. He is desperate not to hurt his mother, though he does, and she is incapable of hearing the truth. Like Dr. Adams and so many others, Krebs will have to live with his secret burden, the unsaid, the lower layer he has discovered but cannot explain, certainly not to his mother.

"Soldiers Home" is not the story of Windemere, but the scene in which Mrs. Krebs forces her son to kneel is—like Hemingway's eviction—the immediate and not the sufficient cause of a fundamental displacement. What lay behind Hemingway's break with his family was not simply the events of July 1920. There was the whole story of Clarence and Grace, sisters and neighbors and friends, of religious and community values in conflict with a developing young artist who loved much of what he learned from his parents but who kept discovering realities his parents could only call blasphemous. And what lies behind Krebs's leaving home is not merely a supposedly dominating mother. There is the whole story of college in Kansas, of veterans who say what society wants them to say, of pretty girls in fashionable clothes who are products of their time and place, and of parents who lead narrow lives and want their son to do the same.

Nonetheless, Krebs at the end of the story and Hemingway in 1920 do not leave home to seek a life of isolation; and when we give excessive weight to Leicester's interpretation of what happened during a single period of two weeks, ignoring the broadranging experiences and stories he also recorded, then we are unfair not only to Grace but also to Ernest. Like Harry in "The Snows of Kilimanjaro," Ernest could, when hurt or angry, blame everything on a convenient woman, even while knowing what Harry Morgan learns, too late, about individual responsibility. In a sense, Ernest Hemingway left home in 1920 and spent the rest of his life trying to rewrite Windemere. He wanted to create in art and in life a home and family devoted to the good values; yet home and family seemed to require or to birth those very illusions and indoctrinations he held in contempt.

Notes

1 See, for example, Constance Montgomery, *Hemingway in Michigan* (New York: Fleet, 1966), pp. 172–82; and Carlos Baker, *Ernest Hemingway: A Life Story* (New York: Scribner's, 1969), pp. 71–73.

2 The Hemingway family letters, housed in the Humanities Research Center, University of Texas, Austin, Texas, are contained in twentyeight Hollinger boxes, the total number to be reduced by a half-dozen or so when current rearrangement is completed. The collection consists mostly of letters within the family—not letters by or to Ernest—but includes stray report cards, business notes, songs and lectures by Grace, and various memorabilia. There is a minimal index consisting of approximately six hundred cards, some with single entries, but usually with brief, multiple listings. The entry on one index card, for example, is "158 letters from Clarence to Grace (1900–1928)." The entry on another card is "31 letters from Clarence to Grace and children at Windemere (1902–1924)." There are letters dated from the 1870s to the 1960s. I am grateful to Leicester Hemingway for his generous permission to quote from the Hemingway family letters. I have silently corrected minor errors, with exceptions noted, but have retained informalities characteristic of correspondence ("&" for "and") and relevant to meaning (capital letters for emphasis).

3 See Baker, *Life Story*, pp. 344, 452, 465, 487, 496–97. The five books are Leicester Hemingway, *My Brother, Ernest Hemingway* (Cleveland: World, 1961); Marcelline Hemingway Sanford, *At the Hemingways: A Family Portrait* (Boston: Little, Brown, 1961); Madelaine Hemingway Miller, *Ernie: Hemingway's Sister "Sunny" Remembers* (New York: Crown, 1975); Mary Welsh Hemingway, *How It Was* (New York: Knopf, 1976); and Gregory H. Hemingway, *Papa: A Personal Memoir* (Boston: Houghton Mifflin, 1976). Also, Hadley gave full cooperation to Alice Hunt Sokoloff's *Hadley: The First Mrs. Hemingway* (New York: Dodd, Mead, 1973).

4 See Richard Drinnon, "In the American Heartland: Hemingway and Death," *Psychoanalytical Review*, 52 (1965), 5–31; David Gordon, "The Son and the Father: Patterns of Response to Conflict in Hemingway's Fiction," *Literature and Psychology*, 16 (1966), 122–38; and Richard B. Hovey, *Hemingway: The Inward Terrain* (Seattle: University of Washington Press, 1968), pp. 36, 212–13.

5 Baker, *Life Story*, p. 474.

6 See my "The Stewardship of Ernest Hemingway," *Texas Quarterly*, 9 (Winter 1966), 89–101.

7 Leicester Hemingway, *My Brother, Ernest Hemingway*, pp. 13–15. Since the first permission for an outsider to study the family letters was granted in 1971, Leicester's selections from and treatment of the letters represented the only version available. Scholars, having to depend on Leicester's presentation of the letters and on remarks by Ernest, have been understandably biased against Grace.

8 An example of Marcelline's lack of influence is Scott Donaldson's *By Force of Will: The Life and Art of Ernest Hemingway* (New York: Viking, 1977), p. 291. Donaldson, in his generally excellent study of Hemingway, cites Marcelline's book as the source for statements about Grace as the negligent mother but ignores Marcelline's testimony that Grace gave singing lessons and earned money with which she hired domestics to do the chores customarily assigned to the wife-mother. Issues not yet fully resolved, however, include the family finances. Marcelline says Grace contributed to the family (*At the Hemingways*, pp. 204–5); Baker says Grace's negligence made domestics a necessity and caused "a steady drain on the family income" (*Life Story*, p. 8). Is Marcelline correct in saying that Grace was ill in 1920, unable to contribute the usual to the family income, and that this is why Clarence could afford only two weeks at Windemere rather than the full summer? It is hoped that the current research of Michael Reynolds will resolve these and other questions.

9 There would be no letters within the family, of course, while the family was together; but Leicester confirms the two-week vacation indicated by the dates of Clarence's letters (*My Brother, Ernest Hemingway*, p. 64).

10 Clarence Hemingway to Grace Hemingway, 18 July 1920, Hemingway Family Letters, Humanities Research Center, University of Texas, Austin, Texas. Hereafter cited as Family Letters.

11 Clarence Hemingway to Grace, 22 July 1920, Family Letters.

12 Clarence Hemingway to Grace, 25 July 1920, Family Letters. Ernest's birthday in 1920 fell on a Wednesday; Clarence made a slip.

13 Leicester Hemingway, *My Brother, Ernest Hemingway*, p. 69.

14 Clarence Hemingway to Grace, 25 July 1920, Family Letters.

15 Clarence Hemingway to Grace, 26 July 1920, Family Letters.

16 Clarence Hemingway to Grace, 25 July 1920, Family Letters. "Bill" is Bill Smith.

17 Grace Hemingway to Clarence, 27 July 1920, Family Letters. "Beumice," or "Beummie," is Theodore Brumback; see Baker, *Life Story*, pp. 70–74.

18 Grace Hemingway, Copy of Letter to Ernest, 27 July 1920, Family Letters.

19 Grace Hemingway, Envelope of Letter to Ernest, 27 July 1920, Family Letters.

20 Clarence Hemingway to Grace and children, 28 July 1920, Family Letters.

21 Clarence Hemingway to Grace, 30 July 1920, Family Letters.

22 Grace Hemingway to Clarence, 28 July 1920, Family Letters.

23 Grace Hemingway to Clarence, 28 July 1920, Family Letters.

24 Grace Hemingway to Clarence, 27 July 1920, Family Letters. Maurice Maeterlinck's *The Blue Bird: A Fairy Play*, a work of sentimental optimism, was popular in America in the early twentieth century. Printed by Dodd, Mead, in 1907, it was reprinted in 1909, 1911, and 1919. By "the *American*," Grace means the *American Magazine*. Dr. Frank Crane was a preacher who left the pulpit for the larger audience available in print. Ernest, in his literary judgment if not in his treatment of his mother, was certainly right. Dr. Crane's superficial optimism in support of Christian capitalism does qualify him as the "moron's Maeterlinck." The fact that Dr. Crane also wrote a small book in which one sermon is entitled "Irony and Pity" and another refers to "The colonel's lady and Julia O'Grady" is surely a trap for the over-eager scholar (Dr. Frank Crane, *Four Minute Essays*, 6 (New York: William H. Wise, 1919), pp. 5–8, 131); but the

fact that his parents liked superficial and commercialized versions of good values was important in Ernest's frustrated attempts to maintain relationships.

25 Baker cites Ernest's remark to Hadley that he might have gone to Princeton if his mother had not spent the money to build Grace Cottage (*Life Story*, p. 78). Montgomery is one of many to repeat the story that Ernest earned his mother's hatred by opposing her plan to spend "two or three thousand dollars to build a new cottage for herself," money that should have been used to send the younger girls to college (*Hemingway in Michigan*, p. 177). As with the eviction of 1920, the standard version of what happened is wrong in part because of a lack of information, in part because of bias. The facts concerning Grace Cottage have not been previously available, but the fact that Ernest did not want to go to college has long been known and has carried no weight in scholarly evaluation of the disputes between Grace and Ernest.

26 Grace Hemingway to Clarence, n.d., Family Letters.
27 Grace Hemingway to Ed Morford, n.d., Family Letters.
28 Grace Hemingway to Ed Morford, n.d., Family Letters.
29 Grace Hemingway to Ed Morford, 15 May 1919, Family Letters.
30 Clarence Hemingway to Ed Morford, 26 May 1919, Family Letters.
31 Grace Hemingway to Clarence, n.d., Family Letters.
32 Leicester Hemingway to Grace, 4 January 1904, Family Letters.
33 Sanford, *At the Hemingways*, pp. 49–67, 235–41.
34 Baker, *Life Story*, pp. 433–34; Donaldson, *By Force of Will*, p. 256; Sanford, *At the Hemingways*, p. 55.

35 Hemingway's lack of flexibility is perhaps the most puzzling part of his relations with his parents. Grace's Dr. Frank Crane wrote with incredible superficiality about the power of happy thoughts and the evil of negative thoughts, and Hemingway wrote with honesty and success—in "The Snows of Kilimanjaro," for example—about a realistic version of affirmative thinking and the destructive nature of despair; but the dogmatism he so resented in his parents is an objectionable characteristic found—according to numerous critics and friends—in his fiction and in his own personality. Perhaps, as we see in *A Farewell to Arms* and *For Whom the Bell Tolls*, Hemingway's rewriting of his parents' dogmatic devotion to virtues consists in his rejection of partisan politics, his devotion to freedom and abhorrence of all tyranny.

36 Grace Hemingway to Clarence, 18 October 1908, Family Letters.
37 Grace Hemingway to Clarence, 17 October 1908, Family Letters.

38 Grace Hemingway to Clarence, 5 September 1914, Family Letters.

39 Clarence Hemingway to Grace, 5 May 1917, Family Letters.

40 For a first-rate exploration of stoicism in Hemingway, see Thomas Barker, "The Stoic Ideal in Hemingway's Fiction," Diss. University of Texas (Austin) 1980.

41 Grace Hemingway to Clarence, 10 August 1917, Family Letters.

42 See Donaldson, *By Force of Will*, pp. 211–15.

43 Clarence Hemingway to Grace, 12 August 1917, Family Letters.

44 Clarence Hemingway to Grace and children, 27 June 1920, Family Letters.

45 Clarence Hemingway to Grace, Ursula, and Sunny, 28 June 1920, Family Letters.

46 Clarence Hemingway to Grace and children, 29 June 1920, Family Letters.

47 Clarence Hemingway to Grace, 1 July 1920, Family Letters.

48 Clarence Hemingway to Grace and children, 16 July 1920, Family Letters.

49 Clarence Hemingway to Grace, 1 September 1920, Family Letters.

50 Clarence Hemingway to Grace and Leicester, 13 September 1920, Family Letters.

51 Clarence Hemingway to Grace and Leicester, 15 September 1920, Family Letters.

52 Letters not quoted here make it clear that while differences and problems—as with all families—continued to occur, the Hemingway daughters loved their mother and enjoyed good relations with her, the summer of 1920 being, for them, a minor rough spot in the process of growing up.

53 Leicester Hemingway, *My Brother, Ernest Hemingway*, p. 68.

54 Clarence Hemingway to Ernest, 18 September 1920, Hemingway Collection, John F. Kennedy Library, Boston, Mass.

55 On Hemingway's inability to respect his father, see Donaldson, *By Force of Will*, p. 296.

56 There is no envelope for Clarence's letter of October 2, but several letters make it clear that Clarence did return to Windemere to secure the cabin; for example, Clarence Hemingway to Grace, 6 October 1920, Family Letters.

57 Clarence Hemingway to Grace, 2 October 1920, Family Letters.

58 Lloyd R. Arnold, *High on the Wild with Hemingway* (Caldwell: Caxton, 1969), p. 79.

59 Ernest Hemingway to Grace, 22 December 1920, Hemingway Collection, John F. Kennedy Library.

60 Other family letters in the John F. Kennedy Library suggest that Clarence and Grace did appreciate their son's writing, at least his journalism; but the evidence would have to be more extensive to be convincing. There was, in any case, a finality about Ernest's reaction to his parents' rejection of *In Our Time*. Since writing literature that would offend Clarence and Grace was to be his life, what hope was there for a relationship?

61 See Delbert E. Wylder, *Hemingway's Heroes* (Albuquerque: University of New Mexico Press, 1969), pp. 40–49.

62 Wirt Williams convincingly describes Hemingway's artful combination of security and the ominous in the opening of *Islands in the Stream*; see his *The Tragic Art of Ernest Hemingway* (Baton Rouge: Louisiana State University Press, 1981), pp. 202–4.

63 See Carlos Baker, "A Search for the Man As He Really Was," *New York Times Book Review*, 25 July 1964, pp. 4–5, 14. Citing a letter from Clarence to Ernest about the authenticity of the story (p. 14), Baker demonstrates the close relationship between an actual event and the fictional account of that event, including the fact that the youthful Ernest was, in actuality, a witness. It is easy to see why critics have been led to believe that Nick is therefore present and that the story is about the unmanning of Clarence by Grace. Two excellent corrective essays which summarize the standard view and then offer much-improved readings are Joseph M. Flora, "A Closer Look at the Young Nick Adams and His Father," *Studies in Short Fiction*, 14 (Winter 1977), 75–78; and Richard Fulkerson, "The Biographical Fallacy and 'The Doctor and the Doctor's Wife,'" *Studies in Short Fiction*, 16 (Winter 1979), 61–65. Stephen D. Fox also avoids the biographical trap and quite rightly emphasizes the importance of Dr. Adams's *assuming* that the stray logs are driftwood and the importance of gentility in contrast with Boulton's outcast status. See his "Hemingway's 'The Doctor and the Doctor's Wife,'" *Arizona Quarterly*, 29 (Spring 1973), 19–25.

64 Hemingway made a sound distinction between describing (repeating) actual experience and making (creating) out of experience and other sources. He also said that a good writer could "make something through . . . invention that is not a representation but a whole new thing truer than anything true and alive. . . ." See George Plimpton, "An Interview with Ernest Hemingway," in *Ernest Hemingway: Five Decades of Criticism*, ed. Linda Wagner (East Lansing: Michigan State University Press, 1974), pp. 36, 38.

65 Sanford, *At the Hemingways*, pp. 50–51.

66 Leicester Hemingway, *My Brother, Ernest Hemingway*, pp. 35–37.

67 See, for example, Joseph DeFalco, *The Hero in Hemingway's Short Stories* (Pittsburgh: University of Pittsburgh Press, 1963), pp. 33–40.

68 Ernest Hemingway, *The Short Stories of Ernest Hemingway* (New York: Scribner's, 1954), p. 102 (italics added). Further quotations from "The Doctor and the Doctor's Wife" and from "Soldier's Home" are from this edition and are cited parenthetically.

69 For an excellent demonstration of how Hemingway moved beyond actual experience to invention, to art, see Robert W. Lewis, Jr., "Hemingway in Italy: Making It Up," *Journal of Modern Literature*, 9 (1981–82), 209–36.

70 For an illuminating exposition of Hemingway's abhorrence of tyranny, see Donaldson *By Force of Will*, pp. 93–124. For Hemingway's revealing comments on Senator Joseph McCarthy, see Ernest Hemingway, *By-Line: Ernest Hemingway*, ed. William White (New York: Scribner's, 1967), p. 450.

7. Millicent Bell

A *Farewell to Arms:*
Pseudoautobiography and
Personal Metaphor

AUTOBIOGRAPHIC novels are, of course, fictions, constructs of the imagination, even when they seem to incorporate authenticating bits and pieces of personal history. But all fiction is autobiography, no matter how remote from the author's experience the tale seems to be; he leaves his mark, expresses his being, his life, in *any* tale. *A Farewell to Arms* can illustrate both of these statements.

Ernest Hemingway's novel is not the autobiography some readers have thought it. It was not memory but printed source material that supplied the precise details of its descriptions of historic battle scenes on the Italian front in World War I.[1] The novel's love story is no closer to Hemingway's personal reality. He did go to Italy and see action, but not the action he describes; he did fall in love with a nurse, but she was no Catherine Barkley. A large amount of the book fulfills the principle expressed in the deleted coda to "Big Two-Hearted River": "The only writing that was any good was what you made up, what you imagined."[2] Still, there is much that must represent authentic recall in the book. Innumerable small details and a sense of general conditions in battle, the character of the Italian landscape, the Italian soldier, the ambulance corps—all impressed themselves upon Hemingway in 1918 in the Dolomite foothills near Schio as surely as they might

107

have further east around the Tagliamento a year earlier. And there are fetishes of autobiography, trophies of the personal, chief among these the famous wounding at Fossalta, which Hemingway often recalled.[3]

Why is this last episode reproduced so exactly as it happened—the shell fragments in the legs, the sensation of dying and coming to life, the surgical sequel? In the coda, Nick—who is Hemingway—had "never seen a jockey killed" when he wrote "My Old Man"; "he'd never seen an Indian woman having a baby" like his namesake in "Indian Camp." But Hemingway had been wounded just as Frederic is. The answer may be that it was a trauma obsessively recurring to mind, irrepressibly present in his writing because of its crucial, transforming effect upon his life.[4] Still, in the novel the wounding is not at all transforming, does not provide the occasion for the "separate peace" declared by Nick at a similar moment in chapter 6 of *In Our Time*, often incorrectly thought to be the novel's germ. It does not even cause the novel's hero to suffer from sleeplessness afterward, the consequence of a similar wounding for the narrator of "Now I Lay Me," written only two years before *A Farewell to Arms*. Perhaps in life as in the novel the wounding was simply a very striking experience, the young man's first brush with death. But as an authentic, indelible memory it was deliberate evidence, in any case, that the fiction was *not* all made up. Perhaps, then, the authentic wounding is chiefly a sign, a signature of the author's autobiographic contract with himself.

Hemingway's style, his realist pose, suggests, guilefully, that much more has been borrowed directly from experience than is actually the case. Perhaps the testimonial incorporation of the real, which guarantees autobiographic realism, may also be mimicked. When the "real" is made up to become the "realistic," when the seemingly accidental detail appears to have been stuck into the narrative for no other reason than that it happened, than that it was there, the writer has deliberately made it look as though he is yielding to memory and resisting the tendency of literature to subdue everything to a system of connected significance. In *A Farewell to Arms*, as elsewhere in his writing, Hemingway made the discovery of this secret of realist effect, and his art, which nevertheless presses toward poetic unity by a powerful

if covert formalist intent, yet seems continually open to irrelevance also. The result is a peculiar tension requiring the strict-
est control. Only a manner which conceals implication as severely
as Hemingway's can nevertheless suggest those coherences, those
rhythmic collocations of mere things, in the manner of imagist
poetry, pretend notation of what the witnessing eye might simply
have chanced to see. And this restraint is reinforced by deliberate
avoidance of the kind of comment that might impose significance
or interpretation. It is even further strengthened by the often-
noted qualities of Hemingwayan syntax, the simple or compound
declaratives lacking subordination, and the vocabulary high in
nouns and verbs and low in qualifiers. The frequency of the
impersonal passive voice that presents events simply as conditions, as in the many sentences that begin with "There were,"
suppresses not only the sense of agency but the evaluating
presence of the observer. If, despite these effects, there is often
poetic meaningfulness it is also true that the poetic is sometimes
renounced altogether and the realistic detail maintains its irrelevance, refusing any signification in order to affirm the presence of the actual, whether or not truly remembered, reported,
historical.[5]

But this stylistic contest only reflects the struggle of the writer
between the impulses to tell it "as it was" and to shape and pattern a story; it is not that struggle itself. The "realistic" style is, in
fact, most conspicuous and most successful in the most "invented"
parts of the book, the war scenes. It is not so evident in those
other scenes where Hemingway draws upon memory—the Milan
and Switzerland sections. Hemingway had been a patient in the
Red Cross hospital in Milan and had spent convalescent weeks in
the city; and he had taken vacation tours in the Alpine lake
region. But the action situated in those places in the novel has no
authenticity to match that of the great Caporetto chapter in
which Frederic participates in events Hemingway had not. Still,
it is the war scenes, probably—to turn our paradox about once
more—that express Hemingway's deepest feelings by way of
metaphor, his sense of the war as an objective correlative of his
state of mind. The love affair located in familiar, remembered
scenes fails of authenticity though it takes something from the
writer's experiences with his nurse, Agnes von Kurowsky, and

something from his love for Hadley Richardson, and even Pauline Pfeiffer's caesarian operation; it succeeds less well than the invented war scenes in achieving either the effect of realism or the deeper autobiography of metaphor. It is as the latter that it can, however, be explained.

Any first-person story must imitate the autobiographic situation, but there is particular evidence that Hemingway gave his narrator his own sense of the difficulty of reconciling *Wahrheit* and *Dichtung*. The novelist's struggles to achieve an appropriate ending to his book are visible in the manuscript drafts at the John F. Kennedy Library.[6] They show that his chief problem was that he felt both that a novel needed formal closure and also that life was not "like that." He rejected, in the end, the attempt to pick up dropped threads and bring Rinaldi and the priest back into the narrative from which they had been absent since the end of chapter 26, a little beyond the novel's midpoint. It may be argued that these two *companions de la guerre* are felt even in their absence, that there are no dropped threads, the priest in particular being absorbed into the transformed conception of love which the American lieutenant and the English nurse discover in the later portions of the book. But there is really no such absorption; Frederic and Catherine remain very much what they were at the beginning, this mentor and the skeptical doctor both being left behind. Of the "three people of any importance in this story" to whom Hemingway referred in the rejected opening for chapter 10, only Catherine persists.[7] Hemingway must have decided this made an ending—the tightening isolation of his hero requires the loss of the larger human world—but in one of the discarded drafts he permits Frederic to express the misgivings of his creator. "I could tell how Rinaldi was cured of the syphilis. . . . I could tell how the priest in our mess lived to be a priest in Italy under Fascism," the pseudoautobiographic narrator observes. But he knows that a story must end somewhere. That he realizes that his closure cannot be complete is due to his awareness that life does not have endings.

Things happen all the time. Everything blunts and the world keeps on. You get most of your life back like goods recovered from a fire. It all keeps on and then it keeps on. It never stops for you. Sometimes it stops when you are still alive. You can stop a story anytime. Where you stop is the end of that story. The rest goes on and you go on with it. On the other hand you have to stop a story. You have to stop at the end of whatever it was you were writing about.[8]

The rejected passage can be read not merely as a device to excuse the odd shape of the novel but as a reflection of Hemingway's personal dilemma, his desire to respect the claim of art and also to get back his own past like "goods recovered from a fire."

Getting back his life by writing fiction was not, in this case, a matter of endings, of plot. The indeterminacy of remembered experience does not matter, because the coherence of events is not so important as the unity of the mind which is the container for them. If Hemingway was to fulfill the autobiographic expectation, the promise made by authentic transcriptions like the Fossalta wounding, it would not be by trying to tell, literally, "the story" of his past. The novelist wrote about himself, and perhaps never so truly as in A Farewell to Arms, but he did so by projecting, lyrically, an inner condition. Mood and tone, not events, provide unity, and these were more intensely the concomitants of the present life of the writer than of his younger self. The novel is about neither love nor war; it is about a state of mind, and that state of mind is the author's.

That plot is not dominant in A Farewell of Arms has not been properly recognized. Critics who have stressed the prevalence of poetic metaphors in the novel have failed, on the whole, to see that such patterns establish its "spatial" composition, minimize progressive effects.[9] In fact, an unvarying mood, established by the narrative voice, dominates everything it relates, bathes uniformly all the images and levels events which are seen always in one way only. That the principal descriptive elements—river, mountains, dust or mud, and above all, rain—are all present in the opening paragraphs suggests not so much that later scenes are being predicted as that the subsequent pages will disclose nothing that is not already evident in the consciousness that has begun its self-exhibition.

The famous wounding is no turning-point in the journey of that consciousness. But even the later "separate peace" in chapter 32 after Frederic's immersion in the Tagliamento is not really a change of direction, a peaking of the plot, though Hemingway's hero does say as he lies on the floor of the flatcar that takes him to Milan, "You were out of it now. You had no more obligation" (p. 232). In chapter 7, even before his wounding, it should be remembered, he has already said, "I would not be killed. Not in this war. It did not have anything to do with me" (p. 37). It is impossible to tell at what point this narrator has acquired his conviction of separateness amounting to alienation from the events which carry him along the stream of time.

By the time he turns away from the war at the Tagliamento in October 1917, Frederick will have had two years in which to acquire the apathy of war weariness. But this is not his malady. Already on the opening page, in 1915, the voice that speaks to us exhibits that attitude psychoanalysts call "blunting of affect," the dryness of soul which underlies its exquisite attentiveness. One has heard of the "relish of sensation" implied in this and other passages of descriptive writing by Hemingway. But "relish" is too positive a word for the studied emotional distance from the perceived world which is in effect here. For the view from Gorizia across the Isonzo, toward the passing troops and the changing weather, this narrator seems hardly to feel anything beyond a minimal "things went very badly." An alienated neutrality governs the reiterated passives, the simple declaratives. "There were big guns. . . . There was fighting. . . . There were mists over the river. . . . There were small gray motor cars" (p. 4). The next year (chapter 2) is the same. "There were many victories. . . . The fighting was in the next mountains. . . . The whole thing was going well. . . . The war was changed" (pp. 5–6). The different character of military events makes for no change in the tone. We are prepared for the personality who emerges into view as he describes his leave. He had not gone to Abruzzi but had spent drunken nights when "you knew that that was all there was," and he had known the "not knowing and not caring in the night, sure that this was all . . . suddenly to care very much" (p. 13), swinging from not caring to caring and back again, from affectlessness to to affect and then again to its loss. If there is something that transcends this alternation, the ecstasy of either love or religion, it is so fugitive as to be almost unnameable: "If you have had it you know. . . . He, the priest, had always known what I did not know, what, when I learned it, I was always able to forget" (pp. 13–14).

"Always" is an important word here. There is no hint that Frederic has at any time had a beginning in illusion, that he ever started out like Stephen Crane's Henry Fleming in *The Red Badge of Courage* (something of a model for *A Farewell to Arms*) with a naive belief in exalted meanings. The well-known passage, "I was *always* embarrassed by the words sacred, glorious, and sacrifice, and the expression in vain" is not the culmination of a process by which these concepts have withered. His embarrassment goes as far back as he can remember. He has had it always. "Gino was a patriot," Frederic continues, "so he said things that separated us sometimes, but he was also a fine boy and I understand his being a patriot. He was born one" (pp. 184–85). And the opposite attitude, disbelief in such things, may also be inborn. Rinaldi has told Frederic that for him "there are only two things"—drink and sex—and his work. Frederic hopes that he will get other things but the doctor says, "No. We never get anything. We are born with all we have and we never learn" (p. 171). If Frederic may be conceived of as having been also born with all he has, this explains why he is described as having enlisted in the ambulance corps for no reason at all, unlike Hemingway who was swept into the wave of American enthusiasm to aid the Allies. Frederic just happened to be already in Italy when the war broke out. He had been studying architecture. He has never had any belief in the big words. "Why did you do it?" asks Catherine, referring to his enlistment. "I don't know. . . . There isn't always an explanation for everything," he answers.

And yet this sufferer from blunted affect can fall in love. It is one of the "givens" of the story, though it seems to demand a capacity which, like the emotion of patriotism, he was born without. "When I saw her I was in love with her," he says when Catherine appears again at the hospital. "I had not wanted to fall in love with anyone. But God knows I had" (pp. 91, 93). Catherine, as well, had experienced this hardly credible conversion. Al-

though we never get so direct a view of her mental operations—
this is Frederic's story, after all—she appears, in the earlier
scenes, to be as incapacitated as Hemingway's other English nurse
who has lost a fiancé in the war, Brett Ashley. There is more than
a hint that she too suffers the dissociation of feeling from sensation that accounts for her unfocused sexuality when Frederic first
makes love to her. But now she feels. The raptures of both lovers,
however, are curiously suspect.

Frederic has only delusively attached himself to an otherness.
Far from the war's inordinate demand upon his reponses, he has
been converted to feeling in the isolation of his hospital bed,
where, like a baby in its bassinet, he is totally passive, tended and
comforted by female caretakers, the nurses, and particularly by
this one. The image is regressive, and the ministering of
Catherine, who looks after all his needs, including sexual, while
he lies passive, is more maternal than connubial. The relation
that now becomes the center of the novel is, indeed, peculiar
enough to make us question it as a representation of adult love.
More often noted than Frederic's passivity is the passivity of
Catherine in this love affair, a passivity which has irritated
readers (particularly female readers) because it seems to be a pro-
jection of male fantasies of the ideally submissive partner. It
results from her desire to please. She is a sort of inflated rubber
woman available at will to the onanistic dreamer. There is, in
fact, a masturbatory quality to the love of each. The union of
these two is a flight from outer reality and eventually from
selfhood, which depends upon a recognition of the other; the
selfhood that fails to find its definition in impingement upon the
world at large and the establishment of distinction from it eventually proves incapable of recognizing the alien in the beloved
and therefore the independent in itself. The otherness that
Frederic and Catherine provide for one another is not enough to
preserve their integral selves, and while the sounds of exteriority
become more and more muffled in the novel, their personalities
melt into one another. It is for this reason that Hemingway's
novel, far from being the *Romeo and Juliet* he once carelessly
called it, is more comparable to *Anthony and Cleopatra*, a play

which shows that the world is not well lost for love, though nothing, of course, can be further from the masterful images of Shakespeare's adult lovers than Hemingway's pitiful pair.

Affective failure, then, shows itself not merely in the war sections of the novel but in the parts where one would imagine it to have been transcended, the love story of Catherine and Frederic. Catherine constantly reminds her lover of her resolution not to offer him otherness but to collapse her own selfhood into his. She asks what a prostitute does, whether she says whatever the customer wants her to, even "I love you." She will outdo the prostitute: "But I will. I'll say just what you wish and I'll do what you wish and then you will never want any other girls, will you. . . . I want what you want. There isn't any me any more. Just what you want" (pp. 105, 106). The idyll of their Milan summer is spent in such games as this: "We tried putting thoughts in the other one's head while we were in different rooms. It seemed to work sometimes but that was probably because we were thinking the same thing anyway" (p. 114). She refuses his offer to marry her, and when he says "I wanted it for you" replies, "there isn't any me. I'm you. Don't make up a separate me" (p. 115).

Their solitariness à deux is only emphasized by their occasional contacts with others who are outside the war, those met in the Milan cafés or at the racetrack who are not the true alienated but the self-serving and parasitic, and even by their encounter with the genuine war hero, Ettore, who is wounded in the foot, like Frederic, and has five medals, and whom they cannot stand. After she becomes pregnant, Catherine says, "There's only us two and in the world there's all the rest of them. If anything comes between us we're gone and then they have us." When the time comes for him to leave for the front, they walk past a couple embracing under a buttress of the cathedral, and she will not agree that they are like themselves. " 'Nobody is like us,' Catherine said. She did not mean it happily" (p. 147). Not surprisingly, they both are orphans of a sort. Catherine has a father but "he has gout," she says to Frederic; "You won't ever have to meet him." Frederic has only a stepfather, and, he tells her, "You won't have to meet him" (p. 154). When they are waiting for the birth of their baby in Switzerland, she asks him about his family: "Don't you care anything about them?" He replies, "I did, but we quarrelled so much it wore itself out" (p. 304).

Book 3, the justly praised Caporetto section, returns Frederic to Gorizia where others have spent a different sort of summer. Rinaldi, depressed, overworked, perhaps syphilitic, says, "This is a terrible war, baby," drinks too much, and is impatient of Frederic's acquisition of a "sacred subject." The priest tells him how the terrible summer has made the major gentle. No one any longer believes in victory. But Frederic confesses that he himself believes in neither victory nor defeat. He believes, he says, "in sleep." It is more than a joke, even though in a moment he apologizes that "I said that about sleep meaning nothing" (p. 179). The regressive process, the withdrawal from reality, the surrender of complex personal being, the limitation of relationship to that with an other who is really only a mirror of self approaches more and more the dreamless sleep of apathy, the extremity of ennui. There is a suggestion of the pathologic in the "I was deadly sleepy" with which the chapter ends (p. 180).

The retreat is reported by a sensibility already asleep, by an emotional apparatus already itself in retreat from the responsibilities of response. "The houses were badly smashed but things were very well organized and there were signboards everywhere" (p. 181). However much this sounds like irony to us, irony is not intended by the speaker, who does not mean more by saying less. His downward adjustment of feeling is the one often made by soldiers—or by concentration camp victims, or long-term prisoners—by which emotions are reduced to the most rudimentary since the others have become insupportable. His battle-weary companions express their own reduction by a preoccupation with food. The entire retreat is a massed legitimization of apathy and a symbol of it.

Frederic's affectlessness is climaxed by his "cold-blooded" shooting of one of the Italian sergeants who has refused to obey his order to move the stalled ambulance. "I shot three times and dropped one," he observes, as though describing the pursuit of game, and Bonello then takes the pistol and "finishes him," as a hunting companion might finish off an animal still quivering where it has fallen (p. 204). One may say that this is simply war—Sherman's war—and feeling has no place in it. But this does not make it less shocking that the perceiving hero is so matter-of-fact. Even Bonello expresses a motive: he is a socialist, and all his life he has wanted to kill a sergeant, he tells Frederic, who expresses no personal motive at all, and who has never felt that it was his war. Yet for giving up his part in it he has also no special motive. His case is not like that of the demoralized soldiers who are flinging down their arms and shouting that they want to go home. He cannot go home. And now a profoundly significant flash of memory comes to him as he rests in the hay of a barn:

> The hay smelled good and lying in a barn in the hay took
> away all the years between. We had lain in the hay and
> talked and shot sparrows with an air-rifle when they perched
> in the triangle cut high in the wall of the barn. The barn
> was gone now and one year they had cut the hemlock woods
> and there were only stumps, dried tree-tops, branches and
> fireweed where the woods had been. You could not go back.
> (p. 216)

The "separate peace" was made long ago. Again we must note the reference to a congenital disengagement when he says with what only looks like a newly acquired minimalism, "I was not *made* to think, I was *made* to eat. My God, yes. Eat and drink and sleep with Catherine" (p. 233). Removing his uniform after his escape, he strips himself of the last vestige of social self. He no longer can interest himself in the war news, as he had in the earlier Milan section, and does not give us summaries of military events. "I had a paper but I did not read it because I did not want to read about the war. I was going to forget the war" he says at the beginning of chapter 34. It is now that he says, "I had made a separate peace." "Don't talk about the war," he tells the barman at the hotel. And he reflects, "The war was a long way away. Maybe there wasn't any war. There was no war here. Then I realized it was over for me" (pp. 243, 255). But how committed to this war has he ever been?

The rest is a "fugue" in the technical psychiatric sense of a period during which the patient, often suffering loss of memory, begins another life from which all his past has been drained. Thus, the "all for love" that remains for Frederic and Catherine is qualified by the lovers' knowledge that the whole empire of normal being has been surrendered. "Let's not think of anything," says Catherine (p. 252). The lover boasts that he has no wish to be separate from his beloved: "All other things were unreal." He tells her, "My life used to be full of everything. Now if you aren't with me I haven't a thing in the world" (p. 257). Their universe of two is reducing itself further, and their games continue to suggest this constriction. He might let his hair grow longer, she suggests, and she might cut hers short so that even their sexual difference may be lessened. "Then we'd both be alike. Oh, darling, I want you so much I want to be you too." He says, "We're the same one," and she, "I want us to be all mixed up. . . . I don't live at all when I'm not with you." He replies, "I'm no good when you're not there. I haven't any life at all any more" (pp. 299–300).

These scenes are a drift toward death, which is why the novel must end in death, Catherine's and the baby's, though Hemingway considered allowing the child to survive. Such a survival would have contradicted all that has gone before by introducing a new otherness when its parents are losing the otherness of each other. The two lovers already live on the margin of life. Count Greffi is an even more mythological figure than Mippipopolous in *The Sun Also Rises*, whom he resembles. The very old man, so close to death, is a fit sentinel upon that border they are about to cross before they pass, by a symbolic boat voyage, out of Italy. Their Switzerland is not on the map, notwithstanding the fact that it resembles the Switzerland of Hemingway's vacation tours. In their chalet, wrapped in the cottony blanket of the winter snow, cared for by their good-natured landlord and his wife, whose lives have a reality with which they make no connection, and in contact with no one else, they are united as before in his hospital bed. Their destiny is out of their own hands as they become, quite literally, patients awaiting surgery, playing bed-games. Perhaps Frederic will pass the time by growing a beard. Their loss of connection with human modes of being produces fantasies of an animal identity, like that of the fox they see in the snow who sleeps with his brush wrapped about his face, curled in the regressive fetal position. What would they do if they had tails like the fox? They would have special clothes made, or "live in a country where it wouldn't make any difference" to have a fox's tail. Catherine says, truly, "We live in a country where nothing makes any difference. Isn't it grand how we never see anyone?" (p. 303). The country is, of course, the country of the dead, toward which she is bound.

If indeed "all fiction is autobiography," no special demonstration is required to support the idea that A Farewell to Arms expresses the author's inner being, his secret life. Yet there is particular reason to suppose this in the case of this novel which is the presentation of a state of mind, a mood and condition of being. These, it may be arguable, belonged to the writer himself at the time of writing. As a war novel, it is curiously late. In 1929, American society was preoccupied with other things than its memories of the battles of the First World War. Hemingway, already the author of a novel dealing with a later period and married for the second time, had come a long way from the naive nineteen-year-old of 1918. Any such analysis is speculative, but there is reason to suppose that for the writer as for Frederic Henry the barn was gone where he had lain in the hay as a boy: "You could not go back." This realization must have been particularly acute when this novel was being written. Since 1925 his life had been one of personal turmoil. He had found himself in love with Pauline Pfeiffer, forced to decide between her and the woman whom he still claimed also to love and who had been, he would declare, a faultless wife. In 1927, he had remarried and, in the following year, while Pauline was pregnant, he was struggling to make progress on this second novel, plagued by various accidental disasters—an eye injury, head cuts from a fallen skylight—such as he always seemed prone to. Pauline's baby was delivered by caesarian section after a labor of eighteen hours during a Kansas heat wave. The first draft of A Farewell to Arms was finished two months later, but before Hemingway began the task of revision, his father, Dr. Clarence Hemingway, who had been depressed for some time, committed suicide by shooting himself in the head.
Beyond the immediate strain and horror of such events must

have been their power to intensify Hemingway's most buried anxieties. His remarriage, which he did not quite understand, created a keen sense of guilt in him along with the recognition that he contained compulsive forces he was powerless to restrain. Marriage, moreover, could be destructive not only because it had resulted in pain and divorce in his own case; as a child he had seen its effects in the secret contests of will between his parents. Pauline's dangerous, agonized parturition seemed to confirm his feeling that death as readily as life was the consequence of sexuality. He may well have felt what he had imagined the Indian father to feel before cutting his throat in "Indian Camp." That early story suggests that Hemingway had always seen something terrifying in the birth process. Now he incorporated a birth process fatal to both fictional mother and child in the conclusion of his novel.

His father's suicide must have awakened further all his most inadmissible emotions, above all his feelings of hostility and guilt toward his parents. Readers of Carlos Baker's biography do not need a review of Hemingway's childhood and youth with its history of rebellions and chastisements.[10] The spirited boy, adoring and striving to emulate his father, also incurred this father's disciplinarian severity, and young Ernest's resentment of his punishment was so intense that he would sometimes, when he was about eighteen, sit hidden in the doorway of a shed behind the house drawing a bead on his father's head with a gun while the doctor worked in his vegetable garden.[11] Yet it was this same father who had taught him to shoot, initiated him in the craft and passion of killing animals. His feelings toward his mother, whose musical-artistic inclinations might be thought to be the source of his own impulses toward the life of art, would, in the end, prove more bitterly hostile. As he grew to manhood he felt, it would seem, more betrayed by her attempts to control his behavior, especially after the war had proved him a man and even a hero. There is the well-known incident of youthful high-jinks in the woods, shortly after his twenty-first birthday, which resulted in his expulsion from the Hemingways' summer cottage at Walloon Lake. But more hurtful must have been his parents' moralistic censure of his writing. First *In Our Time* and then *The Sun Also*

Rises received their uncomprehending disapproval, against which he politely pleaded.

Beneath the politeness there was sometimes a threat. After receiving her criticism of his first novel Hemingway wrote his mother with only half-concealed scorn, "I am sure that it [the novel] is not more unpleasant than the real inner lives of some of our best Oak Park families. You must remember that in such a book all the worst of the people's lives is displayed while at home there is a very lovely side for the public and the sort of which I have had some experience of observing behind closed doors."[12] Behind what doors but those closed upon the conflicts he had known between his parents themselves? Hemingway was prone to hint for years that he might write an Oak Park novel that would tell all: "I had a wonderful novel to write about Oak Park," he said in 1952, "and would never do it because I did not want to hurt living people."[13] After his father's death in 1928 he wrote his mother offering her some advice about how to handle his uncle George, whom he held responsible for his father's money worries, and he also added menacingly, "I have never written a novel about the [Hemingway] family because I have never wanted to hurt anyone's feelings but with the death of the ones I love a period has been put to a great part of it and I may have to undertake it."[14] It is a curious statement, with its slip into the plural "ones" when among his near relatives only his father had died. And was not his mother to be counted among the "ones I love"? There seems to be an unclear implication that she as much as his uncle—whom he had always disliked—might be exposed by his writing. The Oak Park novel was never written. Yet if he rejected the temptation to write about his family life—except in the hints given in such a story as "The Doctor and the Doctor's Wife"—he did not stop writing works that might convey his insight into the "unpleasant" and defy his mother's moralistic hypocrisy. And the covertly autobiographic impulse persisted.

From the time of his father's suicide, he must have felt himself to be just such an orphan, though with a living parent, as Catherine and Frederic describe themselves. "My father is the only one I cared about," he wrote Maxwell Perkins after the doctor's suicide.[15] He then may already have believed what he later stated to Charles Scribner, that his mother had destroyed her husband, and his bitter sense of having been unloved by her fused with his identification with his father: "I hate her guts and she hates mine. She forced my father to suicide."[16] But such liberations from filial love are never quite complete. Underneath must have been the longing for approval, for a lost infantile security. Hemingway's own sexual history, that ultimate personal expression, may have taken some shape from the mixture of need and anger which probably composed his emotions toward his mother. The need to reject as well as the need to be wanted again may explain the course of his love life, with its three marriages and, as his life advanced, its rather greater propensity of promiscuity. Promiscuity, of course, may also be based on the fear that one cannot feel at all. Beneath the intensely expressive, even violent personality of the visible Hemingway there may have been a self that was haunted by the demon of boredom. Apathy, which might seem the least likely affliction of this articulate and active man, may have been what he feared most, knowing his own inner indifference. If so, then *A Farewell to Arms* does have a special relation to the mind of the maker, is autobiographic in a metaphoric way.

Some confirmation of this view may be gained by study of Hemingway's text as the result of revision and excision in accordance with his well-known iceberg theory.[17] In looking for the submerged element that supports a style so economic, so dependent upon implication rather that explication, one is prompted to consider the nature of what has been pruned away. Obviously, the Hemingway esthetic promotes the elimination of the merely redundant, the detail that adds nothing, the explanation that can be supplied by the reader's own surmise, the additional episode which may thicken the reality of the story but also complicates its meaning too much. Some of this discard may well supply autobiographic clues to the intentional process by which the work was molded. Sometimes, one suspects, the rejected matter comes out of the too-exact transcript of memory.

Even before the manuscript of *A Farewell to Arms* had been studied, it was obvious that Hemingway might have planned his novel at some earlier stage to include other elements besides those finally selected. Julian Smith has argued that two stories written in 1926 just after the breakup of Hemingway's first marriage amplify the novel so precisely at certain points that they may have been conceived of as part of it at one time.[18] One of these is "In Another Country," whose title, with its reference to Marlowe's *Jew of Malta* ("Thou hast committed—/ Fornication—but that was in another country; and besides, the wench is dead"), Hemingway once considered using for the novel.[19] The second story linked with the novel is "Now I Lay Me," entitled "In Another Country—Two" in a late draft.[20] Both short stories fulfill the title of the collection in which they were printed in 1927, *Men Without Women*, which attaches them in an interesting way to the novel begun soon after, the novel about the failure, in the end, of the sexual bridge over the gulf of solitude.

Both stories are really about marriage. In "In Another Country" the narrator, recovering from his wounds in a Milan hospital and receiving mechanical therapy—like Hemingway and Frederic Henry—is warned not to marry. An Italian major who has just lost his wife tells him that a man "cannot marry" because "if he is to lose everything, he should not place himself in a position to lose that." Had Hemingway chosen to include the story as an episode in *A Farewell to Arms* it might have served to predict Catherine's death as well as the conclusion that nothing, not even love, abides. In "Now I Lay Me" the hero has been wounded in the particular fashion and with the particular sensations Hemingway remembered from his own experience and attributed to Frederic. He does not sleep well—because of the sound of the silkworms and because he is afraid of dying—and passes restless nights thinking about two kinds of boyhood experience: trout fishing and the quarrels between his parents, with his mother's hen-pecking of his father. He is advised by his orderly *to* marry but does not, and does not intend to, unlike the narrator of the companion story, who tells the major that he hopes to be married.

There are any number of ways in which both stories can be related to Hemingway's personal experience, but it is clear that together they suggest a fear associated with marriage—either one will somehow kill it oneself, as he had done with his own first marriage, or it will kill you, or at least emasculate you, as his mother had emasculated his father. Despite the seemingly positive assurance of the orderly in the second story that marriage will "fix everything," the effect of both tales is to suggest that death and destruction arrive in the end. Love cannot heal the Hemingway hero who longs to return to some presexual condition in the untainted woods of boyhood.

The connection of the two stories with the novel written so soon after them is a matter of conjecture, but Hemingway's manuscript drafts of *A Farewell to Arms* may justifiably be searched for evidence of his compositional intentions and his autobiographic sources. The draft indicates that Hemingway had, for example, included a much more detailed version of the description of wounding already used in "Now I Lay Me" and also a more detailed and more emotional description of Frederic's sensations on waking up in the hospital in Milan. The final version screens out autobiographic irrelevance, for Frederic, in the draft, makes on Hemingway's behalf one of those representative comments that show him struggling against the flood of memory: "If you try and put in everything you would never get a single day done and then the one who made it might not feel it."[21] In the end the writer made these occasions consistent with the rest of the novel as a representation of the state of mind that is the grounding of his hero's being. In the first three books, as Reynolds has observed, the revisions nearly efface Frederic as a personality.[22] He becomes an almost completely apathetic sufferer. Though self-expression is allowed to emerge in the love affair, it does not really make for reversal of this condition, for in the place of the grand afflatus of love, the language of amorous avowal that these lovers speak is self-diminishing.

A complex revision of a crucial passage is the alteration of the conversation between Frederic and the priest in chapter 11. In the manuscript draft Frederic lists some of the things he loves, and adds at the end, "I found I loved god too, a little. I did not love anything too much."[23] In the revision there is no such list or remark, but there is, instead, the priest's statement: "When you love you wish to do things for. You wish to sacrifice for. You wish to serve" (p. 72). Hemingway may be thought to have promoted by this addition the hope of moral growth in his hero, who then asks, in the printed text, "How about loving a woman? If I really loved some woman would it be like that?" He cannot answer his own question nor does the priest answer it, and though, much later, Count Greffi calls love "a religious feeling," Frederic, still dubious, can respond only, "You think so?" (p. 263). Can we analogize the love of God and Frederic's love of Catherine, in fact? Does human love acquire the highest possible meaning for him? Not really. He cannot be said to attain the priest's ideal of service and sacrifice. Nor does the formula apply to Catherine herself. Her death is not redemptive, is not a true Imitation of Christ. It is not voluntarily offered and does not save Frederic from anything or give him faith. Only irony attends the sequel in which the surrender of self seems the consequence of weakness rather than the bounty of strong love. The revision removes the small assertion of faith that Frederic makes, "I found I loved god too, a little," and when the priest declares, "You should love Him," the answer is simply, "I don't love much," or, as the draft has it, "I did not love anything very much," which seems a statement of affective deficiency in general, a general inability to donate emotion.

Frederic's estrangement from feeling is not the consequence of any particular wounding or of war disgust, or of any experience of adulthood, but of deeply founded sense of loss. A passage Hemingway took out of the novel gives confirmation. It begins with the opening sentence of chapter 40, "We had a fine life" (p. 306), followed in the finished novel by a brief description of the way the couple spent their days during the last of their winter stay in the Swiss mountains. Hemingway decided not to use the long passage that originally followed this opening sentence in which Frederic reflects, anticipating the tragic conclusion, "wisdom and happiness do not go together," and declares his reductive certitude: "The only thing I know is that if you love anything enough they take it away from you." In this discarded passage, as in the rejected ending of the novel, Hemingway felt the need to refer once again to Rinaldi and the priest, those seemingly forgotten mentors of contrary wisdom, and it is plain that Frederic cannot accept the latter's faith, though he says, "I see the wisdom of the priest in our mess who has always loved God and so is happy and I am sure that nothing will ever take God away from him. But how much is wisdom and how much is luck to be born that way? And what if you are not built that way?" Earlier in the novel Gino is described as a patriot because he is "born that way" and Rinaldi is a skeptic for the same reason. But here, in the excised passage, Frederic speaks of himself: "But what if you were born loving nothing and the warm milk of your mother's breast was never heaven and the first thing you loved was the side of a hill and the last thing was a woman and they took her away and you did not want another but only to have her; and she was gone, then you are not so well placed."[24] For Hemingway, too, cannot it have been true that "the warm milk of [his] mother's breast was never heaven"? Is this the underwater knowledge of self which supports the poignancy of what remains in the final text of the novel?

Hemingway's difficulties with the ending can now be seen to have been caused by something besides his desire to be true to life's inconclusiveness. His hero's emotional or philosophic *nada* threatened the very process of making sense, achieving illumination. Hemingway decided to eschew any hint of apocalypse, rejecting even Fitzgerald's suggestion that he place at the end the passage in which Frederic describes how all are finished off impartially, though the good, the gentle, and the brave go first—as dark a revelation as one could imagine, but still a revelation of sorts. What would do best, he realized, would be simply the hero's numb survival without insight, his notation without catharsis.

Notes

1 The dependence of *A Farewell to Arms* on Hemingway's research rather than on direct observation is comprehensively demonstrated in Michael S. Reynolds's *Hemingway's First War: The Making of 'A Farewell to Arms'* (Princeton: Princeton University Press, 1976).

2 *The Nick Adams Stories*, ed. Philip Young (New York: Bantam, 1973), p. 217.

3 As related, for example, to Guy Hickok: "I felt my soul or something like it coming right out of my body, like you'd pull a silk handkerchief

out of a pocket by one corner. It flew around and then it came back and went in again and I wasn't dead anymore." "A Portrait of Mister Papa," by Malcolm Cowley, *Life* (10 January 1949), repr. *Ernest Hemingway: The Man and his Work*, ed. John K. M. McCaffrey (New York: Cooper Square, 1969), p. 35.

4 It is Philip Young's influential thesis that "one fact about this recurrent protagonist [the Hemingway hero] as about the man who created him, is necessary to any real understanding of either figure, and that is the fact of the 'wound,' a severe injury suffered in World War I which left permanent scars, visible and otherwise." *Ernest Hemingway: A Reconsideration* (University Park: Pennsylvania State University Press, 1966), p. 6.

5 A typical example of such calculated irrelevance might be the sentences that conclude the opening paragraph of chapter 9 which describes the hero's pause, with his ambulance drivers, on the way to the battle location where he will be wounded: "I gave them each a package of cigarettes, Macedonias, loosely packed cigarettes that spilled tobacco and needed to have the ends twisted before you smoked them. Manera lit his lighter and passed it around. The lighter was shaped like a Fiat radiator." *A Farewell to Arms* (New York: Scribner's 1929), p. 47. All further references to the novel will be to this edition.

6 The variant manuscript endings are described by Reynolds (*Hemingway's First War*) and by Bernard Oldsey, *Hemingway's Hidden Craft: The Writing of 'A Farewell to Arms'* (University Park: Pennsylvania State University Press, 1979).

7 Reynolds, *Hemingway's First War*, p. 22.

8 Reynolds, *Hemingway's First War*, pp. 46–47.

9 The most influential description of the novel as a system of imagery has been Carlos Baker's in *Hemingway: The Writer as Artist*, rev. ed. (Princeton: Princeton University Press, 1963), pp. 94–96. But Baker's constrasted symbology of mountain and plain suggests a dynamics of psychological and moral movement correlated with physical description. In my own view there is no such movement.

10 Carlos Baker, *Ernest Hemingway: A Life Story* (New York: Scribner's 1969).

11 Baker, *A Life Story*, p. 54.

12 *Ernest Hemingway: Selected Letters, 1917-1961*, ed. Carlos Baker (New York: Scribner's, 1981), letter to Grace Hall Hemingway, 5 February 1927, p. 243.

13 Charles Fenton, *The Apprenticeship of Ernest Hemingway* (New York: Farrar, Straus & Young, 1954), p. 1.

14 Hemingway, *Selected Letters*, letter to Grace Hall Hemingway, 11 March 1929, p. 296.

15 Hemingway, *Selected Letters*, letter to Maxwell Perkins, 16 December 1928, p. 291.

16 Hemingway, *Selected Letters*, letter to Charles Scribner, 27 August 1949, p. 670.

17 "If a writer of prose knows enough about what he is writing about, he may omit things that he knows and the reader, if the writer is writing truly enough, will have a feeling of those things as strongly as though the writer had stated them. The dignity of movement of an iceberg is due to only one-eighth of it being above water. A writer who omits things because he does not know them only makes hollow places in his writing." See *Death in the Afternoon* (New York: Scribner's, 1932), p. 192.

18 Julian Smith, "Hemingway and the Thing Left Out," *Ernest Hemingway: Five Decades of Criticism*, ed. Linda W. Wagner (Lansing: Michigan State University Press, 1974), pp. 188–200.

19 Reynolds, *Hemingway's First War*, pp. 295, 296.

20 Cf. Philip Young and Charles W. Mann, eds., *The Hemingway Manuscripts: An Inventory* (University Park: Pennsylvania State University Press, 1969), p. 44.

21 Reynolds, *Hemingway's First War*, p. 33.

22 Reynolds, *Hemingway's First War*, p. 59.

23 Reynolds, *Hemingway's First War*, pp. 286–87.

24 Reynolds, *Hemingway's First War*, pp. 40–41.

Women and the Loss of Eden in Hemingway's Mythology

WHEN we read about the Hemingway hero—Lt. Henry or Jake Barnes or Robert Jordan—we are often told that he is the man who stands alone against the universe, who preserves his sanity and his integrity by a silent rebellion and a private armistice. Yet on closer inspection it is clear that he is seldom entirely alone; he stands armed against the forces of nature with his woman at his side: Catherine or Maria or even Brett. Although we can find in Santiago in *The Old Man and the Sea* and in the matador in *Death in the Afternoon* extreme examples of Hemingway's portrayal of one man pitted against a single beast as antagonist, in the major novels it is a pair of lovers who define the fictional center of interest, and it is the loss of love that represents the chief stakes in the game of life.

There is no question that Ernest Hemingway idealized love, although he was also deeply suspicious of it, and, considering his generation's suspicion of ennobling values, it is significant that love is one of the few survivors of the old value system. In Hemingway's famous statement about the "obscenity" of abstract words in *A Farewell to Arms*, love is conspicuously absent:

> I was always embarrassed by the words sacred, glorious, and sacrifice and the expression in vain. . . . I had seen nothing

sacred, and the things that were glorious had no glory and
the sacrifices were like the stockyards at Chicago if nothing
was done with the meat except to bury it. . . . Abstract
words such as glory, honor, courage, or hallow were obscene
beside the concrete names of villages, the numbers of roads,
the names of rivers, the numbers of regiments and the dates.[1]

Love was not an abstraction used by generals and presidents to
manipulate the innocent but an individual response to the mean-
ingless institutions of modern life. Together with male friendship,
it was perhaps the only individual action still available.

What is characteristic of Hemingway is the mythic, almost biblical, patterns he imposes on relations between the sexes. Indeed,
it is Eden all over again. True, selfless love is the special attribute
of good women like Catherine and Maria. They do more than
serve men; they respond to their souls and, most important of all,
free them from the guilt of male sexuality. The special power of
Hemingway's women lies in their frank and honest enjoyment of
sexuality. Catherine and Maria are prelapsarian Eves in Hemingway's mythology, and they create one of the only values worth
living for. But the Fall is inevitable in Hemingway's view of life:
war and the death of love destroy even the most beautiful Eden.

Hemingway's good women die or their happiness is destroyed
as victims of an unconscious God. The good suffer most, for they
act with more courage and run more risks. Bad women are more
troublesome. Brett is dangerous and untrustworthy in her need
and threatens the male code of honor and stoicism. Good women
fix their love on one man and support him. Bad women use their
sexual power to tempt men and to disrupt the often fragile stability of the male world, where violence seethes just below the surface. It is thus the very strength of the hero's attraction to the bad
woman that represents to him her betrayal. Given this definition
of betrayal, it is very easy for a good woman to turn into a bad
woman, for the transformation requires only that her love induce
conflict in the male world or disrupt the healthy stability of an
earlier Eden, a pattern of response which characterized Hemingway's own affairs with women.

Indeed, Hemingway's best-known heroines are remarkably
similar psychologically. The good and bad women alike have

been injured by love and war. When the novels open, they know
more of the pain of the loss of love than the heroes do. Though
they have suffered violation or disillusionment, Hemingway's
women are characterized by their willingness to risk love again in
order to restore the private world of two. This is part of their
courage. Thus the male code of sport and stoicism has its counterpart in women's willingness to love again, though in both Catherine[2] and Brett it comes very near to compulsion.

When Lt. Henry first meets Catherine Barkley, for example,
she carries the stick of the boy she was planning to marry before
he was killed in the battle of the Somme. She expresses remorse
for not having given herself to her lover: "He could have had anything he wanted if I would have known. I would have married
him or anything. I know all about it now. But then he wanted to
go to war and I didn't know" (p. 19). Given Catherine's devotion
to her dead lover, Lt. Henry is not prepared for the unnatural intensity of their second meeting; she slaps him for trying to kiss her
and yet talks about their future together. She cries and says, "Oh,
darling, . . . You will be good to me, won't you?" (p. 27). It is obvious that she is trying hard to imagine him as her lover who was
lost. He says:

> I thought she was probably a little crazy. It was all right if
> she was. I did not care what I was getting into. It was better
> than going every evening to the house for officers where the
> girls climbed all over you and put your cap on backward as
> a sign of affection between their trips upstairs with brother
> officers. I knew I did not love Catherine Barkley nor had
> any idea of loving her. This was a game, like bridge, in
> which you said things instead of playing cards. Like bridge
> you had to pretend you were playing for money or playing
> for some stakes. Nobody had mentioned what the stakes
> were. It was all right with me. (pp. 30–31)

It is when Frederic Henry first sees Catherine in the hospital in
Milan after his wounding that he knows he is suddenly in love
with her. But there is throughout their love affair the clear sense
that he is her substitute lover. When they first make love she says,
"Now do you believe I love you?" (p. 92), as if to assuage her

earlier regret that she had not proved her love for her fiancé by sleeping with him before he went off to war. Catherine's total accommodation and self-sacrifice have the quality of religious fervor and neurotic symptom. She tells Frederic, "There isn't any me any more. Just what you want" (p. 106), and later, "You're my religion. You're all I've got" (p. 116).

Carlos Baker notes that Hemingway once referred to *A Farewell to Arms* as his *Romeo and Juliet*,[3] and the atmosphere of starcrossed lovers pervades the book. The sense of foreboding is achieved by a subtle amalgam of foreshadowing by the narrative voice and by the intensity of Catherine's brave but obsessive love. Her desire to be "a good girl," to cause Frederic no trouble despite her pregnancy, is evidence not only of her willingness to love again but also of the risks involved. Her every selfless utterance reminds us of how short their time together may be and how inevitable the loss of Eden.

Lady Brett Ashley in *The Sun Also Rises* is another heroine who has been wounded by love and war and yet compulsively seeks to reestablish the special world of lovers. She is one of Hemingway's bad women, a Circe who turns men into swine, but even as she invades and violates the masculine world of the matador she offers to Jake and Romero and Robert Cohn alike the supreme allurement of a beautiful woman aroused to insatiable passion. Hemingway makes clear that she cannot help herself; she, like the men she tantalizes, is sick with unrequited love.[4] She is a threat to men because she forces them to recognize the primitiveness of their desire and the fragility of male bonding when threatened by lust, sexual need, or competition for a woman.

Lady Brett has generally been considered to differ fundamentally from Hemingway's more positive portraits of women. Carlos Baker says, for example, that though Brett and Catherine share nationality and have both lost lovers in the Great War, "here the resemblances stop":

Brett's neurosis drives her from bar to bar, from man to man, from city to city. None of it is any good: her polygamy, with or without benefit of justices of the peace, leads only to more of the same, as one drinks leads to another in the endless round. Brett is not "good" for the men she knows. Romero wants her to let her hair grow out, to become more feminine, to marry and live with him. The basic abnormality at work in Brett opposes such feminization.[5]

It is true that her hair is bobbed, that she likes to wear male dress and to drink like the men she emulates, but beneath her pose Lady Brett bears a striking resemblance to Hemingway's other heroines. That she is sick with love is evident early in the novel when she and Jake escape from their drunken friends at the Bal Musette. Once in the cab, Brett gives up her pretense of brittle gaiety and confesses her misery and her desire for Jake:

> Brett was leaning back in the corner, her eyes closed. I got in and sat beside her. The cab started with a jerk.
> "Oh, darling, I've been so miserable," Brett said.[6]

They both struggle with the desire to be with each other and the realization that they can never be lovers. Their relationship is a study in approach-avoidance. When Brett appears drunk at Jake's flat, and when she seeks him out for help and comfort, she is following the approach arc of this vicious circle. When she goes off with other men, she hopes to find in the drug of sex a way to forget the future and the past. The Paris section of the novel is filled with negative portraits of women, the prostitute with bad teeth, rich and superficial women, and women like Frances, "bitches" who seek marriage when they have lost their looks and who destroy the freedom of men like Cohn who are cowed by them. In this company Brett appears more honest than the rest; her "abnormality" is actually a brave attempt to conceal her pain and to find substitute comforts for true love. The difference between Brett and Hemingway's good women lies not in her desperate need for love nor in her willingness to follow wherever love leads but in the degree of sexual anxiety she arouses. Dangerous as she is, like all of Hemingway's women, she is defined by love. Although she is unreliable and a drunk, she is the mirror image of Hemingway's good girls. She is a good woman the world has broken. Even so, she and Jake Barnes remain a pair: it is he she calls upon when she is in trouble and he responds by coming to her rescue. Neither Brett nor Jake can fully live the stoical code that Count Mippipopolous endorses when he says, "You see, Mr. Barnes, it is because I have lived very much that now I can enjoy everything so well" (p. 60). Being in love does not allow them the luxury of gaining the cool perspective that time and distance could provide. They attempt to fake that perspective as best they can and to keep the pain to themselves.

Brett's attempts to conceal her pain by remaining drunk or by "going off with someone" are relatively successful in the social chaos of expatriate life in Paris. In the traditional world of Spain, however, they are disruptive. Brett's dishonor is that her need for the emotional fix of an affair spills over into the public arena. Although she finally acknowledges the code of honor by sending Romero away, even Jake is stunned by the dangerousness of loving women. His famous response to her comment that they could have had "such a damned good time together" ("Yes, . . . Isn't it pretty to think so?" [p. 247]) seems to suggest his self-disgust and his wish for disengagement.

Maria in *For Whom the Bell Tolls* is a later version of the good woman. It is interesting to see how Hemingway has modified the pattern without fundamentally changing it, even though *For Whom the Bell Tolls* shows a greater degree of support for social engagement. The private armistice of Catherine and Frederic has now become the tragedy of lovers who are denied a future together by the strength of the hero's belief in Republican freedom. At the end of the novel, after Robert Jordan has forced the others to leave him to die, he expresses this belief: "I have fought for what I believed in for a year now. If we win here we will win everywhere. The world is a fine place and worth the fighting for."[7] But although the war is now the Spanish Civil War and the cause is one he is willing to die for, Robert is still an outsider who has come to give temporary help to the Spanish Republicans, just as Lt. Henry served the Italians as a gentleman volunteer, and Jake Barnes was a favored outsider at the festival at Pamplona. Maria has suffered the loss in war of her father and mother, who died courageously defending the Republican cause. Her sexual wounds are not metaphorical, as in the two earlier novels, for she has literally suffered rape and humiliation at the hands of the Fascists. Like Catherine and Brett, she has been made crazy by the violation of her identity as a woman. Rafael, the gypsy, tells

Robert Jordan of Maria's state when she was found by the guerrillas after the train bombing: "When we picked the girl up at the
time of the train she was very strange. . . . She would not speak
and she cried all the time and if anyone touched her she would
shiver like a wet dog. Only lately has she been better" (p. 28).

She has been rescued and protected by Pilar, the guerrilla lead-
er's woman, and gradually healed by Pilar's philosophy that
nothing Maria has not consented to could really touch her. Encouraged by Pilar, she comes to sleep with Robert on his first
night in the camp and shows by this act that she is ready to love
again. She is passionately eager to stay with him and to be his
woman. As in the case of Catherine Barkley, this act of commitment to love can cleanse and heal the good woman; Pilar knows
this when she sends Maria to Robert Jordan. As in Hemingway's
earlier books, in which women show greater experience with
love's pain and yet greater willingness to love again at any cost,
Maria expresses her wish to be Robert's natural "wife" despite the
dangerousness of his mission to blow up the bridge. But although
Robert and Maria imagine their life together in Madrid and in
America, Robert knows his chances for survival are not great, and
Pilar has read his death in his palm. Like Hemingway's other starcrossed lovers, they recognize that they must crowd a lifetime into
their few days together:

> Maybe that is what I am to get now from life. . . . I suppose
> it is possible to live as full a life in seventy hours as in sev-
> enty years. . . . So if your life trades its seventy years for
> seventy hours I have that value now and I am lucky enough
> to know it. And if there is not any such thing as a long time,
> nor the rest of your lives, nor from now on, but there is only
> now, why then now is the thing to praise and I am very
> happy with it. (p. 166)

In her confession of love to Robert, Maria says: "But we will be
one now and there will never be a separate one. . . . I will be thee
when thou are not there" (p. 263), which echoes Catherine Barkley's "There isn't any me any more." When he is wounded at the
bridge, Robert uses the idea of inseparable union to persuade
Maria to leave him: "Listen. We will not go to Madrid now but I

go always with thee wherever thou goest. Understand? . . . If thou goest then I go with thee. It is in that way that I go too" (p. 463).

In Maria, Hemingway has created a child-woman. In contrast to Catherine's and Brett's honest appraisal of their "rotten luck," Maria is carefully protected by both Robert and Pilar and kept uninformed of the danger of Robert's mission. She is encouraged to hope for a future they know will never occur. Her foil is Pilar, the earthy and realistic gypsy, characterized by her power and courage and by her loyalty to the Republic. Together these two characters make one full woman. In the imagery of the book, Maria is a hurt rabbit, a child bride, injured by war and in need of protection, while Pilar is her alter ego, ugly, passionate, and dangerous, especially to men her scorn can wither. Both are good women, but some of Brett's destructive force has been included in Pilar's powerful yet benign maternal concern for Maria and in her leadership of the guerrillas. Only a few hints remain of the dangerous woman who dominates men.

One of those hints is in Hemingway's autobiographical references to the suicide of Robert's father. Lloyd R. Arnold, in *High on the Wild with Hemingway*, records Hemingway's comment that the cause of his father's death had not been illness or debt but domination by his mother:

> She had to rule everything, have it all her own way, and she was a bitch! . . . True, it was a cowardly thing for my father to do, but then, if you don't live behind the eyes you can't expect to see all of the view. I know that part of his view.[8]

In *For Whom the Bell Tolls* Robert traces his courage, his "good juice," to his grandfather, who fought for four years in the Civil War and with Custer at Little Big Horn. It was his gun that Robert's father used to kill himself, as Hemingway's father had done. Robert says:

> I wish Grandfather was here. . . . Maybe he sent me what little I have through that other one that misused the gun.
> . . . I wish the time-lag wasn't so long so that I could have learned from him what the other one never had to teach me.

But suppose the fear he had to go through and dominate and just get rid of finally . . . had made a *cobarde* out of the other one the way second generation bullfighters almost always are? . . .

 . . . Go on, say it in English. Coward. . . . He was just a coward and that was the worst luck any man could have. Because if he wasn't a coward he would have stood up to that woman and not let her bully him. I wonder what I would have been like if he had married a different woman? . . . Maybe the bully in her helped to supply what was missing in the other. (pp. 338–39)

To Robert Jordan, cowardice was "the worst luck any man could have" and the domination by a woman its most humiliating evidence. In the character of Pilar and in her humiliation of Pablo there are clear signs of the dominating bitch, and the mixture of fear and admiration the men feel toward her may echo Hemingway's own childhood ambivalence toward his mother. If so, it would represent another example of the transformation of one kind of woman into another. By separating the powerful woman from the injured girl, he was able to distance the danger and allow Pilar to represent the strength and dominance of the Spanish earth while Maria became the innocent and obedient child-wife, able to be loved without fear of loss of manhood.

 Another evidence that Hemingway applied these views of female power and female betrayal to real women occurs in an early fictional treatment of his love affair with Agnes von Kurowsky, the chief source of Catherine Barkley. After Hemingway's return to Oak Park from the Italian front he waited for word from the nurse he hoped to marry and suffered great pain when she finally wrote that she planned to marry an Italian officer instead.[9] In "A Very Short Story," included in *In Our Time*, there is a brief but bitter sketch of Agnes, whom Hemingway would later transform into the faithful and loving Catherine of *A Farewell to Arms*. In this two-page story, the narrator describes their romantic idyll during his recovery in an Italian hospital:

 Luz stayed on night duty for three months. They were glad to let her. When they operated on him she prepared

him for the operating table. . . . He went under the anaes-
thetic holding tight on to himself so he would not blab about
anything during the silly, talky time. After he got on crutches
he used to take the temperatures so Luz would not have to
get up from the bed. There were only a few patients, and
they all knew about it.[10]

They want to get married before he goes back to the front, "but
there was not enough time for the banns, and neither of them had
birth certificates. They felt as though they were married, but they
wanted every one to know about it, and to make it so they could
not lose it" (p. 65).

After the armistice Luz insists that he go home and get a job so
they can marry, but they quarrel about her unwillingness to come
home with him. With controlled understatement, he describes
the end of the romance:

He went to America on a boat from Genoa. Luz went
back to Pordenone to open a hospital. . . . The major of the
battalion made love to Luz, and she had never known Italians before, and finally wrote to the States that theirs had
been only a boy and girl affair. She was sorry and she knew
he would probably not be able to understand, but might
some day forgive her, and be grateful to her, and she expected, absolutely unexpectedly, to be married in the spring.
(p. 66)

The story's last paragraph is heavy with irony: "The major did
not marry her in the spring, or any other time. Luz never got an
answer to the letter to Chicago about it. A short time after he con-
tracted gonorrhea from a sales girl in a loop department store
while riding in a taxicab through Lincoln Park" (p. 66). The implication of this ending is that a universal revenge will be called
down upon both the betrayer and the betrayed. Luz will never
marry her major, and she will certainly never be able to return to
her first love; he will see to that. His disillusionment is reflected in
the last sentence, in which he is driven by her defection to casual
sex in a taxicab and then punished by gonorrhea.

Female betrayal is also the subject of several episodes in *A Moveable Feast*, Hemingway's memorial to his Paris years. He pictures Zelda Fitzgerald, for example, as a beautiful but bad woman engaged in a jealous struggle to keep Fitzgerald from working and succeeding by keeping him drunk. Finally, in driving him to ruin she drove herself to madness. Hemingway also describes his bitterest memory of the Paris years, the theft of his early manuscripts when Hadley brought them to him in Switzerland. He stops just short of describing this as an act of betrayal and tells instead of Hadley's tears of remorse. Characteristically, he describes his efforts to conceal his grief as "all that stuff you feed the troops."[11]

Most significant of all is Hemingway's description of the breakup of his marriage to Hadley. He pictures their idyllic and healthy life with their son Bumby in the mountains at Schruns and the invasion of "the rich."

> During our last year in the mountains new people came
> deep into our lives and nothing was ever the same again. . . .
> It was that year that the rich showed up.
>   The rich have a sort of pilot fish who goes ahead of them,
> sometimes a little deaf, sometimes a little blind, but always
> smelling affable and hesitant ahead of them. (p. 205)

Hemingway says that the rich are attracted because "the two people who love each other" are happy and gay and are doing good work. They are also inexperienced. "They do not know how not to be overrun and how to go away. They do not always learn about the good, the attractive, the charming, the soon-beloved, the generous, the understanding rich who have no bad qualities and who give each day the quality of a festival" (p. 206).

An even greater danger is "another rich," a wealthy young woman who was, of course, Pauline Pfeiffer, Hemingway's second wife:

> Before these rich had come we had already been infiltrated
> by another rich using the oldest trick there is. It is that an
> unmarried young woman becomes the temporary best friend

of another young woman who is married, goes to live with
the husband and wife and then unknowingly, innocently and
unrelentingly sets out to marry the husband. When the husband is a writer and doing difficult work so that he is occupied much of the time and is not a good companion or
partner to his wife for a big part of the day, the arrangement
has advantages until you know how it works out. The husband has two attractive girls around when he has finished
work. One is new and strange and if he has bad luck he gets
to love them both. (pp. 207–8)

Hemingway describes his trip to New York and his meeting in
Paris with Pauline: "I should have caught the first train from the
Gare de l'Est that would take me down to Austria. But the girl I
was in love with was in Paris then, and I did not take the first
train, or the second or the third" (p. 208). When he finally arrives
in Schruns and see Hadley and Bumby at the station, his feelings
of guilt and conflict are intense:

I wished I had died before I ever loved anyone but her. She
was smiling, the sun on her lovely face tanned by the snow
and the sun. . . .
    I loved her and I loved no one else and we had a lovely
magic time while we were alone. . . . I thought we were in-
vulnerable again, and it wasn't until we were out of the
mountains in late spring, and back in Paris that the other
thing started again. (p. 208)

Hemingway is clearly struggling with his own sense of guilt and
responsibility for his affair with Pauline Pfeiffer, but the narrative follows the familiar pattern: idyllic love betrayed, first by
"the pilot fish" and then by the seduction of the vulnerable artist
by "the rich," especially by "another rich" in the form of a dan-
gerously exciting woman who destroys the idyll with the relent-
lessness of a natural instinct. These threats are described as impersonal forces of nature, not the human misjudgments of a man
in love. The loss of wife and son is seen as the loss of purity and
happiness, the cost of passion. For Hemingway these are the in-
exorable terms of life: pure love in its health and innocent per-

fection cannot withstand the forces of destruction. Women represent both poles of the dilemma. Their love can create an Eden or, with the male as their helpless victim, destroy one. Just as Eve is transformed from Adam's innocent helpmate into his evil temptress, so Hemingway's women are often the subject of a similar sleight of hand. According to both myths, it is in the nature of things that Eden is lost. What is missing in Hemingway's treatment of love is the element of personal choice, all-important in the biblical story. Indeed, his version sometimes seems a convenient means of avoiding responsibility for decisions that are moral choices. Hemingway's susceptibility to romantic love and equally strong fear of the dominance of women predisposed him to see love's failure as one more "dirty trick" in a world gone wrong.

There is a curious male passivity in those novels: women come to men and are initially the sexual aggressors. In their need they accelerate the love affair and raise it to first intensity. There is a telling passage in "Soldier's Home," another story in *In Our Time*, which illuminates this psychology from the male point of view:

> Nothing was changed in the town except that the young girls had grown up. . . .
> Vaguely he wanted a girl but he did not want to have to work to get her. . . . He did not want to get into the intrigue and the politics. He did not want to have to do any courting. He did not want to tell any more lies. It wasn't worth it.
> . . . You did not need a girl unless you thought about them. He learned that in the army. Then sooner or later you always got one. . . . You did not have to think about it. . . .
> Now he would have liked a girl if she had come to him and not wanted to talk. But here at home it was all too complicated. . . . It was not worth the trouble.
> . . . Not now when things were getting good again.
> (pp. 71–72)

This passage expresses a quintessential Hemingway attitude: despite the attraction of women, they come at a very high price. "Now when things were getting good again," it is better to keep control and avoid complications. This deep ambivalence conceals both desire and fear. It also puts the responsibility for love on women as the mysterious and dangerous "other" and sets a premium on male separateness. To remain strong, a man is better off alone for then he is out of emotional danger. Psychologically, the male code Hemingway develops hides a very traditional morality, one that says pleasure and sexual freedom must be paid for by remorse and repentance, that after the release of love or war, the barriers must again be restored and payment must be made.

The cultural stereotypes of Hemingway's world support this pattern. In Western culture the myth of an individual complete in emotional isolation is a male myth. The female counterpart is that women create the web of social relationships and "complications" and are thus ruled by love and destroyed by its loss. In Hemingway's fictional love affairs, under the stress of war the stakes are raised. Women are even more vulnerable, being cut off from their social base, and men must pursue the male pattern of strength, independence, and courage more relentlessly than ever in order to preserve control in the face of death and in the presence of the emotional needs of women. It is important to recognize, however, that despite the prevalence of these myths, they are not laws of the universe. The universe in Hemingway's work has a very familiar look about it. God has not been lost; God is up there punishing to the last.

Hemingway's portrayal of love is a very romantic vision. Real life rarely is an enthralling drama played against cosmic odds. What saves Hemingway's best work from his own stereotypes is his ability to show the tension between what his characters believe in and what they feel. His heroes, despite their celebrated stoic silence, spend a great deal of time thinking out loud about their principles, their pain, and their conflicts. It is this tension between judgment and emotion that makes Jake Barnes and Frederic Henry "real." Hemingway's heroines talk more openly but are seen more externally: with very few exceptions we hear what they say, we do not hear what they think. The conflict in these novels thus resides in the hero and is filtered through the male code. Nevertheless, in his best work Hemingway's unfailing eye for detail and ear for speech rarely fail him. He creates characters struggling against the unrelenting strictness of their own ideals. They find it difficult to live up to the rigid demands of sexuality. Catherine and Maria struggle to be perfect wives but are best presented in their moments of doubt and defeat. Even Brett struggles against her nature and her dangerousness. It is this struggle, finally, that gives these characters their unique sense of reality. The value of Hemingway's picture of love between men and women does not lie in the rigid patterns of gender he imposes on his lovers but in their valiant struggle as complex personalities to fit these patterns. We can all identify with this struggle, especially in the game of love. Given the great odds against which love is waged in these novels, it is no wonder that Hemingway and his readers found relief in the simpler struggles of Santiago against the sea and the matador against the unleashed forces of primeval nature.

Notes

1 Ernest Hemingway, *A Farewell to Arms* (New York: Scribner's, 1969), pp. 184–85. All further references to this work appear in the text.

2 Catherine is often seen either as an unrealistically "good" woman or as a poorly realized character, rather than as a woman compulsively afraid of losing another lover. Leslie A. Fiedler, in *Love and Death in the American Novel* (New York: Stein and Day, 1966), sees Catherine as an example of his contention that the greatest American novelists are incapable of dealing with adult heterosexual love, "giving us instead monsters of virtue or bitchery" (p. 24). Linda W. Wagner, in "'Proud and Friendly and Gently': Women in Hemingway's Early Fiction," *Ernest Hemingway: The Papers of a Writer*, ed. Bernard Oldsey (New York: Garland, 1981), cites approvingly F. Scott Fitzgerald's comment that Catherine is less successful than some of the women in Hemingway's early short stories because "in the stories you were really listening to women—here you're only listening to yourself" (p. 63). Wagner theorizes that Catherine's death is really a substitute expression of Hemingway's bereavement over his father's death, after which he stopped believing "in the romantic, mystic ideal of genuine love, of a man's finding ultimate completion with a woman" (p. 69).

3 Carlos Baker, *Hemingway: The Writer as Artist* (Princeton: Princeton University Press, 1972), p. 98.
4 Robert W. Lewis, Jr., in *Hemingway on Love* (Austin: University of Texas Press, 1965), makes the same point, but sees the lovesickness of Jake and Brett as patterned on Tristan and Iseult, portraying the "tyranny of romantic love" (p. 28).
5 Baker, *The Writer as Artist*, p. 112.
6 Ernest Hemingway, *The Sun Also Rises* (New York: Scribner's, 1954), p. 24. All further references to this work appear in the text.
7 Ernest Hemingway, *For Whom the Bell Tolls* (New York: Scribner's, 1968), p. 467. All further references to this work appear in the text.
8 Lloyd R. Arnold, *High on the Wild with Hemingway* (Caldwell: Caxton, 1968), p. 79. This episode is also mentioned in Carlos Baker, *Hemingway: A Life Story* (New York: Scribner's, 1969), p. 344.
9 See Baker, *Life Story*, p. 59, and Marcelline Hemingway Sanford, *At the Hemingways* (Boston: Little, Brown, 1961), p. 188.
10 Ernest Hemingway, *In Our Time* (New York: Scribner's, 1970), p. 65. All further references to this work appear in the text.
11 Ernest Hemingway, *A Moveable Feast* (New York: Bantam, 1965), p. 74. All further references to this work appear in the text.

PART FOUR

RELATIONSHIPS WITH OTHER WRITERS

9. Peter L. Hays

Exchange between Rivals: Faulkner's Influence on *The Old Man and the Sea*

ERNEST HEMINGWAY'S antagonism to fellow writers, particularly to those who might be considered his equals, is well known, and William Faulkner was among his many targets for vituperation. Hemingway denounced him as "Corncob," "Old Corndrinking Mellifluous," and as the author of stories about "Octonawhoopoo" or "Anomatopoeio County."[1] Yet the situation was not simply one of unmixed antagonism. Hemingway told both James T. Farrell (in 1936) and Jean-Paul Sartre (in 1944) that Faulkner was a better writer than himself.[2] And in *Death in the Afternoon* (1932) he praised Faulkner while mocking *Sanctuary*:

> My operatives tell me that through the fine work of Mr. William Faulkner publishers now will publish anything rather than to try to get you to delete the better portions of your works, and I look forward to writing of those days of my youth which were spent in the finest whorehouses in the land amid the most brilliant society there found.
>
> *Old lady:* Has this Mr. Faulkner written well of these places?
>
> Splendidly, Madame. Mr. Faulkner writes admirably of them. He writes the best of them of any writer I have read for many years.

Old lady: I must buy his works.

Madame, you can't go wrong on Faulkner. He's prolific too. By the time you get them ordered there'll be new ones out.

Old lady: If they are as you say there cannot be too many.

Madame, you voice my own opinion.[3]

When Robert Coates, in his *New Yorker* review of *Death in the Afternoon,* chided Hemingway for his "petulant jibes" at Faulkner, Hemingway responded in a letter: "There weren't any cracks against Faulkner. . . . There was . . . a pretty damned friendly mention. . . . I have plenty of respect for Faulkner and wish him all luck. I'm damned if I wrote any petulant jibes against Faulkner and the hell with you telling citizens that I did."[4] Hemingway wrote Malcolm Cowley (in 1945) that Faulkner "has the most talent of anybody," then qualified that praise by adding:

He just needs a sort of conscience that isn't there. . . . He will write absolutely perfectly straight and then go on and on and not be able to end it. I wish the christ I owned him like you'd own a horse and train him like a horse and race him like a horse—only in writing. How beautifully he can write and as simple and as complicated as autumn or as spring.[5]

Of Faulkner's work, Hemingway wrote Owen Wister (in 1932) that he liked *As I Lay Dying* but that *Sanctuary* was "pretty phony"; in another letter (1956),while calling Faulkner a "no-good son of a bitch," Hemingway praised *Sanctuary, Pylon,* and "The Bear" but condemned *A Fable* as night soil.[6] He did, however, include Faulkner's "Turnabout," Faulkner's most Hemingwayesque tale, in his wartime anthology *Men at War* (1942).

The major contretemps between them occurred in 1947 when Faulkner, questioned by students at the University of Mississippi about his ranking of American writers, put Thomas Wolfe, himself, and John Dos Passos—in that order—ahead of Hemingway for their courage in stylistic experimentation.[7] Hemingway chose to interpret the published remarks as an insult to his physical courage. He asked General Charles T. (Buck) Lanham, with whom he had served in the Second World War, to write to Faulkner, which the general did, praising Hemingway's courage under fire. Faulkner replied, apologizing in separate letters to Lanham and to Hemingway, inspiring this response from Hemingway:

> Awfully glad to hear from you and glad to have made contact. . . . Please throw all the other stuff away, the misunderstanding. . . .
> You are a better writer than Fielding or any of those guys and you should just know it and keep on writing. You have things written that come back to me better than any of them. . . . Have much regard for you. Would you like to keep on writing [letters].[8]

On the other side of the rivalry, Faulkner, as befitted his less bellicose nature, was consistently milder in his comments and more respectful of both Hemingway and his work. Most of his early correspondence deals with the man, not the books: e.g., he thanks Paul Romaine (1932) for a greeting passed on from Hemingway and remarks that he wished he had thought to initiate a friendship; he responds (1945) to Malcolm Cowley's letter about Hemingway's failed third marriage and loneliness, promising to write Hemingway (but not doing so for two years).[9] It is interesting that Cowley begins his correspondence with Faulkner in the spring of 1944 (he writes in February, Faulkner answers May 7), just after Cowley has finished compiling *The Portable Hemingway* and as Faulkner is finishing the screenplay of Hemingway's *To Have and Have Not*. Whereas Cowley mentions Hemingway frequently, Faulkner writes of him only twice: once in the letter of May 7 and once in another version of his much-repeated statement that Hemingway's fiction lacked experimentation.[10]

Elsewhere, however, Faulkner three times wrote high praise of Hemingway. In 1950, in a letter to *Time* magazine, seconding Evelyn Waugh's defense of *Across the River and into the Trees*, Faulkner said, "the man who wrote some of the pieces in *Men Without Women* and *The Sun Also Rises* and some of the African stuff (some—most—of all the rest of it too for that matter) does not need defending."[11] When Harvey Breit asked Faulkner to review *The Old Man and the Sea* for the *New York Times Book Review*, Faulkner declined, but he sent Breit a letter praising Hemingway, repeating many of his *Time* magazine comments (but adding *A Farewell to Arms* and *For Whom the Bell Tolls* to his list of Hemingway's eminent achievements), concluding "that if even what remained [the other, unmentioned work] had not been as honest and true as he could make it, then he himself would have burned the manuscript before the publisher even saw it."[12] Faulkner finally did write a one-paragraph review of *The Old Man and the Sea* for *Shenandoah*, calling the book Hemingway's "best. Time may show it to be the best single piece of any of us, I mean his and my contemporaries."[13]

The two authors' works are also curiously interwined. There is the coincidence of simultaneous publication by the New Orleans *Double Dealer* in June 1922; there is the friendship of both with Sherwood Anderson, the lessons learned from him, and their coincidental mockery of their mentor, Hemingway savagely in *The Torrents of Spring*, Faulkner more gently in his introduction to *Sherwood Anderson and Other Creoles* (both published in 1926) and in his portrait of Anderson in *Mosquitoes* (written in 1926, published in 1927). Then there begin to be instances in their published works where one seems to have learned from, borrowed from, or be poking fun at the other (Hemingway's remarks in *Death in the Afternoon* are one example of the last). Malcolm Cowley makes the first attribution in 1945, saying that there is a suggestion of Hemingway in the way Faulkner presents a trout in a river (in the Quentin section of *The Sound and the Fury*).[14] In 1952, French reviewers noted a similarity between *A Farewell to Arms* and *The Wild Palms*; similarities of theme aside, certain words make the connection obvious: Faulkner writes of "hemingwaves"; on the same page he picks up Hemingway's pun on "armor" (from Swift and Armour in "The Snows of Kilimanjaro") by making one of his own—"armorous"—and even writes of "aficianados" [sic].[15] The protagonist of *The Wild Palms* (1939) bears the same first name, Harry, as do the protagonists of "Snows" (1936) and *To Have and Have Not* (1937), just as the title of the contrapuntal novella within *The Wild Palms*, "Old Man," pre-figures *The Old Man and the Sea*. As Thomas McHaney notes, the last chapter of Faulkner's *The Unvanquished* (1938), "An Odor of Verbena" (written in July of 1937),[16] apparently owes its title to a phrase in Hemingway's "The Short Happy Life of Francis Macomber" (published September 1936), and references to Hemingway by name occur in *Pylon* and *Requiem for a Nun*.[17] George Monteiro suggests that Hemingway, in turn, borrowed from *The Wild Palms* for the masturbation scene and the ending of *For Whom the Bell Tolls*.[18] There also seems to be a passing back and forth of the use of bicycles grotesquely associated with death, probably based in Hemingway's own near-mortal wound after bicycling to the Italian front at Fossalta di Piave. We see this conjunction first with Hemingway's *A Farewell to Arms* (1929); then Faulkner picks it up for the Percy Grimm section of *Light in August* (1932); then Hemingway takes it back for "A Way You'll Never Be" (1933), "The Snows of Kilimanjaro" (1936), and *To Have and Have Not* (1937).[19] And John Howell sees the influence of *For Whom the Bell Tolls* on "The Bear."[20] As Malcolm Cowley has written, "Faulkner and Hemingway read each other's work with close attention."[21]

Their lives, too, reveal curious likenesses.[22] Two years separated their births, one year their deaths. Both boys were taught a lifelong love of the outdoors, of hunting and fishing, by fathers dominated by their wives. Both boys played football in high school (Faulkner even repeated the fall term of eleventh grade to play more football, in spite of his slight size); and both, unable to enlist with American troops, found other means to join World War I forces. What Carlos Baker wrote of Hemingway applies to Faulkner equally well: "Because Hemingway was by nature and inclination and profession a spinner of yarns, not all of the stories relayed in his letters can be trusted as true. He believed and often said that writers are liars and took evident delight in living up to his own dictum in conversation and letters."[23] This love of invention, plus a desire for self-glorification, led to the reports of Hemingway's serving as an infantryman with the Italian army, printed on the back cover of so many Scribner's paperbacks; and to Faulkner's returning from Canada, not in the air cadet garb he should have been wearing, but in British officer's uniform, telling friends of his terrible crash and of the silver plate in his head.[24]

Though their writing styles are very different, both suggest a basic distrust of language. Hemingway avoids flowery rhetoric and highly connotative words; he purposefully omits certain details, trusting to a skillfully managed recording of fact and event to convey what he wants. Faulkner piles up synonyms as though no one word were adequate, insists in his fiction on the power of intuition, insists as well, epistemologically, on the limits of human knowledge by never telling his readers enough for them to be sure of what has happened. Frederic Henry's comment "There were many words that you could not stand to hear and finally only the names of places had any dignity. . . . Abstract words such as glory, honor, courage, or hallow were obscene beside the concrete names of villages" is very similar to Addie Bundren's "words are no good; that words don't ever fit even what they are trying to say at."[25] But the greatest similarity between the two men who hunted all their lives is the display in their fiction of their love of land: both show respect for wild creatures who inhabit wilderness, for the code of the hunter, and for anyone who acts with the dignity that they often ascribe to animals.

Faulkner praised *The Old Man and the Sea* as the work in which Hemingway discovered God and in which "he wrote about pity."[26] Pity had been present before in Hemingway's works, but God does not play a major role in *The Old Man and the Sea*;[27] in fact, the religion in Hemingway's novella, as in Faulkner's "The Bear," is more totemic or animistic than it is formally Christian.[28] If "Turnabout" is Faulkner's work most like Hemingway's, then *The Old Man and the Sea* is Hemingway's work most like Faulkner's—most specifically, it resembles "The Bear." Perhaps at least part of what appealed to Faulkner in this novella was what he had supplied himself. Some of the likenesses between "The Bear" and *The Old Man and the Sea* are obvious. Both stories involve the pursuit of a large, anthropomorphized beast by an old man who has been responsible for the initiation of a boy into the craft of hunting or fishing and for instilling in the boy values, discipline, and a sense of respect. In both works, the authors are at great pains to establish a link between man and nature, a tight, interdependent community; beyond that, both works present social communities within the larger, natural one. And—unusual for both authors—women figure very slightly in *The Old Man and the Sea* and "The Bear," whereas women are the primary complicating figures in both authors' longer works.

Both authors paid tribute to land or seascape repeatedly; such passages are too familiar to need repeating. Both authors hunted or fished all their lives and devoted much of their writing to the subject—Hemingway from "Big Two-Hearted River" through *The Sun Also Rises, Green Hills of Africa,* to *The Old Man and the Sea;* Faulkner in *Big Woods* (which Edward Shenton illustrated, as he had *Green Hills of Africa*) and throughout *Go Down, Moses.* Even the pursuit of other men in their fiction is presented in terms of hunting: in Hemingway's Robert Jordan's discussion with Anselmo about killing men vs. killing bears,[29] or in Faulkner's "Red Leaves" or "Was " The animals pursued in "The Bear" and *The Old Man and the Sea* are clearly elevated and made human (or superhuman). Faulkner says that "the big old bear had earned for himself a name, a definite designation like a living man"; the bear is "widowered childless and absolved of mortality—old Priam reft of his old wife and outlived all his sons." Faulkner describes Old Ben as Ike's instructor: "If Sam Fathers had been his mentor and the backyard rabbits and squirrels his kindergarten, then the wilderness the old bear ran was his college and the old male bear itself . . . was his alma mater."[30] Hemingway emphasizes that Santiago loves and respects the fish as an equal. He has Santiago say of the marlin, "He is my brother. The fish is my friend too," and, "I have killed this fish which is my brother."[31] The identity Hemingway insists on between Santiago and the marlin, common between hunter and hunted, can also be seen between Sam Fathers and Old Ben: both are aged for their kind, both unwifed and childless; both are Ike's tutors (and, like Isaac, were named from the Old Testament: Samuel the prophet and Benjamin, Isaac's youngest grandson, whose name means son of the South).[32] Both are doomed to die with the vanishing wilderness that both live in and represent. Although Hemingway does not deal with the ending of an era as explicitly as does Faulkner, the changing values of different generations are suggested in this passage:

> Some of the younger fishermen, those who used buoys as floats for their lines and had motorboats . . . spoke of [the sea] as *el mar* which is masculine. They speak of her as a contestant or a place or even an enemy. But the old man always thought of her as feminine. (p. 27)

More significantly, both authors make gods or demigods of the animals their protagonists hunt. Faulkner's bear is clearly an incarnation of Frazer's King of the Wood: Old Ben is the object of an attention approaching veneration "in the yearly pageant-rite of the old bear's furious immortality" (p. 194). As many critics have noticed, Sam Fathers is the priest inducting Ike as "novitiate to the true wilderness" (p. 195), but the bear is the symbol of that wilderness, its "apotheosis" (p. 193); it will die when he does (and Sam along with him). Isaac's approach to the bear—fasting one morning, and leaving behind his gun, watch, and compass—approximates the ceremony by which American Indian youth sought their personal totem, their *nigouimes*. Subsequently he confronts the bear "where it loomed and towered over him like a thunderclap . . . : this was the way he had used to dream about it" (p. 211), another element of the *nigouimes* ceremony.[33] Thus Ike does not kill the bear, his personal totem, when the opportunity presents itself, and he buries the bear's mutilated paw in the grave above Lion. Similarly, while Hemingway is content for the most part merely to link Santiago and the marlin in a chain of cruel kill-or-be-killed brotherhood, at one point he literally and symbolically elevates the marlin. For much of the novella, Santiago has been identified with Christ: he bears the name of a fisherman disciple, is scourged by the rope line, earns stigmata (p. 56), carries the mast falteringly, stumbling various times, sleeps in a cruciform position, and makes "a noise such as a man might make, involuntarily feeling the nail go through his hands in the wood" (p. 107). At the death of the marlin, however, Santiago becomes the centurion; and the fish, ICHTHYS, appropriately, assumes the role of Jesus: Santiago drove the harpoon "into the fish's side just behind the great chest fin that rose high in the air to the altitude of a man's chest" (p. 94). The subsequent line, "showing all his great length and width and all his power and his glory" (p. 66, the only page where "Christ" is used as an expletive), echoes "The Son of man coming in a cloud with power and great glory" (Luke 21:27) or the more familiar "For Thine is the kingdom and the power and the glory" of the Lord's Prayer.[34]

Also significant for comparison's sake is the moment of death itself for both animals, a moment Hemingway describes as seeming like a dream, with "some great strangeness" (p. 98). Santiago's marlin "came alive with his death in him and rose high out of the water. . . . He seemed to hang in the air over the old man in the skiff. Then he fell into the water with a crash" (p. 94). Similarly, Old Ben and his pursuers, also fixed in time for an instant by Faulkner, "almost resembled a piece of statuary." Then, as Boon probes and finds the bear's heart with his knife, "the bear surged erect," and finally "crashed down . . . all of a piece, as a tree falls" (p. 241). Thus both authors attempt to capture what Faulkner's favorite poem, "Ode on a Grecian Urn," describes: the fixing of a moment in time for all time, the permanent presentation of the momentary and ephemeral.

Continuing with the totemic rites appropriate to both beasts, one should note that both are killed not at a distance, but by hand, with knives, as is appropriate for totemic sacrifices. Both inductors-into-the-rites, Sam and Santiago, initiate their hierophants into the mysteries of the hunt with blood. When Ike killed his first buck, "Sam Fathers had marked his face with the hot blood" (pp. 209–10); and when Santiago first took Manolin into his boat, the boy was nearly killed when Santiago brought "the fish in too green and he nearly tore the boat to pieces." Manolin remembers "feeling the whole boat shiver and the noise of you clubbing him like chopping a tree down and the sweet blood smell all over me" (p. 12).

The Old Man and the Sea is the only long work by Hemingway published in his lifetime in which the protagonist is not close to the author's own age: rather, Hemingway makes Santiago as old as Sam Fathers so that the fisherman can pass on a lifetime of values and experience to the boy. "The old man had taught the boy to fish and the boy loved him" (p. 10), as is evident in the boy's taking care of his tutor, feeding him, providing bait for him, being willing to steal for him, and crying over his wounds and his loss. So too in "The Bear." Sam teaches Ike safety in shooting, woodlore, the craft of "hunting right, upwind" (p. 207): Ike "lay in wait for the buck at dawn and killed it when it walked back to bed as Sam Fathers had told him" (p. 210). And when Sam wants to die, Ike stays with Boon, to care for Sam, to help him to death and to an Indian burial. And just as Santiago addresses the fish as relative, brother, so Sam addresses a buck: "Oleh, Chief, . . . Grandfather" (p. 184).

There are other, smaller similarities between the works. Though "The Bear" is landbound, the surrey in which Ike approaches the big woods is likened by Faulkner to a "solitary small boat [that] hangs in the lonely immobility, merely tossing up and down, in the infinite waste of the ocean" (p. 195), a sentence redolent of Conrad, who influenced both authors. Santiago's hero, Joe DiMaggio, is crippled with a bone spur on his foot and Ike's hero, Old Ben, has lost toes on one foot. In both works also, the totemic religion is celebrated with alcohol drunk in communion. "The Bear" begins with "a bottle present, so that it would seem to him that those fierce instants of heart and brain and courage and wiliness and speed were concentrated and distilled into the brown liquor which not women, not boys and children, but only hunters drank, drinking not out of the blood they spilled but some concentration of the wild immortal spirit" (p. 198). This emphasis on the communion between initiates into shared mysteries appears also in *The Old Man and the Sea*:

> . . . the boy said, "Can I offer you a beer. . . ."
> "Why not?" the old man said. "Between fishermen."
> (p. 11)

Both books emphasize this sense of shared knowledged denied outsiders. To underscore the contrasts, the authors bring in awkward spectators: the tourists at the end of *The Old Man and the Sea* who mistake the marlin's skeleton for a shark's, and the uninitiated hunters in "The Bear": "In camp that night—they had as guests five of the still terrified strangers in new hunting coats and boots who had been lost all day until Sam Feathers went out and got them" (p. 225).[35]

The presence of these onlookers is a reminder of the social nature of the hunt in "The Bear"; indicative of the many ties are the opening communal drink, the shared social status of the land- and slave-owning DeSpains, Compsons, and McCaslins, and their shared values. The social structure—Ike's coming to grips with his grandfather's actions and determining a place for himself in the South alongside his white and black cousins—is central to "The Bear." Ike's relationship with Sam, Cass, and even Old Ben are metaphors in the novel's study of tangled human relationships and man's social responsibilities. Hemingway has the reputation of being primarily concerned with the individual, but as critics have noted, he is much less so in his later works, especially *The Old Man and the Sea*. Most obvious, of course, is Santiago's close relationship with Manolin, which opens and closes the novella, and which Santiago calls to mind throughout his attempts to catch the fish when he needs strength and inspiration. This small circle of two is concentrically surrounded: Santiago is fed on credit by Martin (p. 29); Pedrico saves newspapers for Santiago and cares for his skiff and gear (pp. 17 and 125); Santiago knows that the older fisherman will worry about his absence (p. 115); and even the Coast Guard searches for him in boats and planes (p. 124). Then Hemingway surrounds this human community with a natural one in which Santiago feels kinship with green turtles, small birds, and the marlin.

Hemingway builds two other forms of social organization into his story: baseball and Santiago's dream lions. Although sport has long been a metaphor in Hemingway's work, usually it has been man against man—boxing—or man against beast—bullfighting, hunting, fishing. But in *The Old Man and the Sea* it is baseball, a team sport, and Santiago's code hero is Joe DiMaggio, the ultimate team player. Furthermore, lions are the only cats that are social, rather than solitary, a group of them being called a pride, an important virtue in both works.[36] (The natural habitat of lions is not the ocean beach. Perhaps these strong figures in *The Old Man and the Sea* were suggested to Hemingway by the strong dog named Lion in "The Bear.")

Finally, the basic likenesses of the two books lie in the similarity of themes discussed and virtues praised. Faulkner's ideal virtues are explicitly stated throughout "The Bear": "will and hardihood to endure and the humility and skill to survive" (p. 191), "humble and enduring enough" (p. 192), "the humility and the pride" (p. 233), "pity and humility and sufferance and endurance" (p. 257), "honor and pride and pity and justice and courage and love" (p. 297). "Humility" and "pride" appear over and over, in paradoxical juxtaposition. Hemingway's ideal virtues have always been less explicit, usually left for the reader to infer from characters' actions. Endurance has always been present in Hemingway's work from "The Undefeated" (1924), through Jake's acceptance of his lot, through Hemingway's favorite motto—*"Il faut (d'abord) durer"*—to Santiago's three days in his skiff; in Faulkner's work, however, it is a later addition. Endurance is not central or highly important in *Soldiers' Pay* (1926), *Mosquitoes* (1927), *Flags in the Dust* (1929), *The Sound and the Fury* (1929; the "They endured" of the "Appendix" dates from 1945, not 1929). It first becomes explicit in Addie's single monologue in *As I Lay Dying* (1930), is not major in *Sanctuary* (1931), or *Light in August* (1932). Endurance first becomes a major theme in *Absalom, Absalom!* (1936). Often the demands Hemingway makes of his characters' endurance is unrealistically superhuman, from Romero's willing himself not to be knocked out by Cohn, to Jack Brennan's sustaining Jimmy Walcott's foul, all the way to Santiago's twenty-four-hour arm wrestling match and his declaring that "pain does not matter to a man" (p. 84). Although these are exaggerations of probability, they clearly underscore the value of endurance throughout his work.

Pride, skill in one's ability, is also present throughout Hemingway's work, in his bullfighters, boxers, fishermen, and writers. He always admired those "who were pretty good in there." But there is not another work where humility is praised as it is in

The Old Man and the Sea; good manners and decorum are virtues in Hemingway's works, but not meekness and humility. Thus it comes as a surprise, especially after the statement in *A Farewell to Arms* that "abstract words . . . were obscene," to read this description by Hemingway of Santiago, not only mentioning humility but (like Faulkner) coupling it with pride: "He was too simple to wonder when he had attained humility. But he knew he had attained it and he knew it was not disgraceful and it carried no loss of true pride" (pp. 13–14). These many similarities are evidence that Hemingway's long, close reading of Faulkner led him to include some Faulknerian elements from "The Bear," that good hunting story, into his own account of a man's attempt to subdue a great beast. As he wrote Faulkner in 1945, "You have things written that come back to me better than any of them."

There is another link between the two men at this point in their career, a similarity that perhaps explains why Faulkner began emphasizing endurance. *Go Down, Moses*, of which "The Bear" is a part, is Faulkner's last major work. He will follow it with *Intruder in the Dust, Requiem for a Nun, A Fable, The Town, The Mansion*, and *The Reivers*; but he will win the Nobel Prize for what was written up to and including *Go Down, Moses*, and he will never write with such power and sustained authority again. For Hemingway, *The Old Man and the Sea* would be the last book he would publish in his lifetime. In 1952, when Faulkner read and reviewed Hemingway's book, both felt themselves, in their own fifties, enduring, hanging on, wondering whether they could write well again. Responding to her questions about Faulkner's review, Hemingway wrote Lillian Ross: "You ask if I know what he means. What he means is that he is spooked to die."[37] In those years, as Carlos Baker records, so was Hemingway.

Of the two works, Faulkner's is the richer, the more complex, the more rewarding. Stylistically, there is the same demanding reader-involvement, epistemologically significant incomplete information, and moving rhythms of the hunt. Chapter 4 of "The Bear" also encapsulates most of Western history, and the whole work presents many of the primary emotions: desire, fear, anger, ambition, disgust. It uses the Bible, both in the allusions of the book's title, *Go Down, Moses,* and in chapter 4 of "The Bear" and in the Genesis-like genealogy of that same chapter. It also uses ritual—the ancient patterns of the hunt and of initiation, and Frazer's more modern highlighting of them. Though these patterns are obvious, they are never so baldly asserted as Hemingway's use of Christ's Passion. Cass's role, however, is unclear: is he meant as a foil for Isaac—a wise and practical role model whom Isaac repudiates when he repudiates the land? Or is he (like Ike himself) another of Faulkner's failed heroes, in this case one who raises his cousin well but not well enough to preserve Ike's social responsibility? Certainly Faulkner succeeds admirably in presenting Ike's conflicting desires to prevent the continuing abuses of slavery and of the wilderness, to preserve his lot, his identity, his honor, and his marriage—those truths, as Faulkner has called them, of "the human heart in conflict with itself." It is with regard to internal conflict that *The Old Man and the Sea* is especially lacking. (Whether Hemingway's style in this book is a return to the famous earlier style or a parody of it seems impossible to resolve.)

Though *The Old Man and the Sea* is a moving tribute to the human spirit and to dignity, it describes no internal conflict. Santiago, in this touching parable, represents puny man against the might of nature. But Santiago never seriously questions his task, never doubts whether he should fish, never debates at length whether he should have allowed Manolin to accompany him. When he does question himself—over his right to kill the fish— the results are maudlin. Without this dimension of human conflict—of the heart in conflict with itself—Hemingway's novella remains a parable.

On the other hand, although Faulkner said in his Nobel Prize acceptance speech that man will prevail, this optimistic note is not evident in Faulkner's fiction. Hemingway, though he presents man as inevitably doomed, as fated for destruction, shows his protagonists fighting fate: even as they suffer they establish man's dignity and capacity for love. In the two works in question, Santiago and the Ike of "Delta Autumn" are much alike, but the similarities should not be overstated. Aged, father to none but uncle to many, both men are noble failures. Ike failed to reconcile his natural and social inheritances, failed to find an effective way to repudiate his grandfather's sin and to help his black cousins; as a carpenter, his emulation of Jesus adds to the spoliation of the woods he loves. Dignified in old age, still more in touch with nature than anyone else around him, he has failed through lack of nerve, lack of courage, lack of commitment. Tennie's Jim's granddaughter excoriates him for forgetting in practice what he has said love means—sharing. Santiago also fails, but not through want of nerve or effort. In Hemingway's cosmology, what the gods grant, they also take away. Santiago catches his fish and has the evidence to prove it, even though his victory is only symbolic—in the skeleton of the fish and in his example of man's courage. But he knows—as Uncle Ike does not—that love involves sharing, and he shares his knowledge and himself with the boy who loves him.[38]

Notes

1 Carlos Baker, *Ernest Hemingway: A Life Story* (New York: Scribner's, 1969), pp. 661, 532, 495, 503.

2 Baker, *Life Story*, pp. 297, 439.

3 Ernest Hemingway, *Death in the Afternoon* (New York, Scribner's, 1932), p. 173. On a drive with Bumby to Piggott, Arkansas, subsequent to the publication of *Death in the Afternoon*, Hemingway found himself in a hotel in Oxford, Mississippi. Realizing that he was on Faulkner's turf and the disparaging nature of his remarks, he sat up all night beside Bumby, guarding the door with a shotgun. See Baker, *Life Story*, p. 605, amplified in "Faulkner: An Orientation, 1940" *Faulkner Studies*, 1 (1980), 10.

4 *New Yorker*, 5 November 1932, pp. 74–75; reprinted in *Ernest Hemingway: Selected Letters, 1917–1961*, ed. Carlos Baker (New York: Scribner's, 1981), pp. 368–69.

5 Hemingway, *Selected Letters*, p. 604.

6 Baker, *Life Story*, pp. 227, 534.

7 *Lion in the Garden: Interviews with William Faulkner*, ed. James B. Meriwether and Michael Milgate (New York: Random House, 1968), p. 58.

8 Hemingway, *Selected Letters*, pp. 623–25.

9 *Selected Letters of William Faulkner*, ed. Joseph Blotner (New York: Random House, 1977), pp. 61, 203. Cf. *The Faulkner-Cowley File* by Malcolm Cowley (New York: Viking, 1966), pp. 29, 32.

10 Cowley, *The Faulkner-Cowley File*, p. 104. Cowley also talked Robert Linscott of Random House into having Hemingway write an introduction to a new edition of *Sanctuary*. Faulkner told Linscott no. See Cowley, *The Faulkner-Cowley File*, p. 87; Faulkner, *Selected Letters*, pp. 229–30.

11 William Faulkner, *Essays, Speeches, and Public Letters*, ed. James B. Meriwether (New York: Random House, 1965), p. 210. The letter was published in *Time* on November 13, 1950. Since Faulkner first learned of the Nobel Prize on November 10 of that year, this letter must have been written before he knew of the award.

12 Faulkner *Selected Letters*, pp. 333–34. Breit passed the letter on to Hemingway, who once more misread Faulkner and believed himself again insulted. See Baker, *Life Story*, p. 503.

13 Faulkner, *Essays*, p. 193.

14 Malcolm Cowley, ed., *The Portable Faulkner* (New York: Viking, 1946, 1967), p. ix.

15 William Faulkner, *The Wild Palms* (New York: Random House, 1939), pp. 97 and 263. I am indebted to Thomas J. McHaney's close study of the two authors, *William Faulkner's "The Wild Palms"* (Jackson: University of Mississippi Press, 1976), pp. 12–20. The critic who first noticed Faulkner's pun on Armour from "Snows" was Melvin Backman, "Faulkner's *The Wild Palms*: Civilization against Nature," *University of Kansas City Review*, 29 (Spring 1962), 199–204.

16 Faulkner, *Selected Letters*, p. 100.

17 McHaney, *Faulkner's "The Wild Palms,"* p. 21. William Faulkner, *Pylon* (New York, Random House, 1935), p. 50; William Faulkner, *Requiem for a Nun* (New York: Random House, 1950, 51), pp. 154, 158, 159–60.

18 George Monteiro, "Between Grief and Nothing: Hemingway and Faulkner," *Hemingway Notes*, 1 (Spring 1971), 13–15.

19 Cf. Peter L. Hays, "Hemingway, Faulkner, and a Bicycle Built for Death," *NMAL*, 5 (Fall 1981), Item 28. See also Fred D. Crawford and Bruce Morton, "Hemingway and Brooks: The Mystery of 'Henry's Bicycle,'" *Studies in American Fiction*, 6 (1978), 106–9.

20 John M. Howell, "Hemingway, Faulkner, and 'The Bear,'" *American Literature*, 53 (1980), 115–26.

21 Malcolm Cowley, —*And I Worked at the Writer's Trade* (New York: Viking, 1978), p. 6.

22 Cf. Cowley, *The Faulkner-Cowley File*, pp. 159–60.

23 Hemingway, *Selected Letters*, p. xii.

24 David Minter, *William Faulkner: His Life and Work* (Baltimore: Johns Hopkins Press, 1980), p. 32. Cf. Meta Carpenter Wilde and Orin Borsten, *A Loving Gentleman* (New York: Simon & Schuster, 1976), p. 46; John Faulkner, *My Brother Bill* (New York: Trident, 1963), p. 138. John Faulkner also records the presence of a family friend who taught law at the University of Mississippi when Bill was enrolled there after the war—one Judge Hemingway (pp. 144–45).

25 Ernest Hemingway, *A Farewell to Arms* (New York: Scribner's, 1929), p. 185. William Faulkner, *As I Lay Dying* (New York: Random House, 1930, 1964), p. 163.

26 Faulkner, *Essays*, p. 193.

27 Hemingway didn't think so. When Lillian Ross sent him Faulkner's review, he responded to her: "The Old Man in the story was born a Catholic in the island of Langa Rota in the Canary Islands. But he certainly believed in something more than the church and I do not think Mr. Faulkner understands it very well" (Hemingway, *Selected Letters*, p. 807).

28 Cf. Claire Rosenfield, "New World, Old Myths," *Twentieth-Century Interpretations of "The Old Man and the Sea,"* ed. Katherine T. Jobes (Englewood Cliffs: Prentice-Hall, 1968), pp. 42–44.

29 Ernest Hemingway, *For Whom the Bell Tolls* (New York: Scribner's, 1940), pp. 39–41.

30 William Faulkner, *Go Down, Moses* (New York: Random House, 1942), pp. 193–94, 210. All subsequent quotations from this work will refer to this edition and will be in parentheses in my text.

31 Ernest Hemingway, *The Old Man and the Sea* (New York: Scribner's 1952), pp. 54, 59, 75, 95. All subsequent quotations from this work will refer to this edition and will be in parentheses in my text. See the discussion by Herbert Wilner, "Aspects of American Fiction: A Whale, a Bear, a Marlin," *Americana-Austriaca*, ed. Klaus Lanzinger (Vienna: Wilhelm Braumüller, 1966), p. 235.

32 *The Oxford Annotated Bible*, ed. Herbert May and Bruce Metzger (New York: Oxford University Press, 1965), p. 45n.

33 Claude Lévi-Strauss, *Totemism*, trans. Rodney Needham (Boston: Beacon, 1963), defines *nigouimes* on p. 18. For initiation ceremonies, see *The Encyclopedia of Religion and Ethics*, ed. James Hastings (New York: Scribner's, 1961), vol. 12, p. 405; and J. G. Frazer, *Totemism and Exogamy* (London: Macmillan, 1910) vol. 1, pp. 49–51. See also Francis Parkman, *The Jesuits in North America* (Boston: Little, Brown, 1895), pp. lxviii–lxxi.

34 Cf. Arvin R. Wells, "A Ritual of Transformation: *The Old Man and the Sea*," originally printed in *University Review*, 30 (Winter 1963), 95–101, reprinted in Jobes, *Twentieth-Century Interpretations*, pp. 56–63.
35 This device of contrasts between initiates and outsiders is of course not new to *The Old Man and the Sea* and not dependent on Faulkner: Hemingway had used it in *The Sun Also Rises*, if not even earlier in "Indian Camp."
36 Cf. Clinton S. Burhans, Jr., *The Old Man and the Sea:* Hemingway's Tragic Vision of Man," *American Literature*, 31 (1960), 451–52.
37 Hemingway, *Selected Letters*, p. 807.
38 I am indebted to my colleague Karl Zender for many helpful suggestions regarding Faulkner.

Ernest and Henry: Hemingway's Lover's Quarrel with James

T HAT Henry James was a figure in Ernest Hemingway's works is apparent to anyone who reads the novels and non-fiction. Indeed, with the recent publication of Hemingway's letters and the holdings of the Key West and Finca libraries,[1] his varying attitudes toward the older writer can be documented. James entered directly by name into the first two novels. *The Torrents of Spring* (1926) includes a Henry James anecdote used in a parodic scene. Scripps speaks of his interest in James to Mandy, that unlikely waitress who has an anecdote to tell about James:

> "Let's hear it," Scripps said. "I'm very interested in Henry James." Henry James, Henry James. That chap who had gone away from his own land to live in England among Englishmen. Why had he done it? For what had he left America? Weren't his roots here? His brother William. Boston. Pragmatism. Harvard University.[2]

Mandy then relates how Professors Gosse and Saintsbury came with the man who brought the Order of Merit to James's death-bed. After they had left, Henry James spoke to the nurse and "never opened his eyes." "'Nurse,' Henry James said, 'put out the candle, nurse, and spare my blushes.' Those were the last words

165

he ever spoke," and Scripps, "strangely moved by the story," said, "James was quite a writer."[3]

How did Hemingway know such an anecdote? He tells us. "Would it be any violation of confidence if we told the reader that we get the best of these anecdotes from Mr. Ford Madox Ford?"[4] It is indeed a fanciful anecdote from Ford Madox Ford, who had known both James and Hemingway. James met the young Ford in 1896 at Rye and, although not inclined to trust him, did become friendly with him and his wife. Ford published four stories by James in the *English Review*, "The Jolly Corner" and "The Velvet Glove" among them. It may be that Ford introduced Hemingway to the James stories even as he was publishing Hemingway in his new *transatlantic review*.[5] From the Key West library list we know that Hemingway owned seven of Ford's published volumes by 1940 (in the Finca list there are only five), including *Portraits from Life* (1937), although Ford's *Henry James* (1913) does not appear in the earlier list.[6]

In *The Sun Also Rises* Bill Gorton refers ironically to a contemporary argument that expatriation impoverished a writer's art and leads to creative impotence. Answering Jake's response that "I just had an accident," Gorton says, "That's the sort of thing that can't be spoken of. That's what you ought to work up into a mystery. Like Henry's bicycle."[7] That Henry is Henry James. Fred D. Crawford and Bruce Morton have identified the source of the anti-expatriate comments in Van Wyck Brooks's *The Pilgrimage of Henry James* and Hemingway's response to that volume.[8] Alluding to the role of a bicycle in causing James's injury, Barnes continues,

> "It wasn't a bicycle," I said. "He was riding horseback."
> "I heard it was a tricycle."
> "Well," I said, "A plane is sort of like a tricycle. The joystick works the same way."[9]

That passage suggests that Jake became impotent as a result of an accident, his plane shot down in a battle during World War I, "on a joke front like the Italian."[10]

Actually James had received *his* "obscure hurt," as he recounts in *Notes of a Son and Brother*, when he was about eighteen years old, "at the outbreak of the Civil War," while helping to extinguish a fire. "Jammed into the acute angle between two high fences . . . I had done myself . . . a horrid even if an obscure hurt." But what was significant to him about his "hurt" is that it was associated with Civil War battles. There was "the queer fusion . . . established in my consciousness . . . by the firing on Fort Sumter" and his "physical mishap." He comments on "the undivided way in which what had happened to me . . . kept company . . . with my view of what was happening . . . to everyone about me, to the country at large: it so made of these marked disparities a single vast visitation." He had the sense of an "ache," and he could not tell at times

> whether it came most from one's own poor organism . . .
> which had suffered particular wrong, or from the enclosing
> social body, a body rent with a thousand wounds and that
> thus treated one to the honour of a sort of tragic fellowship.
> The twenty minutes had sufficed . . . to establish a rela-
> tion—a relation to everything occurring round me not only
> for the next four years but for long afterward.[11]

When the statement is separated from its many qualifiers, it seems clear that James felt that his accidental wound, occurring when it did just when the other young men were suffering battle wounds, made him one with them, and he had the feeling that he had been wounded as they had been in the very thick of battle. Thus the identification of James's "obscure hurt" with Jake's unmentionable injury was even greater than Hemingway may have known. (The general assumption is that James's "obscure hurt" was impotency, given his celibacy and his ambiguity as to what had actually taken place.)

As Crawford and Morton nicely put it, "In the process of refuting Brooks, Hemingway combined Henry James', Jake Barnes' and the critic's 'impotence' into one central image, using the bicycle allusion as a focus."[12] However, they are wrong in postulating that he found the bicycle incident that occurred late in James's life in the Lubbock edition of *The Letters of Henry James*, for the newly published letters now show that when Hemingway used the bicycle image he knew that James had suffered a more serious accident in his youth. When Hemingway was cautioned not to mention complete names in *The Sun Also Rises*, since he might be sued, he wrote to Maxwell Perkins: "But I believe that it is a reference to some accident that is generally known to have happened to Henry James in his youth." In that same letter (5 June 1926) he continued,

> To me Henry James is as historical a name as Byron, Keats, or any other great writer about whose life, personal and literary, books have been written. . . . As I recall Gorton and Barnes are talking humourously around the subject of Barnes' mutilation and to them Henry James is not a man to be insulted or protected from insult but simply an historical example.[13]

On August 21, 1926, they decided that Henry James would be indicated simply by "Henry," along with other changes.[14]

More revealing of Hemingway's attitude toward James is Bill Gorton's comment "I think he's a good writer, too." He then continues, "And you're a hell of a good guy."[15] Bill thus relates Jake to James. More important in this context is that just as Jake's injury arose during the war, so Henry James identifies his wound with the shared wounds of thousands of fellow youths of his own age.

In *Death in the Afternoon* (1932), James is the "favorite author" of a Mrs. E. R., a discriminating lady who develops "unerring judgment for a matador's class." Her preference for James proves she is a superior woman.[16] Early in *Green Hills of Africa* (1935), James, Stephen Crane, and Mark Twain are cited as "the good writers" in America.[17] In *A Moveable Feast* (1964), James appears as an example of the impeccable literary taste of Hadley,[18] and again when Ford Madox Ford is said to have considered him to be "very nearly" a gentleman.[19] James thus appears at intervals in Hemingway's oeuvre as a historical literary figure with a benign, almost mythological, presence.

As for his reading in James, Hemingway had a lifelong enthusiasm for *The American*, which he owned in the 1877 edition,[20] and he had two copies of *The Portrait of a Lady* as well as

Blackmur's edition of Henry James's prefaces that Perkins had given him. Hemingway took both novels along with him when he moved from Key West to Cuba.[21] The five James entries in the Key West list grew to thirteen entries in the Cuba list.[22]

Finding evidence of the influence of James's work on Hemingway's is another matter. A typed page that Sheldon N. Grebstein found between the manuscript pages of *A Farewell to Arms* (1929) in the John F. Kennedy Library contains an interview with James which Preston Lockwood published in the Book Review section of the *New York Times*, March 21, 1915. Leon Edel tells us, quoting Theodora Bosanquet, that the interview was completely written by James himself.[23] The passage possibly significant for *A Farewell to Arms* contains the following: "The war had used up words; they have weakened, they have deteriorated like motor car tires, . . . and we are now confronted with a depreciation of all our terms, or, otherwise speaking, with a loss of expression through increase of limpness, that may well make us wonder what ghosts will be left to walk."[24] Grebstein thinks that this clipping has more than an accidental connection with the writing of *A Farewell to Arms*. He sees in a passage from the novel an echo of the lines from James's interview:

> I was always embarrassed by the words sacred, glorious, and
> sacrifice and the expression in vain. . . . There were many
> words that you could not stand to hear and finally only the
> names of places had dignity. . . . Abstract words such as
> glory, honor, courage, or hallow were obscene beside the
> concrete names of villages, the number of roads, the names
> of rivers, the numbers of regiments and the dates.[25]

One is tempted to make a further correlation between an early Hemingway tale and a late James tale. There is a striking similarity of basic theme and a repetition of certain key phrases in James's "The Great Good Place" (1900) and Hemingway's "Big Two-Hearted River." James's lead story in *The Soft Side*, his collection praised by Pound, was reprinted in the New York Edition, owned by Gertrude Stein, and in 1925 Hemingway could have had easy access to her books.

"The Great Good Place" concerns an overburdened writer

who, to escape from his world, retreats in a dream to an ideal haven for tired writers and artists where they can rest and recharge their creative batteries. Nick, in Hemingway's tale, has also found his "good place" (using James's very phrase, or parts of it, four times), after his wartime experience with death and destruction. "He had made his camp. He was settled. Nothing could touch him. It was a good place to camp. He was there, in the good place."[26] After eating Nick thinks how this place is the good place: "There were plenty of good places to camp on the river. But this was good."[27]

For James's hero, "the Great Good Place" is "the scene of his new consciousness";[28] for Nick it is the scene of the perfect fishing expedition. Hemingway seems to realize and actualize James's metaphors. The images of feeding that are put into similes and metaphors in James's tale become the real dinners and breakfasts that Nick makes for himself in Hemingway's story.[29]

Before James's hero, George Dane, came to his Great Good Place, he had "been in danger of losing" what he called his "genius," which was "held by a thread that might at any moment have broken. The change was that, little by little, his hold had grown firmer, so that he drew in the line—more and more each day—with a pull that he was delighted to find it would bear."[30] In "the Place" he found "he had got his soul again. He had drawn in by this time, with his lightened hand, the whole of the long line, and that fact just dangled at the end. He could put his other hand on it, he could unhook it, he was once more in possession."[31]

This long fishing image is James's metaphoric way of showing the worth of the peace that came to his hero. Hemingway does it by having Nick actually fish and find a peace he never had before. Nick, too, in Hemingway's tale, after "the tug on his line," allows a couple of trout to slip away. After this loss, Nick gets over his disappointment. He says, "It was all right now."[32] These are more or less the words which the Brother says to Dane when he is about to go back: "Oh, it's all right!"[33] When Dane returns to his now uncluttered life he agrees with the Brother, and in the last words of the story he repeats, "It *was* all right."[34] Hemingway seems to have noticed that. Above all Dane hooks his soul and Nick hooks his trout. A further similarity occurs when Nick decides to leave alone that part of the river that corresponds to the hectic contemporary world that George Dane inhabits. Nick has no need for danger at this time, just as danger is excluded from Dane's "Place." Is this kind of possible conversion of James's tale what Hemingway meant when he wrote to Hadley on 25 November 1943, "Maybe I'll turn out to be the Henry James of the People or the comic strips"?[35]

There is also an interesting relationship between James's *The Ambassadors* and *The Sun Also Rises*. It is well known from Toklas's correspondence that Gertrude Stein admired the last novels of James. Hemingway must have heard those late novels, of which *The Ambassadors* is the first, praised by her, by Ford Madox Ford, and by Hadley. Be that as it may, the correspondences are very striking. In fact, Hemingway's is the only novel about Americans in Paris after James's that is also considered a masterpiece.

The opening of *The Sun Also Rises* is so close to the opening of *The Ambassadors* that it is hard to believe that Hemingway had not read it. Robert Cohn's life, summarized in the early pages of the book, is close to Strether's. Both now have been taken up by forceful women who own journals that both men edit. At the beginning of each novel that particular relationship is approaching its end as the men start really "living." Robert's speech to Jake about wanting to live is a striking condensation of Strether's speech to Little Bilham at Gloriani's party in *The Ambassadors*:

> "Listen, Jake," he leaned forward on the bar. "Don't you ever get the feeling that all your life is going by and you're not taking advantage of it? Do you realize you've lived nearly half the time you have to live already?"[36]

Strether says: "Live all you can; it's a mistake not to. It doesn't so much matter what you do in particular, so long as you have your life. If you haven't had that what *have* you had? . . . One lives in fine as one can."[37] Yet Strether himself refuses life and love in Paris because of a kind of emotional impotence. It is possible that Hemingway entertained the notion that Strether cannot respond to the advances of Maria Gostrey or Marie de Vionnet because of a "horrid" hurt, a real as well as spiritual impotence. This is where Robert Cohn ceases to be the only character based on

Strether, for now Jake takes over the James model of the impotent writer.

As in *The Ambassadors*, all the characters in *The Sun Also Rises* are expatriates. The only important foreigner in both novels is the *femme fatale*, in one Lady Brett and in the other the Countess de Vionnet, and desperation is a characteristic of both. Marie de Vionnet says, "the only certainty is that I shall be the loser in the end."[38] Nor is she the only loser in the book. Maria Gostrey, who loves Strether, also loses, but it is Strether who is the prime example of the "winner take nothing" motif of all Hemingway's work. At the end of *The Ambassadors* Strether rejects Miss Gostrey's proffered love: "But all the same I must go. . . . To be right. . . . That, you see, is my only logic. Not, out of the whole affair, to have got anything for myself."[39]

When Brett goes off with the "bullfighter chap," Jake's reaction to it is like Strether's reaction to his discovery that Marie and Chad are actually lovers. Brett summons Jake, just as, after her exposure as the mistress of Chad, Marie summons Strether. Both women want to be seen through the separation from their lovers by the hero. Although their methods of enslavement vary, they tangle erotically with all the characters and have a blocked sexual relation with the impotent heroes, Strether and Barnes.

The piece that Glenway Wescott wrote for the *Hound and Horn* issue on James in 1934 is interesting in this connection for it sheds light on the attitudes of Hemingway's group toward James's late novels. According to Wescott, they seem "to have originated in . . . excitement about some bold, sad, and scabrous problem, some overt perversity or real bad behaviour. . . . In regard to the motherly heroine, the match-making Circe, James's allusive handling raises a moral issue: if he had not somewhat expurgated his conception of her conduct as he went along, would she not have seemed simply villainous?"[40] This point of view, which seems today too hard on Marie, may offer an understanding of the kinship between Brett and Marie, both of whom play havoc with expatriate and castrated heroes. Lady Brett is actually called Circe in the novel.

Hemingway's references to James in his letters show clearly that he had a love-hate relationship with both the figure of James and with his work. We must remember that Hemingway, as well as wanting to be "the Henry James of the People," wondered "what Henry James would have done with the materials of our time,"[41] and as early as 1926 Pound could accuse him of following too much "in the wake of H. J."[42]

From a letter to Waldo Peirce, 13 December 1927, we know that Hemingway's new wife, like his old one, liked James:

> Pauline has been fine and has read Henry James (The Awkward Age) out loud—and knowing nothing about James it seems to me to be shit. . . . The men all without any exception talk and think like fairies except a couple of caricatures of brutal "outsiders." You have read more and better ones than this doubtless but he seems an enormous fake in this. What ho? Was he a fake? He had obviously developed a fine easy way for himself to write and great knowledge of drawing rooms but did he have anything else?[43]

Although Hemingway claimed he knew "nothing about James" we must view this remark, in the light of the continuing references to James in his work, with a certain amount of skepticism.

Hemingway wrote to Charles Scribner (6–7 September 1949) that he had "tried for Mr. Turgenieff first and it wasn't too hard. Tried for Mr. Maupassant . . . and it took four of the best stories to beat him. . . . Mr. Henry James I would just thumb him once the first time he grabbed and then hit him once where he had no balls and ask the referee to stop it."[44] Since he made a similar remark about Shakespeare, one sees he took on only the toughest competition. At this time James is very much on Hemingway's mind, for he wrote again to Charles Scribner on October 4, 1949, "Of Henry James you would like, I think, Madame de Mauves. It's quite short. There are a couple of other good ones too. But the greater part of it is rather snobbish, difficultly written shit."[45] The story was reprinted in Philip Rahv's The Short Great Novels of Henry James (1945), which appears in the Finca library list.

Hemingway advises a way of traveling in Italy for one of his sons, a way involving lots of drinking and a motorbike that "is sort of different from Henry James in a way."[46] The next year he wrote to Scribner, "Henry James was not faced with these same problems," that of having to "clip" people who "start to paw your wife" in night clubs.[47] He continues to jibe at James's inactivity in a letter to Scribner, 9–10 July 1950, when he reports on his own night life:

> I do not imagine this is the type of life which would have agreed with Henry James but fuck all male old women anyway.
> He wrote nice but he lived pretty dull I think. Too dull maybe and wrote too nice about too dull.

He then tries to imagine James as a boy without athletic skills and contrasts his own sons.[48]

It is James's personality that seems both to fascinate and to annoy him, especially the problem that his "obscure hurt" created. He sent to Harvey Breit on 21 June 1952 an extract from a reconstructed humorous journal of earlier years: "Thursday:—Commenced writing a new novel. It is to be called A Farewell to Arms and treats of war on the Italian front which I visited briefly as a boy after the death of Henry James. A strange coincidence."[49] He continued to connect his war wound with James's wound, even in 1952. The association here shown in Hemingway's mind between *A Farewell to Arms* and Henry James puts more value on the clipping from the James interview discovered among the manuscript pages of the novel.

From 1952 to 1954 there are five references to Henry James in the *Selected Letters*, for now Hemingway wants to write like James. In 1954 he wrote an affectionate letter to Adriana Ivancich, the young girl who had entered *Across the River and into the Trees* as Venice herself:

> Pretty soon I will have to throw this away so I better try to be a calm like Henry James the writer. Did you ever read Henry James? He was a great American writer who came to Venice and looked out of the window and smoked his cigar and thought. He was born too early and never saw you.[50]

In this image he seems to be remembering a passage devoted to Venice from James's *Portraits of Places* (1883), which is found in

a 1948 edition at the Finca: "If you are happy, you will find yourself, after a June day in Venice (about ten o'clock), on a balcony
that overhangs the Grand Canal, with your elbows on the broad
ledge, a cigarette in your teeth, and a little good company beside
you."[51] This reminder of James in connection with Venice and
with the heroine of *Across the River and into the Trees* (1950)
seems not to be accidental. In James's *The Wings of the Dove*, the
major theme is love and death in Venice. It was just before Hemingway wrote his novel that the spate of books on James was
published after his centenary in 1943, many of which appear in
the Finca list. Among them is F. O. Matthiessen's *Henry James:
The Major Phase* (1944), one of the first and best books to
reinstate the late James novels in the canon.

The name of the heroine of *Across the River*, Renata, indicates
a rebirth of the Colonel's feeling of love and is related to the name
Adriana (derived from Adriatic, the sea wedded to Venice in the
age-old ritual ceremony). "I love Venice, as you know," the Colonel says, and the novel is the story of his love affair with Venice.
In the first chapter of James's *Portraits of Places* on Venice (1882)
we read:

> The place is as changeable as a nervous woman, and you
> know it only when you know all the aspects of its beauty.
> . . . You become extraordinarily fond of these things. . . .
> The place seems to personify itself, to become human and
> sentient, and conscious of your affection. You desire to em-
> brace it, to caress it, to possess it, and finally a soft sense of
> possession grows up, and your visit becomes a perpetual
> love-affair.[52]

In 1882 James thought of loving Venice in terms of loving a
woman.

Throughout the 1950s James's name crops up in Hemingway's
letters. He wrote to Dorothy Connable, 17 February 1953, about
writing something relating to Toronto: "We ought to get Henry
James to write it."[53] The same year he wrote to Bernard Beren-
son, 20–22 March 1953, "We would have to check the dates but I
think I was wounded badly before Henry James received the
O. M. for his patriotic sentiments."[54] Yet he remarks to Harvey

Breit during the following year, on 3 January 1954, from Kenya, "It's like this. You sit down to write like Flaubert, H. James (not Jesse) etc. and two characters with spears come and stand easy outside the tent."[55] Hemingway now wants openly to write like James.

The course of Hemingway's interest in James, the figure and the artist, indicates an appreciation that seems to become more intense as his work progresses, for his last novels show a general kinship with James's themes. The thrust of *The Old Man and the Sea* (1952) is the pursuit of an alter ego ("the fish my brother"). The type for that in modern literature for Hemingway might well be James's "The Jolly Corner" (1908), a story praised by Pound and included in Rahv's collection. *Islands in the Stream,* with its set of doubles, suggests James's *Roderick Hudson.* The main character, Thomas Hudson, has James's hero, Roderick's, last name; and Roger Davis, the man Carlos Baker thinks can be viewed as Thomas's alter ego, would correspond to Roderick himself. Yet Thomas Hudson has rather the character of Rowland Mallet, the sober, steady, alter ego in James's novel, for he is the adviser and counselor to Roger, the romantic writer, and the equivalent of James's sculptor, Roderick. Thomas Hudson is, on the other hand, a hard-working and successful painter, and the way in which his character is handled indicates a habit of conversion not only typical of Hemingway's craft but also of James's fictional strategies.

When Hemingway was awarded the Nobel Prize, he paid tribute to the two great sources of his literary heritage. As a Nobel winner he regretted "that it was never given to Mark Twain, nor to Henry James."[56] In that sentence he linked the two figures of late-nineteenth-century American literature who, although poles apart, most richly nourished his imagination, reconciling his long lover's quarrel with James.

Notes

1 *Ernest Hemingway: Selected Letters, 1917–1961,* ed. Carlos Baker (New York: Scribner's, 1981); Michael S. Reynolds, *Hemingway's*

Reading, 1910–1940 (Princeton: Princeton University Press, 1981); James D. Brasch and Joseph Sigman, *Hemingway's Library: A Composite Record* (New York: Garland, 1981).

2 *The Hemingway Reader*, ed. Charles Poore (New York: Scribner's, 1953), p. 50.

3 *Hemingway Reader*, p. 51.

4 *Hemingway Reader*, p. 57.

5 Carlos Baker, *Hemingway: The Writer as Artist* (Princeton: Princeton University Press, 1973), p. 418.

6 See Reynolds, *Hemingway's Reading*, and Brasch and Sigman, *Hemingway's Library*.

7 Ernest Hemingway, *The Sun Also Rises* (New York: Scribner's, 1926), p. 118.

8 Fred D. Crawford and Bruce Morton, "Hemingway and Brooks: The Mystery of 'Henry's bicycle,'" *Studies in American Fiction*, 6 (1978), 108.

9 Hemingway, *The Sun Also Rises*, pp. 118–19.

10 Hemingway, *The Sun Also Rises*, p. 31.

11 Henry James, *Autobiography* (New York: Criterion, 1956), pp. 414–15.

12 Crawford and Morton, "Hemingway and Brooks," p. 109.

13 Hemingway, *Selected Letters*, p. 209.

14 Hemingway, *Selected Letters*, p. 215.

15 Hemingway, *The Sun Also Rises*, p. 119.

16 Ernest Hemingway, *Death in the Afternoon* (New York: Scribner's, 1932), p. 467.

17 Ernest Hemingway, *Green Hills of Africa* (New York: Scribner's, 1935), p. 22.

18 Ernest Hemingway, *A Moveable Feast* (New York: Scribner's, 1964), p. 38.

19 Hemingway, *A Moveable Feast*, p. 87.

20 See Reynolds, *Hemingway's Reading* for *The American* (1877), 1169.

21 See Brasch and Sigman, *Hemingway's Library*, for *The American*, 3337; *The Portrait of a Lady*, 3342 and 3343.

22 Brasch and Sigman, *Hemingway's Library*, 3337–3348.

23 Leon Edel, *Henry James: The Master, 1901–1916* (New York: Avon, 1972), p. 527.

24 Sheldon Norman Grebstein, *Hemingway's Craft* (Carbondale: Southern Illinois University Press, 1973), p. 206.

25 Ernest Hemingway, *A Farewell to Arms* (New York: Scribner's, 1929), p. 196.

178 *Adeline R. Tintner*

26 *Hemingway Reader*, p. 9.
27 *Hemingway Reader*, p. 10.
28 *The Complete Tales of Henry James*, XI, ed. Leon Edel (Philadelphia: Lippincott, 1964), p. 19.
29 *Hemingway Reader*, p. 10.
30 *The Complete Tales of Henry James*, XI, p. 30.
31 *The Complete Tales of Henry James*, XI, p. 35.
32 *Hemingway Reader*, p. 18.
33 *The Complete Tales of Henry James*, XI, p. 40.
34 *The Complete Tales of Henry James*, XI, p. 42.
35 Hemingway, *Selected Letters*, p. 556.
36 Hemingway, *The Sun Also Rises*, p. 11.
37 Henry James, *The Ambassadors* (New York: Bantam, 1969), pp. 173–74.
38 James, *Ambassadors*, p. 427.
39 James, *Ambassadors*, p. 454.
40 Glenway Wescott, "A Sentimental Contribution," *Homage to Henry James, 1843–1916* (New York: Appel, 1971), p. 187.
41 Baker, *The Writer as Artist*, p. 193.
42 Reynolds, *Hemingway's Reading*, p. 22.
43 Hemingway, *Selected Letters*, p. 266.
44 Hemingway, *Selected Letters*, p. 673.
45 Hemingway, *Selected Letters*, p. 678.
46 Hemingway, *Selected Letters*, p. 679.
47 Hemingway, *Selected Letters*, p. 709.
48 Hemingway, *Selected Letters*. p. 703.
49 Hemingway, *Selected Letters*, p. 768.
50 Hemingway, *Selected Letters*, p. 830.
51 Henry James, *Portraits of Places* (London: Macmillan, 1883), p. 38.
52 James, *Portraits of Places*, p. 8.
53 Hemingway, *Selected Letters*, p. 806.
54 Hemingway, *Selected Letters*, p. 811.
55 Hemingway, *Selected Letters*, p. 826.
56 Carlos Baker, *Ernest Hemingway: A Life Story* (New York: Avon, 1980), p. 668.

11. Jacqueline Tavernier-Courbin

Ernest Hemingway and Ezra Pound

ZRA POUND escapes almost unscathed from Ernest Hemingway's somewhat disparaging portrayal of his contemporaries in *A Moveable Feast*. Granted that Hemingway portrays him as a man whose literary judgment and choice of friends are poor, and whose manhood leaves something to be desired, he still is one of the very few to whom Hemingway grants admirable qualities and with whom he claims an enduring friendship. Hemingway's portrait of a Pound undone by his virtues does not manifest the malice apparent in his portrayals of Gertrude Stein, Ford Madox Ford, Ernest Walsh, or F. Scott Fitzgerald. No one appears in an entirely flattering light in the book, not even Hadley, whom Hemingway would not have wanted to hurt, as evidenced by the concern expressed in the many drafts of the preface.[1] While Hemingway clearly wanted to portray her as the perfect spouse, she comes across as a perfect nitwit whose vocabulary and thought patterns are hardly above those of a five-year-old. This is a very inaccurate portrayal, one might add, for in her correspondence with Hemingway and others Hadley appears as intelligent, mature, and quite witty. Thus, by comparison with almost every other person presented in the book, Pound gets a rather good deal.

Hemingway's friendship with Pound did not suffer the same fate as his friendships with other writers of his generation or older, in particular those who had helped him along in his career. One reason for this continuity of friendship may be that, despite his established reputation as a poet in England, France, and the United States, Pound presented no threat to Hemingway in the literary world. Another reason is no doubt related to the personality of Pound and his uncanny ability to handle as explosive a package as Hemingway's ego. As was his wont on similar occasions, Hemingway's first reaction after meeting Pound was to mock him. He thus wrote a satire, ridiculing Pound's wild hair, his unclipped goatee, his open Byronic collar, and his pretentious Bohemianism.[2] Unaware of Hemingway's reaction, Pound showed immediate appreciation for his work and took six of his poems to submit to the *Dial* and a story for the *Little Review*. While both story and poems were eventually rejected by the two journals, Pound had unerringly found the shortest way to Hemingway's heart. A friendship was sealed that would last to the end of both men's lives. During the early years of that friendship Pound was probably the only literary friend to whom Hemingway could say almost anything, and one of the only writers, if not the only one, who could advise Hemingway, and even criticize his work, without incurring his wrath. While they would share some of the same prejudices, they would also respect each other's right to prejudices and friends not shared by the other, and they would gossip endlessly. In fact, the Hemingway/Pound correspondence is by far the most entertaining to be found in the Hemingway manuscript collection. Among its gems are ones which illuminate some of the episodes narrated by Hemingway in *A Moveable Feast* as well as events of both authors' lives.

Douglas Goldring, who was assisting Ford Madox Ford with the *English Review* in the early 1900s, described Pound as he appeared to him at first:

> I was a bit suspicious of Ezra at first, and, though I am rather ashamed to admit it, perhaps a trifle jealous of him. He struck me as a bit of a charlatan, and I disliked the showy blue glass buttons on his coat; indeed, his whole operatic outfit of "stage poet," stemming from Murger and Puccini. . . . But one day I happened to see round Ezra's pince-nez, and noticed that he had curiously kind, affectionate eyes. This chance discovery altered my whole conception of him.

Perhaps it reveals part of the secret of his hold over Ford.
Ezra could be a friend, and not merely a fair-weather one.[3]

This may also have been part of the secret of his hold over Hemingway, for Pound so clearly wanted what was best for his friends that Hemingway himself could not help but recognize the unselfishness of his attitude. This characteristic of Pound, which Hemingway later stressed in A Moveable Feast, was one of the main points of his "Homage to Ezra" published in the first number of This Quarter, a special number dedicated to Pound after he had settled in Rapallo in February 1925:

> So far, we have Pound the major poet devoting, say, one fifth of his time to poetry. With the rest of his time he tries to advance the fortunes, both material and artistic, of his friends. He defends them when they are attacked, he gets them into magazines and out of jail. He loans them money. He sells their pictures. He arranges concerts for them. He writes articles about them. He introduces them to wealthy women. He gets publishers to take their books. He sits up all night with them when they claim to be dying and he witnesses and dissuades them from suicide. And in the end a few of them refrain from knifing him at the first opportunity.[4]

In a letter to Charles A. Fenton, Hemingway once claimed that Pound has never seen more than a half dozen things he had written, if that, but, particularly in letters addressed to Pound himself, he acknowledged Pound's influence on his writing.[5] For instance, he wrote in November 1925, in a long letter explaining why he wanted Ezra to review In Our Time, that Pound had been the only person who had given him practical advice about prose and that he, Hemingway, not having seen Ezra for some time, felt the need of his judgment.[6] In a later letter, Hemingway again acknowledged his debt, saying that he had learned more from Pound than from any other person. He acknowledges that Gertrude Stein was also an influence on him, primarily in their conversations.[7]

There is little doubt that Pound advised Hemingway on his writing, and it seems to have been good advice, but it was advice so cleverly given that it was in no way an assault on Hemingway's ego. Pound knew how to flatter at the same time as he was criticizing. For instance, he writes concerning a story which Hemingway had submitted to him for his new magazine, the *Exile*:

> Will you have another look at this thing?
> I mean if you aren't in the middle of some important job? I don't think it wd. be any kindness if one wuz trainin a man for a race to fake the time on him and tell him he wuz doing 100 yds. in 9 flat, when his time wuz 11½. Wd, merely lead his thinkin he cd. win easy.
>   Etc. Also job of editor is to EDIT. I.e. keep a man from rushing into royal audience with his flies unbuttoned.[8]

The approach, so far, is that of one who is looking out for his friend's best interest. The simile used is one that Hemingway could readily identify with, and the pose one which Hemingway would often adopt later vis-à-vis other writers. Pound then moves toward flattery to help the pill go down:

> I think you are more intelligent than this mss. As you know, I think you are intelligent some times, and a damn fool others (not therein differing from man, woman, or any other animal). . . .
>   HELL, I want stuufffff that'll END discussion. I want to say: me frien Hem, kin knock yew over the ropes; and then I want to see the punch delivered. I dont want gentle embraces in the middle of the ring.

Again the simile is one familiar to Hemingway; but more important, Pound caters to Hemingway's self-image. Later, Hemingway would often refer to himself as a writer who had figuratively knocked down other great writers such as Stendhal or Turgenev. For instance, he wrote to Charles Scribner: "For your information I started out trying to beat dead writers that I knew how good they were. . . . I tried for Mr. Turgenieff first and it wasn't too hard. Tried for Mr. Maupassant . . . and it took four of the best stories to beat him. He's beaten and if he was around he would know it.'"[9] To William Faulkner he also indicates that they can both beat Flaubert, their most honored master.[10] Hemingway explained his acceptance of the Nobel Prize to Pound in similar terms saying that receiving the Nobel Prize was a shock but that since inferior writers had already received it, characters he could "write the ass off of" before he turned thirty, it seemed all right to take it.[11]

Pound also knew how not to put himself forward or make demands. While he wanted to publish Hemingway in the *Exile*, he always told him to take the best offer available in terms of cash, even if it deprived the *Exile* of a good piece:

> Anyhow, IF you can improve this, DO. Goddamn it, DO improve it. After you have combed out the front end. IF you can sell it to the Bicth-bass-iniano for 40 quid, fer Xt's sake grab the 40 quid. If not, come back to your pore ole uncle. . . .
>
> I want, hell yes, I want a story. TOO. But I DONT want 40 quid sacrificed.[12]

Pound provided concrete advice on how to improve a given story. In a letter dated December 21, 1926, referring to a story Hemingway had sent him for the *Exile*, probably "An Alpine Idyll," which Hemingway had already submitted to *Scribner's Magazine* in May, Pound advised him not to be literary:

> An now let's see the bulls.
> This is a good story (Idyl) but a leetle litterary and Tennysonian. I wish you wd. keep your eye on the objek MORE, and be less licherary.
>
> Do you onnerstan what I mean about bein licherary. Bein licherary mean that the reader (even the interested and in my case abnormally HOPING reader) has to work to keep his eye on the page during the introductory pages.[13]

He also suggests that Hemingway get rid of extraneous material: "ANYTHING put on on top of the subject is BAD. Licherchure is mostly blanketing up a subject. Too much MAKINGS. The subject is always interesting enough without the blankets."

In a letter, dated January 25, 1927, Pound also recommends balance in the telling of a story: "IF the actually story were longer, you might praps use all this lead up. But the lead up OUGHT to have some sort proportion with the 'to-which-one-is-led.'"14 He also advises Hemingway not to be self-conscious and to write more simply: "P.4. these short repeating sentences, TOO DAMN IMPRESSIVE. You'd git the sak for telegraphing in that manner." This letter is probably a follow-up on the December 21 letter, and it seems relatively unlikely that Hemingway had submitted another story to the *Exile*. In any case, Pound concluded his comments of December 21 by accepting the story with the following reservation: "Yes, I vil be glad to print your story. Hoping the subject matter is 'unsuitable' for Scriblers. But you can do it better. I said it. You can do it better. It is a good story and I am not content with it." In the letter of January 25, he finally offered to do the editing himself if Hemingway was too lazy to tackle the job. Whether these letters both deal with "An Alpine Idyll" or with two different stories, Pound never published a Hemingway story in the *Exile*; Hemingway's contribution to it remaining limited to the publication of the "Neo Thomist" poem in the first issue. Amusingly, Pound seems to have been quite fond of Hemingway's poems, which might have endeared him to Hemingway in a special way, for almost no one else appreciated them. After criticizing "An Alpine Idyll," in his December 21 letter, Pound wrote: "I vish you wd. a story in the plain and simple language of your neo-thomist poem."

Despite Pound's straightforward criticism of his story, Hemingway did not take offense, as evidenced by a letter of January 1927 in which he admits that Pound was right and the story was not good enough.15 Thus, while Pound had his *franc-parler*, it is clear that he knew how to handle Hemingway's authorial pride. Again, a little indirect flattery probably helped smooth things over, as Pound suggested that there was much more to criticize in the pieces Archibald MacLeish had sent him: "To Mr. McLeish I am sending 8 pages of griticism; you are invited to descend in a phalanx and poison my afternoon tea."16 Even when, in later years, Pound could no longer be considered Hemingway's mentor, and his criticism of Hemingway's work had become more acerbic, Hemingway still accepted from Pound comments that would have aroused his ire against anyone else, as evidenced by a letter dated August 13, 1933:

> You take orders/ you get coerced/ and as fer your being able to git along in present or any recent system /// yaaas, yaa as, and what gits you along is just what AINT the best of yr/ writin, I dont mean by chunk but by factor.
> An thet is purrhaps az narsty as I can putt it.[17]

Amazing as it may seem, this letter did not end their friendship. One reason for this unwonted tolerance on Hemingway's part may be that Pound had always insisted that, between friends, they should not pull their punches provided they presented a united front against the enemy: "There is no use in our speaking to each other in veiled langwidg. I mean if the review is to exist as a LIFE, we have to parody each others weaknesses, tread on each others toes, pop our air guns at each others fat chickens, etc. (keeping when possible a united front to the enemy)!"[18]

In general, Pound's advice regarding Hemingway's career was good, and, above all, disinterested, which Hemingway could not help knowing. It is Pound who advised Hemingway in 1926 to write and publish another novel rather than concentrate on another book of short stories:

> I.E. as to making Scribblers publish some short stories NEXT.
> Now, mong cher ami. You will do no such GOD DAMND thing. You will publish ANOTHER NOVEL next, and *after* that, and NOT UNTIL AFTER THAT you will make them pub. the sht. stories.
> Wotter yer think yer are, a bloomink DILLYtanty???????[19]

Pound never exhibited the professional jealousy Hemingway believed he saw in Stein. When she had refused to review *In Our Time*, Hemingway wrote to Pound to say that Stein had warned him that there would be no review since she preferred to wait for his novel. Hemingway protested that books should be reviewed one at a time and that Stein was afraid to praise his stories since she might be embarrassed if his novel failed. Hemingway did not like the bitter taste of this attitude.[20] Pound appointed himself as Hemingway's defender against such professional jealousy after the publication of *The Sun Also Rises*: "Az I see you among the six best sellers in the list in the N.Y.H.T.; I feel that I shall now have to pull myself together and defend you against the licherary gents who had thought of being your 'friend' until the funeste occurance."[21]

Indeed Pound's professional attitude toward Hemingway was one which could only please. He knew how to flatter under the guise of banter, and, while he almost always spoke his mind, he knew how to do it in a positive and light-hearted way Hemingway could hardly object to. He also knew how to encourage and urge him on: "DAMN IT ALL; send on your copy. Send on every bloody thing you've got. Not a time for personal feelings, modestry, shame, reclusion, pride, mercy, justice, or mere question of literature statecraft, hygiene disin or disaf-fection, etc."[22]

Knowing how understanding Pound would be in most instances, Hemingway felt free to express much of his true feelings in his letters to him. The sharp contrast in the tone of his letters to Pound and Gertrude Stein, for instance, is revealing of the difference in the relationships. While Hemingway would defer to Stein and flatter her and at the same time criticize both her and her work in letters to others, he would be quite irreverent toward Ezra but rarely write an unkind word about him to others.[23] In fact, Hemingway tended to make Ezra a party to his prejudices, dislikes, feelings of persecution, and more or less honorable intents.

For instance, he wrote to Pound concerning *The Torrents of Spring* that he had written a funny book, the first adult work he had done, and he had written it to destroy Sherwood Anderson. He felt it would show up the "fakes" of Anderson and Lewis, Gertrude Stein, Cather, Hergo, and the rest. He felt that it was the funniest book since *Joseph Andrews*.[24] He then goes on to point out that the comic writer should least of all deviate from nature because "life everywhere furnishes an accurate observer with the ridiculous" and confides that he intends to write a *Joseph Andrews* every ten years on every masterpiece. He felt that Anderson would never be able to write again. He would not have to show up Gertrude Stein, he could simply quote from her work. Hemingway had accurately guessed that Pound would not object to the novel on moral grounds. In fact, with Pauline, Pound is probably the only one in Hemingway's circle who did not object to it. Rather, Pound seems to have appreciated the aggressiveness of *Torrents* and encouraged Hemingway in that line: "I see by Sherwood's sotory in the Sept. Am. Merk. that you *haven't* done him any good, or 'destroyed' anything. Not unless that tale was writ. before The Torrents."[25] Or in the same vein: "The only disserptmnt. I has re/Torrents wuz that you didn't land a few more bots to the jaw. But there is time, oh, hell, as sez Misser Elyot, there is time."[26] It even seems that Pound actually believed that *Torrents* was a good book; at least he certainly gave Hemingway the impression that he did: "I prefer 'Torrents of Spring' to the dying torrero or to the Old Man. IF you have a bunch of stuff like 'They all made peace', that wd. go fine. I mean nacherly with the addred machurity that you now possess."[27] That Pound should have preferred *Torrents* to "My Old Man" and "The Undefeated" suggests that Hemingway might have been right when he wrote in *A Moveable Feast* that Pound's literary taste was poor.

That Pound did not object to Hemingway's attacks on Stein and Anderson, however, did not come from an absence of awareness of a streak of meanness in Hemingway's character. As he wrote to Archibald MacLeish, Hemingway had little tolerance for other writers and was not of a kind disposition:

Do you know anyone that can write? Hem. don't. He is most explicit on that point. But then he demands so much of a writer (I mean . . . yes, I mean about that . . . the Chinese feeling that the character of a man is manifest in everyone of his pen strokes . . . and in Hem.'s case having no wish to look at the penstrokes until he has been previously satisfied as to the character, past, present, and future.) . . .

Let me see ALL the stuff of yours, or of any one you tolerate, that you can scrape together. Also prod Hem. I'll even stand bulls. if the torreros aren't TOO bloody noble. But prefer him on humans. + the intelligentzia or /ig. lif. In fact. a prime cover draw wd. be "Mr. Hemingway on High Life."[28]

Pound, in fact, probably enjoyed Hemingway's attacks on Gertrude Stein for he was not particularly fond of women writers himself, in particular one whose influence over young writers in Paris was a challenge to his own. Actually, Pound tended to encourage Hemingway in his literary parodies. For instance, he suggested that if Hemingway wrote something "narsty" for Number 3 of the *Exile* an honored seat would be reserved for him. He also indicated that "a whoozoo of presidenshul candydates, in style of Orl made Peace" would be a "pleezink feechure" for Number 4.[29]

The exchange of letters that took place in late 1926, at the time when Pound had decided to start the *Exile*, is hilarious but revealing of the prejudice shared by both writers against women writers—prejudice to which Hemingway added his own against homosexuals. Pound suggested that he was not in favor of publishing lady writers and that, as far as he was concerned, it would be mostly a question of insulting them.[30] Responding happily to the idea, Hemingway wrote that Pound should put him down for a contributing membership in the organization against women writers, except for the very wealthy.[31] In another letter, which was probably a reply to one in which Pound was wondering "who the hell they (COULD) insult,"[32] Hemingway writes he would suggest they insult all "fairies," the deceased Mr. Walsh, and the living Carnevalli. He would be happy to insult Gertrude Stein but preferred to do it in a publication of wide circulation.[33]

That Pound and Hemingway shared some of the same prejudices does not always mean that they shared the same friends or the same interests, but Pound knew how to defend his own, when necessary, without offending Hemingway. Their main difference in taste was probably Hemingway's love for bullfights and hunting and Pound's love for music. As Pound amusingly put it: "I feel about bulls and Blasco Ibanez rather as you do about bassoons."[34] Similarly, he disapproved of Hemingway's hunting: "AN if you are goin to be a nacherlist// thass o/ĸ/ but ef yew air goin to Afrik fer to annoy a tranquil family of man eatin lions etc // I reprobate you."[35] Friends, however, were a more sensitive topic. With various degrees of intensity, Hemingway disliked Ford Madox Ford, Ernest Walsh, Robert McAlmon, Cheever Dunning, and others. He was often virulent in the expression of his dislikes and would not let go of his rancor whatever the circumstances. Pound was less devoid of human sympathies and seems not to have harbored such deadly grudges. Their relationship to Ernest Walsh is reveal-

ing of their difference of attitudes. While Pound had expressed his
sadness at the news of Walsh's death, Hemingway would not
allow himself to express any painful emotion of sympathy. Pound
writes, "I am sorry Mr. Walsh is dead, an he shudn't have writ
that article about you, but thats no reason for a little goat turd
like Moss, to keep a two inch obit. out of the Herald. Wot te hell,
the paper's there to print the news."[36] Hemingway apparently replied that he was not sorry Walsh was dead, except in the sense
that he lamented any death. He had known too many good men
who had died to be able to weep at the death of a "shit."[37] But
Pound stood his ground and intimated that, while he recognized
Hemingway's right to personal feelings, he wanted his own feelings respected too: "Please ACQUIT me of wanting people or anyone to share all my feelings. I did not suggest that YOU shd. or
ought to regret Monsieur Walsh. Alow me to understanding M.
Carnevalli's feelings in the matter, however. EHEM!!"[38]

While Pound was not always amused by Hemingway's negative
relationships with others, he knew how to handle them and retain
openly both Hemingway's friendship and his own friendship with
others whom Hemingway considered as enemies. As the editor of
the Exile, Pound had an interest in keeping the peace between his
literary friends, a situation Hemingway understood.[39] Pound
once thanked Hemingway for his generosity in not withdrawing a
short story submitted to the Exile, probably "An Alpine Idyll," in
somewhat ironic terms: "Your resolution re/mss is moss noble.
Especially when you realize that I am goink to print a lot of yr.
pet aversions."[40]

One friend Hemingway and Pound did not have in common
was Cheever Dunning. When Pound had left Paris for good,
Hemingway was somehow entrusted by him to look after Dunning. In one of his letters to Pound telling him the news of the
Latin Quarter, Hemingway narrates an interesting story which
authenticates beyond question one of the chapters in A Moveable
Feast. In the letter Hemingway says that Pound's old concierge
had shown up at seven o'clock on a Sunday morning with the
news that Dunning had come back the night before. Dunning had
climbed upon the roof and insisted on sleeping there but had
finally been persuaded to come down. He claimed that Pound
had stolen all his money and had only pretended to be his friend.

The concierge asked Hemingway to see if he could be of assistance, and Hemingway brought along a small jar that Pound had left. Dunning threw the jar at Hemingway, along with a milk bottle. As Hemingway retreated down the stairs Dunning had thrown a broom.[41] In the rest of the letter and a following letter, Hemingway explains how McAlmon took care of Dunning, and how he is now doing well in a "maison de santé," but indicates that he has no intention of ever seeing Dunning again.[42]

Clearly Hemingway respected Pound's concern for others, even if he did not share that concern personally. But then after Pound left Paris Hemingway missed him,[43] and chatting about others who had stayed in Paris was a major link between them.[44] Much of the correspondence of these years was aimed at telling Pound the news of the Latin Quarter, including juicy gossip, updates on other writers' work,[45] comments on other people's attitudes toward him, and news about his own life and work.[46] Thus, despite Pound's departure from Paris, he and Hemingway remained in close touch through the mail. Whether their correspondence dealt with literary problems related to Hemingway's manuscripts or with Parisian gossip, it was always characterized by mutual understanding and trust, mutual respect and acceptance, and a certain complicity in a critical view of others.

When Hemingway left France to settle in Key West, the correspondence between them began to flag. Each was absorbed by his own life and problems, and, as time passed, they had less and less in common. Later on Hemingway claimed that he had not received a letter from Pound since 1935–36 and that he had seen Pound for the last time in 1933 or 1934. Hemingway's interest in Pound, however, was suddenly revived by a letter from Archibald MacLeish in early 1943 inquiring about his opinion on Pound's war activities. Subsequently, Hemingway became involved in the crusade to save Pound from being brought to trial and condemned as a traitor and in the attempt at securing his release from St. Elisabeths hospital. A draft of a letter intended for Julien Cornell, Pound's lawyer, exemplifies at an early stage the attitude Hemingway would take toward the problem of Pound's broadcasts. In it he states that he had last seen Pound in Paris in 1934. Pound had changed a good deal and James Joyce was convinced that Pound was mad. Hemingway felt that Pound had not been himself mentally for at least a decade and that his work was testimony to his progressive degeneration. Hemingway regarded Pound as one of the greatest poets ever to write and as a generous and kind friend. Ezra had been exploited by unscrupulous people who took advantage of his condition. Hemingway had never felt bitterness toward Pound during the war because he knew that Pound would never have done what he did had he been sane.[47] This is clearly a testimony of friendship. The idea of pleading insanity as Pound's defense was one Hemingway expressed immediately after hearing from MacLeish and one shared by a number of Pound's friends. The same idea was discussed between Pound and Cornell and agreed upon unanimously by the four physicians who examined him at St. Elisabeths hospital.[48]

While Hemingway was certainly not the most active in securing Pound's final release or in defending his cause, he nevertheless stood by his old friend and helped substantially. Instead of turning against him as he so often had done against others, he continually professed his devotion to him, as in a letter to Dorothy Pound in which he declared that he was Ezra's loyal friend and would work for his release. He did not care what the fools and crackpots had done and would not believe any report that Pound had denounced him any more than he could believe that they had not lived in Paris in the old days.[49]

That Hemingway did not turn against Pound is an interesting comment on human nature, for Pound's treason clearly weighed less with him than Ernest Walsh's idle promise of $2,500 or Ford Madox Ford's repulsive (to Hemingway) physical appearance or Fitzgerald's drunkenness. Pity must have had a share in Hemingway's tolerance, for Pound had long been, to borrow Marsden Hartley's 1940 words, "an old man without a branch to sit on."[50] Having chosen the wrong branch, he clearly was even more alienated in the late 1950s than in the 1940s, thus perhaps qualifying better for Hemingway's pity. But, if undeserved misery has a claim on human pity, then Fitzgerald and Walsh would have qualified even more. Thus, one must conclude that Pound had known how to endear himself to Hemingway in a unique way.

Appendix

Via Marsala 12 int. 5
28 Oct. 1926

My Dear Colonel
                Have you anything unsaleable and
too good to be hidden in the Queerschnitt ?
Just in case I shd. slip my .... and
start a review ON my own. Very small ,
qualitative , and to appear *regularly* but not
very often.

I shd. not hold up mss. Indefinitely (I mean
your mss.) shd. say clearly what I mean to
use (on receipt of mss. .

and also know whether or not I am going to bother
with show at all . I mean I orter know by
noo yearz whether there is enough stuff lying round
apart from my own reserve , to make it worth
while .
        I have had three years lay off . an'
REALLY I do NOT see that the pantink pooblik
has gained grtly. by my silence .

        (this may be senile nevrosity on my part.
Dont HESITATE to say so, if that is yr. hnrd.
opinium.)

        NO art. I mean no reprods. of baintings.
If letters cant stand on their own ... we will
leave the matter ; apart from occasional editorial
word by yrs. v. t.

At ennyrate , we INVITE correspondence. The
proposition is not intended to deepen anyone's gloom
or add to his sense of responsibility.

                        yrs.
                        E.P.

Via Marsala, 12 int. 5

3 Nov. 1926

Reverend Colonel :

          I am too old to APPEAL . I mean
appeal for funds . I , yr. honour , wd. propose to keep
the magazine so small that I could pay the printer
myself ;

          and I shd. refuse to pay any contributor who
couldn't prove he wrote better-n I do , or hadn't
did more wuk fer the uplift of licherchure than wot
I have.

          Of course if some sonovabitch wants to give me
money , I wunt refuse . But the only form of support
I propose to suggest is that sustainers who feel
like giving a heave should take block subscriptions ,
i,e, in return for which they wd. git 20 copies of
the mag. to give to their ignorant n tightfisted friens.
Thus the appearance of the promt review wd. be
arssured and no favours axd.

I am glad to hear you approve ; I thought you-d
prob. say : gjheezus Hell , wot , another ov these
goldarn reveews !!!!!!!!!

I dont suppose I'll git off the mark vurry quick
so dont send anything you can sell or place to
advantage ; I mean anything you dont want tied up
for six monfs.

but if you feel like writing a life of Calidge Colvin
or doing some other IMPRACTICAble or unpractical
half sheet of verse , like the Peace Conference ; dont
sqush the impulse jess cause there aint no where
to go .

I thought you wuz in Spain. If you're in Paree ;
you might let out to Arcimbaldo that I'm cogitating.
The rich bastards has got to pay their way . I
aint waitink for Arcimbaldo. If you hadn't tole me he
wuz rich, I shd. prob. have axd. you if he had any
mss. (dont Poetry say Mr McLitch is a mistick or
sumfink ....? I aint long on misticks ...)

    Still, keep yer eye pealed for manuscritti , and
skeckels , of course if there are sheckels to be

had ; or if Mr McLeisch wants to correct proofs ;
there's a sub-ed job going CHEAP (IF Darrantiere's
estimate is lower than Milan price ... might be with
the lire sailing over the franc.)
      Perhaps you wd. yourself .... but ...
   I can not assure you an abs. non-musical review ,
but I assure you , mon cher collegue , there shall
be absolootly no neo-Thomism (will thot content you ?)
///
   Re yr own stuff . az I sez , there is no use
me paying a printer for to set up stuff you can
sell to Scribner .
What one wants fer this kind of show , is short stuff,
so short that space rates cant make it worth while
carrying to market ; and odd sizes , and unvendable
matter .
   I aim to go a bit easy (I mean as easy
as I can without feeling cramped , for first number
or so ; to please ... as far as we without hypocracy
can ... I mean without changing the size of our
feet to put fort the least darned sock .
   SO , I shd. like to SEE anything you' got ;
now IF you like ; and cd. let you know to onct
what I think will use? be useful for opening
amunition , and in what order I shd. want to use it.
   cont-utto rispetto.
But as to money , there aint as yet NO
   money wotever ; only the printers bill foresawn .
(my credit is good in Rapallo , and not on the
state railway , so I cawnt git away from here)
IF anybody has money , HOOray , but NOT wif strings
on it.
If McLeish wants the inestimable value of being
edited by me , all right , he can show a interest
in the venture . but I am going to run the thing
as I damn please . I have been ass-sociated with
too many reviews . all the push coming from the hind
legs. If anybody wants to associate with this one ,
let 'em PUSH.
as the Armenian rug merchant remarked : Mrs Cramp
has expressed her sympathy , but ze sympathy of Mrs

Cramp does me no good. "

I aint wrtink this to ask you seek McLeish . I
thought you wuz in Spain , out of reach of Arcimbaldo.
But you can let drop , that I am thinking of a
review , and will start if I see anything fit to print
, I mean enough to fill three numbers, and if I
git any support.

///

What is yr. candid opinium of distribution in Paris :
Titus or Sylvia, or both. I can deal with Titus .
What is yr. estimate of the number of copies that
cd. be consumed in Paris. Direct subs. being of
course bettern bookstall sales. (It wdnt. be a
Tory orgum of course , and couldn't count on the French
tory party very heavily.)

Scribner's I take it, wd. prob. NOT care
to take an Amurikun agency ? I have wrote to
a enthusiast in amurika to see if he can answer
that problim. I mean the Amurikun end.

We should need a circulation of 500
to cover the expenses of printing. I know that
is demanding a lot, but one should hitch ones wagum
to somfink.

I shd. like to see a guaranteed , or at
least probable sale of 200 copies before setting
sale . price 50 cents , 2 shillings, 10 francs.
according to climate.

A thing of this kind CANT pay , and there is no
use being a -ox and pretending it can , or
kidding or Fording yerself into the idee that it is
going to PAY.

If it keeps the perpetrators from dying of
boredom and gives one a chance to bash in boko
now and then , thass all , thass all an there isnut
any more, an thass all .

Of course it is monstrous that I am not
to be paid a high salary, and Morgan ought to buy
me a ranch in Colorado , where I dont want it , etc...
but thass all an there isnut any more , and thass
all.

And its a wunner we're alive ennyhow .

I am sorry Mr Walshh is dead , an he shudn't have
writ that article about , but thats no reason
for a little goat turd like Moss , to keep a two
inch obit. out of the Herald . Wot te hell , the paper's
there to print the news.

///

Pull yerself together, and help me think whotell is
our fellow contributors . Yes, hell . CONTRIBUTE .
I am alas afraid that is the word .
There's poor ole Bill Williams, representing Rutherford
Noo Jersey ; and Mr MCAlmon , representing the panama
canal .... but we are all leaders, an hell we
want a little cannon fodder .
I am not personaly in favour of having lady writers ,
at least not to start with (not unless Miss
Fife herself writes .) In fact , even if she does,
I am not sure it wdnt. be better to START without
lady writers .
    (It is i admit damned unjust to
several of 'em . and I dont mean seereeusly to
make it a "plank" ; but it might be a tour de force
to see how long one cd. silently run without 'em.

I mean , we prob. omit , Thos. Hardy , and Y eats
and May Sinclair . in fak people over 50.
Apart from which there is Moorhead's prison stuff , which
belongs in the New Masses .
    After which I am afraid the question
of lady writers, becomes a matter of personal insult.
    There are so few that one cd. consider at all.
Still , the ladies , gawdblessum.

Perhaps , we cd. announce .

    The third number of this periodicle
        WILL BE OPEN TO WRITERS
                OF
        BOTH SEXES.

Merrdre . I ought to keep that I my desk , till
the time comes.

Less know wot yuh see on the horizum.

[11/10/26]

THE EXILE WILL PAY ITS WRITERS

In our war against stupidity we have observed certain
people " of established position " who maintain
and keep up the general dulness , who support
the existing electroplates against living authors
regardless of quality ; and who may be designated
as plague spots.
We therefore propose the following scale of payment
to our own critical writers
      per essay note or article
  5 pounds stg. for the death, by suicide or
    accident of one of these plague sp ots
    spots , when same can be shown to be
    result   said essay etc.
  1 pound stg. for sending plague spot to hospital
      for longer or shorter period , with jaundice
    or similar ailment , when same is manifestly
    result of an essay apperaing in our pages.

This head or carcass money is not to be taken as an
incentive to intern ecine war or
vendettas among rising authors ; it will be paid only
for definite effect upon persons of established
position and whos evil activities have extended over
a sertain period of time ; in no case will it be
paid as counter-insurance for damage to any man under
26 years of age.

Apart from sharpening the pens of our collaborators ,
we trust this measure will be provocative of precision
on their part ; and will lead them to consider
carefully what the mean ; and what value they
attatch to good letters , evil motive in writing ,
etc. before rushing to verbal manifestation.

Notes

1 See Jacqueline Tavernier-Courbin, "The Manuscript of *A Moveable Feast*," *Hemingway Notes*, 6 (Spring 1981), 9–15.
2 See Carlos Baker, *Ernest Hemingway: A Life Story* (New York: Bantam, 1970), p. 114.
3 See Charles Norman, *Ezra Pound* (New York: Macmillan, 1960), p. 51.
4 Ernest Hemingway, "Homage to Ezra," *This Quarter*, 1, No. 1 (May 1925), 221–25.
5 Ernest Hemingway to Charles A. Fenton, 23 September 1951, Charles A. Fenton Collection, Beinecke Library, Yale University, New Haven, Conn.
6 Ernest Hemingway to Ezra Pound, November 1925, Ezra Pound Manuscript Collection, Beinecke Library, Yale University. The exact date of this document has not been established. Actual spelling has been retained.
7 Ernest Hemingway to Ezra Pound, 22 July 1933, Ezra Pound Manuscript Collection, Beinecke Library.
8 Ezra Pound to Ernest Hemingway, 25 January 1927, Ernest Hemingway Manuscript Collection, John F. Kennedy Library, Boston, Mass.
9 *Ernest Hemingway: Selected Letters, 1917–1961*, ed. Carlos Baker (New York: Scribner's, 1981), p. 673.
10 Hemingway, *Selected Letters*, p. 624.
11 Ernest Hemingway to Ezra Pound, 6 November 1954, Ezra Pound Manuscript Collection, Beinecke Library.
12. Ezra Pound to Ernest Hemingway, 25 January 1927, Ernest Hemingway Manuscript Collection, John F. Kennedy Library.
13 Ezra Pound to Ernest Hemingway, 21 December 1926, Ernest Hemingway Manuscript Collection, John F. Kennedy Library.
14 Ezra Pound to Ernest Hemingway, 25 January 1927, Ernest Hemingway Manuscript Collection, John F. Kennedy Library.
15 Ernest Hemingway to Ezra Pound, January 1927, Ezra Pound Manuscript Collection, Beinecke Library. The exact date of this document has not been established.
16 Ezra Pound to Ernest Hemingway, 21 December 1926, Ernest Hemingway Manuscript Collection, John F. Kennedy Library.
17 Ezra Pound to Ernest Hemingway, 13 August 1933, Ernest Hemingway Manuscript Collection, John F. Kennedy Library.
18 Ezra Pound to Archibald MacLeish, 19 November 1926, Ernest Hemingway Manuscript Collection, John F. Kennedy Library. Copy sent to Hemingway.

19 Ezra Pound to Ernest Hemingway, 30 January 1926, Ernest Hemingway Manuscript Collection, John F. Kennedy Library.

20 Ernest Hemingway to Ezra Pound, 8 November 1925, Ezra Pound Manuscript Collection, Beinecke Library. Pound, apparently, did not review *In Our Time* either.

21 Ezra Pound to Ernest Hemingway, 29 January 1927, Ernest Hemingway Manuscript Collection, John F. Kennedy Library. In November 1925, Hemingway wrote to Pound concerning the attitude of his literary friends, saying that they regarded him as something "fairly scabrous" because he had published with an established firm. His friends seem to regard this act as betrayal. The exact date of the November document has not been established. Ezra Pound Manuscript Collection, Beinecke Library.

22 Ezra Pound to Ernest Hemingway, 22 November 1926, Ernest Hemingway Manuscript Collection, John F. Kennedy Library.

23 Even when he criticized Pound, it was never with a mean purpose. See, for instance, the following comments in a letter to Archibald MacLeish dated November 22, 1930 that Pound was an "ass" but that he had written lovely verse. If Pound made a fool of himself in his personal life, he was at his best in his poetry and deserved the Nobel Prize more than Sinclair Lewis.

24 Ernest Hemingway to Ezra Pound, 30 November 1925, Ezra Pound Manuscript Collection, Beinecke Library.

25 Ezra Pound to Ernest Hemingway, 22 November 1926, Ernest Hemingway Manuscript Collection, John F. Kennedy Library.

26 Ezra Pound to Ernest Hemingway, 15 February 1927. Ernest Hemingway Manuscript Collection, John F. Kennedy Library.

27 Ezra Pound to Ernest Hemingway, 18 November 1926, Ernest Hemingway Manuscript Collection, John F. Kennedy Library.

28 Ezra Pound to Archibald MacLeish, 19 November 1926. Copy in the Ernest Hemingway Manuscript Collection, John F. Kennedy Library.

29 Ezra Pound to Ernest Hemingway, 1 August 1927 and 26 December 1927, Ernest Hemingway Manuscript Collection, John F. Kennedy Library.

30 Ezra Pound to Ernest Hemingway, 3 November 1926, Ernest Hemingway Manuscript Collection, John F. Kennedy Library. See Appendix to this chapter for full text of this letter, together with letters from Pound to Hemingway of 28 October 1926 and 10 November 1926.

31 Ernest Hemingway to Ezra Pound, Ezra Pound Manuscript Collection, Beinecke Library. The date of this document has not been established.

32 Ezra Pound to Ernest Hemingway, 8–9 November 1926, Ernest Hem-

ingway Manuscript Collection, John F. Kennedy Library.

33 Ernest Hemingway to Ezra Pound, Ezra Pound Manuscript Collection, Beinecke Library. The date of this document has not been established.

34 Ezra Pound to Ernest Hemingway, 8–9 November 1926, Ernest Hemingway Manuscript Collection, John F. Kennedy Library.

35 Ezra Pound to Ernest Hemingway, 13 August 1933, Ernest Hemingway Manuscript Collection, John F. Kennedy Library.

36 Ezra Pound to Ernest Hemingway, 3 November 1926, Ernest Hemingway Manuscript Collection, John F. Kennedy Library.

37 Ernest Hemingway to Ezra Pound, 1926, Ezra Pound Manuscript Collection, Beinecke Library. The exact date of this document has not been established.

38 Ezra Pound to Ernest Hemingway, 8–9 November 1926, Ernest Hemingway Manuscript Collection, John F. Kennedy Library.

39 Ernest Hemingway to Ezra Pound, 1926, Ezra Pound Manuscript Collection, Beinecke Library. The exact date of this document has not been established, but this is a different letter from the one referred to in Note 37.

40 Ezra Pound to Ernest Hemingway, 15 February 1927, Ernest Hemingway Manuscript Collection, John F. Kennedy Library.

41 Ernest Hemingway to Ezra Pound, 15 October 1942, Ezra Pound Manuscript Collection, Beinecke Library.

42 Ernest Hemingway to Ezra Pound, 22 October 1924(?), Ezra Pound Manuscript Collection, Beinecke Library.

43 Ernest Hemingway to Ezra Pound, 22 October 1925, Ezra Pound Manuscript Collection, Beinecke Library.

44 Ernest Hemingway to Ezra Pound, 16 March 1925, Ezra Pound Manuscript Collection, Beinecke Library.

45 Ernest Hemingway to Ezra Pound, 7 October 1925, Ezra Pound Manuscript Collection, Beinecke Library.

46 Ernest Hemingway to Ezra Pound, 14 October 1925, Ezra Pound Manuscript Collection, Beinecke Library.

47 Ernest Hemingway to Julian Cornell, draft, 11 December 1945. This letter has probably not been sent to Cornell but a copy of it is in the Hemingway Manuscript Collection at the John F. Kennedy Library.

48 Their report is reprinted in Norman, *Ezra Pound*, pp. 410–11.

49 Ernest Hemingway to Dorothy Pound, 8 October 1957, Ezra Pound Manuscript Collection, Beinecke Library.

50 Marsden Hartley to Robert McAlmon, 19 December 1940. This letter is now at the Beinecke Library.

12. James D. Brasch

Invention from Knowledge: The Hemingway-Cowley Correspondence

MALCOLM COWLEY once tried to write a full-length biography of Ernest Hemingway, and it took the combined
fury of both Hemingway and his wife to dissuade him. Perhaps he
knew too much. His poetic memorial suggests that he was closer
to the man and to the writer than most:

ERNEST

Safe is the man with blunderbuss
who stalks the hippopotamus
on Niger's bank or scours the veldt
to rape the lion of his pelt;

but deep in peril he who sits
at home to rack his lonely wits
and there do battle, grim and blind,
against the jackals of the mind.[1]

Hemingway as "the man with blunderbuss" who battled against
"the jackals of the mind" seldom appears in the biographical
record to date, and Cowley's failure to produce an extended biography of Hemingway is a great loss. Hemingway, writing from
Italy in 1951, admitted to Cowley, "I think you know more about

my writing than anybody probably except possibly me."² Their correspondence and friendship lasted many years and survived many arguments.³ The exchange of seventy-one letters began with two random letters in 1937 and 1940, gathered momentum in September 1947, after Cowley had edited *The Portable Hemingway*,⁴ continued through the period when Cowley was commissioned to write a major article on Hemingway for *Life* magazine,⁵ and progressed through the publication of *Across the River and into the Trees* (1950) until it ended shortly after the publication of *The Old Man and the Sea* (1952).

The period during which this correspondence took place started with the Spanish Civil War and centered largely on the post-World War II era. They discussed the surge of postwar fiction, the Korean War, and the McCarthy menace. The correspondence ranged far and wide over the landscape of these events and included comments on John Horne Burns, John Dos Passos, James Jones, Norman Mailer, Maxwell Perkins, J. D. Salinger, Charles Scribner, and Thomas Wolfe, among others. They discussed the relation of the new "war poets" to their experience and the old problems about how critics misunderstood writers and how editors mismanaged authors. In addition, they drew each other out on subjects as diverse as Dante and copyright laws, gardening and Hürtgenwald, the Rambouillet affair and Robert Lowell's paranoia.⁶

Hemingway was undoubtedly lonely for literary conversation in Cuba, and his letters to Cowley frequently took the place of informal conversations about literature and literary personalities. Beneath all of the exchanges runs a mutual concern for the literary scene that Hemingway and Cowley explored with depth and reflection. Since Hemingway considered himself a "world-class" writer, he frequently reflected on his writing in the context of other important writers and their works. He was willing to discuss the process by which his fiction emerged in the same manner that Henry James explained the germ or origin of his fiction. Taken as a whole, the correspondence focuses on two major issues: "invention" and concern for biography as it affects "invention." In the exchange an esthetic emerges which challenges many of the easy biographical assumptions that have been made about Hemingway's novels and short stories, and Cowley's perceptive challenges to Hemingway provide an explanation of how, in great writers, invention proceeds primarily from knowledge. There has frequently been an assumption that Hemingway's desire to protect his private life was actually a cover-up for criminal or sexual activities better left unspecified. A number of Hemingway's own comments about his military and private life give some basis for these suspicions. What emerges from the correspondence with Cowley is an entirely different foundation for Hemingway's wish to protect his early life. At the very least this new view deserves to be given equal weight with the earlier one. At stake is a theory about the sources of Hemingway's fiction.

Hemingway referred to the process of writing fiction out of experience and other knowledge as "invention."[7] What Hemingway meant by "invention" will emerge from his use of the word, but it should be understood here that it was closely linked to the classical definition of *inventio* as recorded by Cicero in *De Inventione*: "taking care for the matter," as distinct from "elocution," which was "taking care for the words and style." Hemingway had no fears at the time of this correspondence about his ability to handle the words and style. The "matter" and the topics he wanted to write about out of his own experience, however, were of deep concern to him. Primarily, this concern resulted from the fact that there were very few incidents that he wanted to write about out of his past and that as time passed it was always more difficult for him to keep them accurately in his mind. This led to his fear that inaccurate biographies would only make it more difficult for him to remember "what really happened." For Hemingway, as for Cicero, a sharp recollection of incidents was the first step of successful "invention."

Accurate recall was important because Hemingway was aware that not all of his stories came from his personal experience. Some stories were based on his reading or were expansions of tales told to him by friends in Upper Michigan, Paris, or Italy during World War I. In his correspondence with Cowley he distinguished carefully between *A Farewell to Arms*, which was an "entirely made-up novel,"[8] and "In Another Country" and "A Way You'll Never Be," which were related to him by other people.[9] Hemingway's distinction between the two categories reveals the necessity for keeping an accurate account of his own experience.

Hemingway's lifelong quarrel with the press was caused primarily by his attempt to maintain this distinction. The more he read about himself, the less he knew about himself. Allegations, gossip, casual contempt, critical jealousy, and the false photographic image presented in the popular press contributed not only to the public's misconception of Hemingway but, more importantly, to Hemingway's conception of himself.[10] Edmund Wilson was typical of those who embraced the popular image presented in the popular press:

> Bunny Wilson's whole theory that I started out to publicize myself as a hunter and fisherman by pictures, *etc.*, is truly false. Max Perkins was always after me for pictures. I was always hunting and fishing ever since I can remember, and the only times we took pictures were then. You don't take pictures looking at Mantegna, Piero della Francesca, Giotto, learning Spanish, French, navigation, English, aerodynamics or inside the Prado, the Luxemburg, the Jeu de Paume or the Louvre. You wouldn't tolerate anybody interrupting your working, taking pictures, but inevitably when you win events, set records, *etc.*, or have a fine trophy someone takes pictures.[11]

Hemingway's list of activities that occupied his time when no one was standing by with a camera has escaped critical attention until very recently; the list itself reveals the triviality of much of the biographical criticism written about Hemingway and why he objected to it.

In addition to the circulation of misinformation, all of the biographical enquiries wasted a great deal of Hemingway's time:

> That's why I don't want any biography. Literary, yes. I have written it and stand by it, but unless I checked on everything

and told you what was true and what was false you would
run into all kinds of shit, printed as well as verbal.

   Also it is bad for me. Makes me think about myself instead
of about writing which is what I should do. I should write
and if I am ever dead then people can write about life. But
while alive, I should be a writer and the hell with anything
else.[12]

Continual intrusion into his personal and public life by Baker,
Fenton,[13] Young, Max Eastman, and Edmund Wilson,[14] among
others, caused him no end of anger and confusion.

   When Cowley was commissioned by *Life* magazine to write a
feature article on Hemingway, he joined the group of biographers
who were intruding on Hemingway's domain. As part of the
agreement, *Life* offered to pay Cowley's expenses for a trip to
Havana to interview Hemingway, and Cowley could not resist
the opportunity. Hemingway was immediately cooperative,[15] although suspicious, and invited Cowley to Havana, suggesting
that he stay at the Ambos Mundos Hotel. Hemingway also advised Cowley to contact General "Buck" Lanham if he wanted to
get "the straight dope" on the role Hemingway played in the war.
Cowley, his wife, Muriel, and his son, Rob, spent two weeks in
Havana during February of 1948.[16] Hemingway and Cowley got
on very well together. Cowley reported that they "got drunk
together and exchanged confidences (none of which went into the
profile)."[17] When the correspondence resumed after Cowley's
return to Connecticut, he began to ask questions about information collected both in Cuba and from General Lanham. Among
other matters, the letters that followed concerned "very bad
trouble" in Italy,[18] the Rambouillet affair,[19] Hemingway's activities off the Cuban coast during 1943–44, and Hemingway's
World War I wounds. These were uncomfortable episodes in
Hemingway's life, and he wanted to make certain that Cowley
would not violate any confidences exchanged during their meetings in Havana. Moreover, he clearly wanted to write about some
of the incidents himself, and he was beginning to suspect that
Cowley would have to be added to his growing list of intruding
meddlers. Owing to Cowley's impeccable taste, and his decision

not to violate any personal confidences, Cowley and Hemingway remained good friends and continued their correspondence for many years.

Cowley had shown an unusual measure of sympathy for Hemingway's concern for biography, and Hemingway was generally appreciative of the fact that Cowley was primarily interested in his works. Cowley had to walk a fairly narrow line between Hemingway and the editors of *Life* in order to get the portrait published, but when Thomas Bledsoe, an editor at Rinehart, asked Cowley to read Philip Young's manuscript for a new book, Cowley was barely able to manage the balancing act required. On the one hand, Cowley defended the book to Hemingway, arguing that Young might as well go ahead since he would be able to manage some control over him. On the other hand, if Hemingway prohibited Young's manuscript from being published, someone else would do a similar book and then neither of them would have any control. Control was necessary because Cowley mistrusted Young's confusion of Hemingway with the heroes of his novels.[20] Cowley felt he could correct the manuscript sufficiently so that both Hemingway and Bledsoe would be satisfied. Young and Bledsoe were not impressed, however, and eventually Hemingway became furious with Cowley for tolerating the whole business. Cowley's insistence that someone was going to do the job anyway carried little weight with Hemingway. Eventually Cowley tried to extricate himself, but he always found that his loyalty to Hemingway required that he try to mediate and bring pressure to bear on the editors at Rinehart.

An earlier incident stemming from the *Life* portrait had made Hemingway exasperated with Cowley, and his implication in the Young book sounded like a rerun of the old problems with the *Life* article. The earlier incident had involved Oak Park, which always made Hemingway angry. Cowley had it all wrong; Hemingway tried to set him straight about parts of the *Life* article:

> I know how good and friendly and careful you were in that piece just as I know there are lots of things you don't know and things people told you that weren't straight and plenty things I didn't tell you. Other things you draw out a strange

interpretation from like not going to dances. Do you know how that works? My older sister . . . was not popular until her last year in school and then only with the jerks. I was not allowed to ask any girl I liked to any formal dances until my sister had been asked. Was in reserve as her escort. All girls you would want to ask are asked a long time ahead. Marg would be asked about the last two or three days before the dance. No girls you were fond of left by then and I would say the Hell with it.[21]

In spite of Cowley's misinterpretation of some data, Hemingway was actually flattered by Cowley's idea that he would like to expand the *Life* portrait into a full-length biography, but he ended the discussion of the *Life* article by saying

I truly think that we suffer in our times from an exaggerated emphasis on personality and I would much rather have my work discussed than the offence of my life. It is OK to have a record of what you have done and it should be made before the people who know what has happened are dead. But I think that it is very bad for the man involved and could be extremely bad for his writing if he ever started to think of himself as a character rather than simply someone trying to write a story as well as he can. I am afraid that I may be stuffy or righteous in expressing this so please forgive me if there is any stuffiness or righteousness or chicken in this attitude.[22]

This controversy over the Young book went on for many letters and finally Cowley had to give in and admit, "I wish to God I had never seen the Philip Young manuscript. . . . It has got me into the damndest hippocritic, hypocitic and hypocritical situation. . . . This is my last will and testament on the subject, signed Malcolm Cowley, so help me God, Amen."[23] This was the end of Cowley's projected biography of Hemingway.

All of Hemingway's fears on the subject of biography were exacerbated as he watched with some horror what Arthur Mizener was doing to F. Scott Fitzgerald. What happened to "poor Scott" could also happen to him. Ultimately, Mizener did a job on Fitz-

gerald, Hemingway wrote to Mizener, which compared favor-
ably with the job the undertaker had done on Hemingway's
father's face after he had shot himself. "One remembers the face
better as it actually was. But the undertaker pleases those who
come to the funeral."²⁴ As part of his research into Fitzgerald's
life, Mizener initiated a substantial correspondence with Hemingway which ran from July 6, 1949, to January 11, 1951, and
which included eight letters from Hemingway to Mizener. *The
Far Side of Paradise* was published in 1950, and an article based
on Mizener's research appeared in *Life* in January of 1951.²⁵ Although Fitzgerald was already dead, Hemingway's concern for
biographical intrusion was heightened by what Mizener had done
to his one-time friend. "Mizener's shameful performance in
Life,"²⁶ Hemingway wrote to Cowley, was based on what Hemingway called "grave robbery":

> Mizener deceived me completely by his letters. I thought he
> was a straight guy and then came that unspeakable piece of
> grave robbery he wrote for *Life*. When a man and a fellow
> writer has a daughter married and with children living to
> hang a heritage of insanity into them for money, seems
> hardly a Christian act. Poor Scott!!²⁷

Mizener had quoted freely from personal letters which Scott had
written to and about Zelda and their daughter, and Hemingway
obviously could not see what any of it had to do with an understanding of Fitzgerald's work. When Mizener ended his *Life*
article with an assumption that biography was the major source
of fiction and proved his point by quoting Malcolm Cowley,
Hemingway felt he had to be careful lest his letters and conversations with Cowley would be treated in the same way.²⁸

The distasteful intrusion of the critic into the personal affairs of
Fitzgerald resulted in a totally false impression of the writer.
Hemingway complained that both Cowley and Edmund Wilson
had tried to turn Fitzgerald into the Henry James of the 1920s.²⁹
This was too much for Hemingway, especially since Fitzgerald
couldn't even spell "Hemingway":

He couldn't be blamed for misspelling my name. He couldn't spell anything, and that spelling is a complicated social problem; two "m's" means "bastard." Hemenway means "silk company" and such a long name as Hemingway was really asking too damn much of Scott.[30]

As any reader of the Hemingway-Mizener correspondence knows, Hemingway had a great admiration for Fitzgerald both as a friend and as a writer with "golden talent." His reservations were based on the distinction between invention and knowledge. Cowley had earned Hemingway's suspicion by reediting *Tender Is the Night*;[31] Hemingway felt that Fitzgerald's first published version was far better than Cowley's reedited text. Hemingway received the reedited version on November 19, 1951. The next day he was ready for Cowley:

> Truly I did not want the reforms to turn out as I was afraid they might, but I'm afraid the whole idea was just a bad idea of Scott's.
> In the straight chronological order the book loses the magic completely. Starting off with a case history there is no secret to discover and no mystery and all sense of a seemingly magical world (the world of Sara and Gerald Muphy) being destroyed by someone that is unknown and lost.
> By the time the bathroom incident goes off the reader knows everything which was to come as a shock. In the form it is now it is simply a pathological [*sic*] and not a nice one at that. It has all the dullness of all the stories of the insane and where it had the charm of the strange mixture that was Scott it is now about as much fun to read as *The Snake Pit*. I know you did it for Scott and it was what he wanted, but I think if he had been completely sane I would have argued him out of it.
> It is just like taking the wings off a butterfly and arranging them so he can fly straight as a bee flies and losing all of that dust that makes the colors that make the butterfly magical in the process.[32]

Readers of *A Moveable Feast* will recall the butterfly metaphor for Fitzgerald in the headnote to section 17:

> His talent was as natural as the pattern that was made by the dust on a butterfly's wing. At this time he understood it no more than the butterfly did and he did not know when it was brushed or marred. . . . Later he became conscious of his damaged wings and of their construction and he learned to think and could not fly any more because the love of flight was gone and he could only think of when it had been effortless.[33]

The manuscript of this published version in the John F. Kennedy Library reveals the more sober and critical view that Hemingway actually held on Fitzgerald in a sentence eliminated by the editors from the published edition: "He even needed professionals or normally educated people to make his writing legible and not illiterate."[34] As Hemingway wrote Cowley, Fitzgerald was one of "the worst educated writers who ever wrote prose,"[35] and worse, Cowley was one of those who had perpetuated what Hemingway considered to be a false image of the writer.[36] Clearly, Fitzgerald had little knowledge to build on after his meteoric rise to fame.[37]

When Cowley edited the new version of *Tender Is the Night* according to notes left by Fitzgerald, Hemingway was annoyed because he felt that Cowley did for Fitzgerald what Max Perkins had done for Thomas Wolfe. As a result, both writers had been credited with knowledge and skill which they did not possess: "But Malcolm, what do you really think of all this editing of writers? For instance, what would Wolfe be if they let him publish as he wrote it and corrected it himself? Shouldn't the books have been by Thomas Wolfe and Maxwell Perkins: Now Scott comes out tidied properly by you and knowing both French and Italian in both of which languages he was completely comical."[38] Hemingway reminisces about a time when writers knew something:

> Wasn't there ever a time when a writer wrote, re-wrote, corrected his punctuation and spelling and decided himself what his characters were going to do? Now it seems to me to

be like the two platoon system in football. Are we to look
forward to when they have offensive and defensive writers?
It seems sort of comic to me. Charlie Scribner told me that
several of his authors do not even read their proofs. No
wonder writing is going on the bum. Charlie put someone
over my proofs before they were returned to me. The going
over consisted in querying place names which the go-over
had not been able to locate in a Rand-McNalley [sic] atlas.
He could find no Fossalta di Piave. Thought because
Monastir was in Serbia there could not be one in Venito. He
said only Fornaci was on the Po River. Of course Fossalta
means a town built behind a sunken road. There are
hundreds of them, but only one is famous. Monastir is
spelled three different ways. Fornaci is a town or village
where there is a furnace or lime kiln.

I had to explain all that. But the editor would have
changed them because those reference points on the military
map one to ten thousand were not in the Rand-McNalley
[sic] atlas. Now maybe I misspelled McNalley in a letter. But
in galley-proofs I would look it up or accept the corrections
of a proofreader. But ninety per cent of the corrections of
proofreaders I have to strike out. When I first started with
Scribners, eliminating the interference with my punctuation
and sentence structure by proofreaders was a lot of work. I
got very angry and told Max they would have to stop fooling
with my galleys. I told him to have them put question marks
on anything they did not understand and if it was as I meant
it to be I would rub out their question marks and he could
believe that was how I wanted it. I want to be checked on
the use of the apostrophe and on any obviously misspelled
words or printer's errors, but at the start honest to christ
proof readers used to try to fix your stuff up the way they
would have written it.[39]

When Hemingway read Cowley's defense of his version of
Tender Is the Night, he was even more critical. Attention to detail
had escaped both Fitzgerald and Cowley. Hemingway decided to
set them straight:

Errors: relizing for realizing on page 194. Cavear with an e for caviar (this spelling is obsolete and is a bastard one at best, but is used throughout), also you can't see Valais at night, described as a short way out of Zurich. There are other small things you will catch in any future edition and if you want to spell caviar as cavear that is a question of taste. It is legal.

None of the above is important unless everything is important in writing, but truly I think the changing about of material is.[40]

The relationship with Fitzgerald was a long and difficult one for Hemingway. As much as he admired Fitzgerald, he knew that Fitzgerald did not take care of his talent.[41] Alcoholism was only one of the aspects of mismanagement, and he always saw his own career as being perilously close to Scott's. Hemingway knew that he personally did not have the charm that saved Fitzgerald,[42] but what his comments on Fitzgerald and Cowley's version of *Tender Is the Night* make clear is that Hemingway felt that he himself did have the knowledge and a sense of invention that were necessary for a good writer. He guarded these qualities ruthlessly. He knew they were what separated him from most other writers, and he did not want them jeopardized by meddling critics, arrogant editors and proofreaders, or his own failure to recognize what knowledge he actually had and from which he could invent. In the final analysis, it was Fitzgerald's career that taught him so much, that made him so suspicious of biographical criticism, and that forced him to protect what made invention possible. As Hemingway wrote to Cowley, it was the confusion of invention and knowledge that had worked so hard against his friend Scott:

Scott caught the surface in the people that he knew or met with a fine brightness, but he always used to interrogate everybody. "Did you sleep with your wife before you were married?" I've heard him ask that to someone the first time he met them. How could he expect to get the truth that way? . . .

There are writers to whom people come all their lives and tell things that writers would give everything not to know. But he hears them and never uses them except as the knowledge he invents from. But Scott would mix up as in *Tender Is the Night* himself and Zelda with Gerald and Sara and they were very different. He got balled up inventing from mixtures of opposites in people instead of inventing from his knowledge of people themselves.[43]

In addition to giving Hemingway perspective on Fitzgerald's career, Hemingway's concept of invention from knowledge had very definite positive implications for his own work. Although there are numerous references to the process throughout the letters, particularly as they apply to other writers, it was the publication of *The Old Man and the Sea*[44] that resulted in a spirited exchange between Hemingway and Cowley and that allowed Hemingway to give Cowley a lecture on just what invention was all about.

The spirited exchange was initiated by Cowley about a year earlier while he was reading Jay Leyda's *The Melville Log*.[45] On this occasion Cowley was responding to Hemingway's accusation that he had given Fitzgerald a credibility that he did not deserve. Cowley was sensitive on the point. In defending his own version, he recalled Melville's reaction to his editors. In a long and fascinating passage Cowley reviewed the entries in the *Log* that parallel many aspects of Hemingway's strictures:

I had been reading a big collection of documents called *The Melville Log* in which Melville's life is recorded from day to day. So far as the records survive. His daughter Fanny hated him and burned most of the family papers so that people thought for a long time there weren't any records at all. But the scholars have been working on them for the last twenty years and now they've collected so many documents that merely to quote the pertinent pages from them makes up a two-volume work of 933 pages. In November 1851 Melville had finished *Moby Dick*. He had written it in a little more than a year; written it twice in a high state of elation but after he finished it he was dead tired, morose, suicidal, then without giving himself a chance for rest he plunged into *Pierre.* Worked on it from eight o'clock to dark each day in a cold room in Pittsfield, didn't eat until he staggered out of the room in the dusk. It was a crazy book when he finished it and was such a complete failure (362 copies sold in twenty years) that he was never again able to earn a living as a writer. He had himself a long breakdown, stopped seeing his friends, tried to earn a living as a magazine writer but failed at it, tried to earn a living as a lecturer but failed at it, finally gave up the writing game completely (he was trying to learn to be a poet, some of his poems were very good but he regarded that as a private matter); got a job in a customs house at $5.00 a day and lived in retirement for thirty years, then other writers who admired him, there were a few, looked him up in his retirement. He gave them the brush-off and apparently most of his family came to regard him as a mean old man.[46]

Cowley concludes the long recitation of Melville's woe with reference to Melville's text: "He had no education beyond age twelve, or no education but the very best, the sort to be had by shipping before the mast. He read enormously. He couldn't spell and his grammar was shaky but his sisters used to copy his manuscripts for him in those days before the typewriter and they peppered the text with commas and changed don't to doesn't. But later when his wife copied his manuscripts he taught her not to use any punctuation whatever. He put it all in himself in the final revision."[47]

Cowley had patiently recounted the whole Melville situation so that he could set up his own theory about editing:

So we're back at the big question. How much should an editor do? I think it all depends whose manuscript he is working on. When a writer knows what he wants to do then the editor should keep his hands off the manuscript strictly and the copy reader and the proofreader should confine themselves to queries and questions of spelling. When a

writer is worth publishing like our late friend Lil Abner
[Wolfe], but doesn't know when to stop then an editor like
Max Perkins can certainly help him (and help the public
more by saving them the trouble of reading packing boxes
full of tripe). Scott's a different matter. Generally speaking
he knew what he wanted in a big way and in small ways
too, but he was always running into trouble about questions
of spelling, especially proper names. He called you Himin-
way and always misspelled the name of Ginevra King with
whom he had been in love for three years desperately. He
called her Genevra. Grammar, geography, chronology is
when a man named McKibben in Tender "unscrewed two
bloody wire hairs from a nearby table and departed." On the
next page he was still there, still talking. He hadn't any
theory about those details, he just wanted them to be con-
ventionally right and hadn't the sort of eye that caught them
on the page. For some damn reason he never put the book
through Scribner's copy-editing department where those matters would have been caught and queried. He simply turned
it over to Miss what's-her-name, his nice secretary, to
handle. Scott himself got a Frenchman to fix up the French
quotations, though a couple must have slipped past the
Frenchman, but had no help on the Italian. What I did to
the book was just what Scribner's proofreading department
would have done if the manuscript had passed through their
hands. I thought it was the only fair thing to do for Scott
because otherwise people were privileged to think that he
was the only illiterate author in the United States. They
ought to see some other manuscripts. People like you who
work over every detail of the manuscript are rare as hell in
the country these days. They are the last individual handi-
craftsman. Most of our so-called writers just do part of their
work as if they had only one job on the production line
before the manuscript moves into the varnish room.[48]

Hemingway's reply is swift.[49] His sympathy is immediate for
Melville. Melville, for Hemingway, *knew* something that those
around him and later the scholars (he returns in this letter to the

buzzard image for the critics and adds the hyena for good measure) did not. The key word is "knew." Cowley's implied compliment in the comparison did not stop Hemingway from establishing his own criteria. In one sense Hemingway's reply is a restatement of the "iceberg" theory of *Death in the Afternoon,* but here he is more precise about what it means. Beneath the surface of his short novel lies a foundation of knowledge, Hemingway insisted, that neither Scott nor Faulkner could manage and which constitutes that seven-eighths that lies beneath the surface.[50] It is not sufficient that a certain part of the plot stick up above the surface, leaving the reader free to imagine a fund of possibilities and probabilities beneath. What is fundamental for Hemingway is that what is beneath the surface is a foundation of information and knowledge which informs every word he chooses to expose.[51] Hemingway's theory was best stated by Henry James in his famous dialogue with Walter Besant. Considering the plight of the young novelist, James struck a balance between experience and knowledge: "The power to guess the unseen from the seen, to trace the implication of things, to judge the whole piece by the pattern, the condition of feeling life in general so completely that you are well on your way to knowing any particular corner of it—this cluster of gifts may almost be said to constitute experience."[52] For James and for Hemingway, invention is not simply a matter of personal experience recollected in tranquility or passion. It is what emerges when a person tries to be "one of the people on whom nothing is lost." A novel must have a "truth of detail" that rises above all other characteristics. That is, in fact, "the supreme virtue of the novel" and the singular "merit on which all [the novel's] other merits . . . helplessly and submissively depend." This process whereby knowledge informs experience is at the heart of James's essay and labels precisely what Cowley and Hemingway were writing to each other about.

Knowing, therefore, was an obsession with Hemingway. Knowing about people, knowing the competition of other writers, knowing about war, fish, witchcraft—the list is endless. Hemingway always returned to the same theme: "I just tried to invent from what I know. . . . I try to invent . . . as straight as what I have known."[53] The first thing, of course, was to know.

His library shows that his thirst for knowledge was insatiable.[54] According to those who knew him best, he was constantly reading and attempting to expand the fund from which he could invent.

One of the many writers who according to Hemingway failed to combine knowledge with experience was Norman Mailer. Hemingway was critical of the experience that Mailer brought to the craft of writing; he felt that Mailer's knowledge of warfare was particularly thin. *The Naked and the Dead* (1949), he wrote to Cowley, was "so phony it couldn't hold the pace. Full of frustrated sadism and all combat faked." Hemingway recognized Mailer as a skillful writer who had produced "several good passages based on at least one patrol and there was some evidence that he had been a general's aid . . . but not for long." What particularly bothered Hemingway was the "General giving coordinates off map without looking at map."[55] The whole scene lost credibility for Hemingway because the general assigned coordinates 439.56 and 440.06 from "a mental image of his battle map."[56] Hemingway concluded that Mailer had been on the scene only a short while. He admits:

> Mailer may be a very good writer. Is certainly skillful as hell and it is a much better book than *Three Soldiers*. But since when do they split up a patrol to take back a mortally wounded (gut shot and dying before they picked him up) man and have him die for two hundred pages. *C'est pornagraphique. Mais, c'nest ce pas la guerre*. . . . I felt all the time I was reading a book by an infant protégé who had read everything.[57]

Invention from knowledge, therefore, had to be based on extensive knowledge of the subject but also had to be filtered through a writer who had experience. The rest is pornography.

Early in August 1952, after reading an advance copy of *The Old Man and the Sea*, Cowley wrote to Hemingway:

> *The Old Man and the Sea* is pretty marvelous. The old man is marvelous and the sea is too and so is the fish. I'm proud of them all and of you and glad that I am reviewing the

book for the *Herald Tribune*. As yet I don't know what I am going to say because I'm getting a lot of space to write about such a short book, but it will be a pleasant task to fill the space. Maybe among other things I can talk about your prose which has that quality here as elsewhere of being absolutely fresh with the words standing out separately on the pages, as if nobody before had ever used the simple words of the English language. And to point up what you do in that story, I can talk about the present rage for symbols and myths, and the kids saying, "Go to!" I will use symbols "go to," I will create the myth, and all of them forgetting that if a character doesn't live it, it can't be a myth. So you give us a character and a story, and the reader is privileged to read them whatever symbolic or mythical qualities they suggest to him. But, meanwhile, the characters in the story have their own life.[58]

Hemingway was, of course, flattered by Cowley's use of the term "myth." He responded by explaining what he knew and how all of it went into the background of *The Old Man and the Sea*. Hemingway's reply is a twentieth-century statement of what Henry James was writing about in "The Art of Fiction":

I'm glad it is short. If I wanted to I could have put in that everybody lived on the same road, and what they did and what they thought. And how they lived and how they put in the dinghy race and bootlegging days and revolution and civil, medical and religious trouble and every change in death and marriage and birth and economic thing I know about the village and the time we killed the whale (sperm) and the time we caught the whale shark and Gregario's five daughters and the time we found gold down at the cove and my girl Smokey was in love with me since she was nine and always sat on the seawall to watch our boat come in and didn't let me know about it until she was seventeen, and all that stuff that make up what you call a novel. Maybe you can do it better. But it has been done well and life is short, no matter how long it is. And why should you do what had already been done well? Especially, if there is something else that you have been working for since the chapters in the first *in our time.* This story, Malcolm, is what I knew and had figured out in those early chapters with what I have learned since. When I wrote those I had learned that when I read novels I would read one part or section or incident in the whole novel that truly convinced me and made me feel that I had been there. But they were always wrapped in these layers of writing and rhetoric and all and I tried to write those chapters to get down the inner true thing. They weren't exercises. I always wrote everything as though it were all and everything I would ever write. But when I wrote this *Old Man and the Sea,* I knew more and I could write with the same degree of concentration and elimination, and tell what the kids, as you say, call the myth, but making it a simple, straight and believable story. You see they cannot have a myth without having a hero. A hero has to face things no one else can face. Things have to be un-believable to make a myth, but they have to be made absolutely believable. Now in our time, the hero has to be made believable too. He has to be someone who has suffered and been defeated. You start out with him on a day when he has been defeated 84 times straight. That seems unbeliev-able, if it is really true, and you make it perfectly believable. You make him an absolutely believable man. Then as he moves out into the sea, which is an unbelievable place, you make it soundly believable. To do what he has to do you have to show how he has been a great man and a champion, and you make that unbelievable. Combat with the Negro from Cienfuegos (which was true) becomes believable. But what the hell? You said all this in your first paragraph. But it is hard not to talk matter when I have no one to talk it with.[59]

Cowley had expanded his own comment on myth in the context of their earlier discussion of Melville. He continued his letter by expanding their earlier exchange on Melville:

There is a curious contrast with *Moby Dick*, when the whole comes to stand for the impersonal power and malignity of

Nature. Your fish and your fisherman are equally parts of
Nature. "Brothers" as the old man says. Each of them plays
his assigned role as in a ritual drama. The old man loves and
honors the fish and one suspects that the fish loves and
honors the old man. And in the end, the fish and man have
collaborated (like bull and matador) to make life on this planet
seem more dramatic than it was before their battle started.[60]

As Hemingway considered this flattering analogy and comment
on the mythological dimensions of his new novel, he responded to
the Melville contrast with a notation focusing on his visual
concept of what he had been writing about. He revealed a knowledge not only of the sea and the character he was writing about
but of how the sea appeared in art:

That thing you speak about of Melville and the malignity of
Nature is interesting because in the other books I try to
show, never having thought of that, that the sea is a *puta*
[whore], but she is our mother. The whole conception of the
malignity of Nature always seems to me to belong to those
Doré [Paul Gustave Doré, 1832?–83] illustrations. I can
remember in some of the other books where the boys were
arguing about the ocean. How she did nothing wrong. It was
always the things that were done to her, the way they were
done to a woman by the moon and the winds. She traps you
by seeming so fair and attractive, but you are a fool if you
are trapped.[61]

Hemingway was very close here to chapter 42 of *Moby-Dick*,
"The Whiteness of the Whale," where Melville meditates on the
union of purity and beauty and terror inherent in the color white.
Hemingway's use of "seeming," perhaps Melville's favorite word
(the whale only "seemed" white), suggests a closeness and an
appreciation for Melville that went beyond the parallel use of a
marlin and a whale. Hemingway's choice of the great fish had not
been taken casually. He continued to develop the background of
his short novel for Cowley: "Once I thought I would like to write
about whales. I've ironed four sperm whale, and lost them and

killed one. But Melville wrote about whales and whaling was a wonderful thing then. But I'm not sure he really loved them, although he went whaling and he certainly studied them."[62] Since whaling and whales were no longer a part of Hemingway's time, he felt he could not have made the relationship meaningful. As he gently questioned Melville's relationship to whales, Hemingway carefully explained to Cowley the difference between his own concept of the sea and the world of whaling that surrounded Melville:

> But I promise you the relationship as it grows, between the old man and the fish, is not a false one. Nor is anything the old man did impossible nor something that has been done by other people. I am so happy that you like it, and if you have to wander off about prose, there is little to wander off about that the boys don't know, just as there is a lot that could be in this story that I did not put in to keep it to the old sound proportions of the iceberg; one-eighth that shows and seven-eighths underwater to give it balance.[63]

One aside by Cowley gives a measure of his desire to help Hemingway and his genuine esteem for the man. They had had many exchanges about editing, and Cowley, unable to resist his professional background, adds almost as a postscript: "The albacore on page 43–44 turns into a bonito on page 64 when the old man eats him."[64] This is a casual comment in a paragraph on other matters concerning the story. Hemingway was not amused:

> It is all right about the bonito; actually the fish could be any one of three. But the fishermen call them all bonito, and when he was tired, the old man would think of it by the shortest name. They are all canned and packed under the one name "bonito" and none of the three is the fish they call the bonito from Florida north. It's okay, I checked the reference and the transferring on page 44, bottom of the page, and 62–63–64. Thanks for mentioning it though, maybe I should have explained it, but when he said, "albacora" he meant that he judged it to be that type of fish which they

generically call "bonito." That doesn't even hold all the way
around the island, because some fishermen have Canary
Island ancestry, (like the old man). And others come from
the Balearics or from Catalonia. And still others from
Galicia. And the Basque country and a few from Asturias.
My point is that when he caught him he would classify him
as a special type of "Bonito" and when he was tired, he
would just be a "bonito."[65]

In the margin, Hemingway added in his own hand, "This fish
was a small tuna, but the old man being from the Canaries,
would call him 'albacore' and think of him generally as "Bonito.'" The point here is not whether the information Hemingway produces is accurate as far as the classification of fish in
Cuban waters is concerned, but how important it was to him that
what shows above the surface of the story rest on knowledge
below the surface. But Hemingway was not finished:

> If I made the fish so he is seen and felt by the reader, then
> my responsibility ends as long as I have the old man speak of
> him properly, or as he would speak. If the reader has
> erudition everything is there for him to use it on, but if I
> start hitting him with erudition, then it is almost as bad as
> using footnotes in a story. I would have to then explain that
> broad-billed swordfish are called "bonito" off Peru and
> Chile, while they are known as "Imperador" off Cuba, and
> "Pez Espada" off Spain. And then we would be explaining
> the differences between broadbill and marlin which nobody
> agrees on yet, etc.[66]

Hemingway is no doubt becoming somewhat tedious, but the
point of Cowley's comment is that it questions Hemingway's
knowledge rather than merely pointing out a copy editor's slip.[67]
Hemingway did not drop the idea of erudition lest Cowley had
not understood his earlier treatise on "bonito":

> I think you should know all this and much more when you
> write a story. Erudition shouldn't show. You know Ezra

[Pound] can't leave any erudition true or false out of a poem and what the results are sometime. Ideally a man should know everything, but when he writes [he should] make something so that it will really happen to the reader; be *made* (not described); so that afterwards the reader will have had the experience; not seen it or heard about it; then he cannot clutter at all.[68]

It is this use of the word "made" (not described) that is the key to Hemingway's technique, as outlined in these letters to Cowley. Knowledge of all the variations of bonito is as necessary for the writer as knowledge of the muscles beneath the skin is necessary for the classical sculptor. The knowledge that lay beneath invention was as solid and necessary as the cones, cylinders, and cubes beneath Cézanne's mountains and apples. Neither Cézanne nor Hemingway could paint the surface or "make a scene" without the knowledge of what lay beneath.[69]

Cowley apparently never answered this remarkable letter, but when his review of *The Old Man and the Sea* appeared in the *New York Herald Tribune*,[70] it was clearly based on their exchange. Cowley used the differences between Hemingway's novel and *Moby-Dick* as structure for the review. After making a passing reference to what had become known as "the poor man's *Moby-Dick*," Cowley was quick to focus on the differences between the two novels. He saw the new short novel as a classic (a work that accepts "limitations of space, subject and treatment while trying to achieve faultlessness within the limitations") but carefully showed the distance between the two novels as Hemingway had explained them to him a month earlier. *Moby-Dick* had accepted no limits, was certainly not short, and was essentially romantic in its portrayal of Ahab as a Titan in search of the unattainable. Cowley continued:

Hemingway's hero is an old man reduced to living on food that is begged or stolen for him by a young boy. . . . Although he goes out further than anyone, there is no sense that God is immanent in nature because when the man prays, he addresses a transcendent God. Both Hemingway's old man and the marlin are *in* nature: "they are even brothers in nature."[71]

Moreover, they are equals, and the strength of one is matched against the intelligence of the other. Following Hemingway's lead, Cowley insisted that *The Old Man and the Sea* was as different from *Moby-Dick* as anything ever written.

The second focus of Cowley's review was Hemingway's language and its relation to classic constraint, simplicity, and concentration:

> There is no attempt in it [*The Old Man and the Sea*] to express the inexpressible by inventing new words and turns of phrases; instead Hemingway uses the oldest and shortest words, the simplest constructions, but gives these new value —as if English were a strange language that he had studied or invented for himself and was trying to write in its original purity.[72]

Cowley continues by analyzing a short passage, finding in it what Hemingway told him to find, and ends with a personal aside which reveals his correspondence with Hemingway and which anyone who has read some of Hemingway's original letters will appreciate. He notes in his review the double and triple spaces between words in Hemingway's typical typewritten style and admits that they *may* come from a defective space bar: "But I like to believe that it has something to do with his feeling that each word has a special value and should stand out separately and clearly on the page. That is what the words seem to do in *The Old Man and the Sea*. The writing has the quality of being familiar and yet perpetually new that is the essence of classical prose."[73] On Hemingway's insistence, Cowley had "read it again" and detected that the prose was a "transparent medium" for revealing the story beneath the surface. Cowley admitted that as he read *The Old Man and the Sea* again, the layers of meaning, patterns in the transparency, musical tone, and values emerged for him as solidly as "turquoise set in silver."[74]

On the basis of Cowley's praise and the generally good reception of *The Old Man and the Sea,* Hemingway felt he still had that old thing, the ability to "make" from "knowledge." He wrote Cowley:

> This new book that I have is a concentration of everything I have learned and focused on all my life, but I hope none of that shows. But if it seems too simple, when you read it, please read it again. . . . But this time I have tried without one trick and yet with all the knowledge I should have acquired by now, to make something that I would stand on as I wanted to do. . . . It is a good lode and it hasn't run out and when it has faulted, we have always been able to tap it again. And it will last as long as I will, and I want to last forever.[75]

Hemingway seems to have gained confidence from his correspondence with Cowley. Shortly after their correspondence ended Hemingway wrote to Charles Poore at the *New York Times* about the sources of his work and how he saw himself as working in the manner of Tolstoi:

> Remember Charlie in the first war all I did mostly was hear guys talk; especially in hospital and convalescing. Their experiences get to be more vivid than your own. You invent from your own and from all of theirs. The country you know, also the weather. Then you have a map 1/50,000 for the whole front or sector; 1/5 000 if you can get one for close. Then you invent from other people's experience and knowledge and what you know yourself.
> Then some son of a bitch will come along and prove you were not at that particular fight. Fine. Dr. Tolstoi was at Sevastopol. But not at Borodino. He wasn't in business in those days. But he could invent from knowledge we all were at some damned Sevastopol.[76]

Here is the most forceful statement of Hemingway's contempt for biographers. The biographers made assumptions that were downright false and demeaning to literary craftsmanship. Seldom did they have any sense of a writer's knowledge. They not only made invention difficult but destroyed the fundamental possibility of invention and its ultimate imaginative excitement.

Five days after "the man with blunderbuss" had lost his battle with "the jackals of the mind" Cowley wrote to Conrad Aiken:

> I mourn for Hemingway. He could be as mean as cat piss and as sweet as a ministering angel. It's hard to think that so much vitality, vanity, unflagging zest, eagerness to excel in everything, willingness to learn and study and finally teach everything, ability to participate in other people's lives— that all this should simply vanish. Sometime I'll tell you some of the curious things I found out about him that he didn't want the world to know.[77]

What was still important to Cowley was that Hemingway himself "knew" and that from what he knew he had been able to "invent."

Appendix: Location of the Letters

Key: N = Maurice Neville, Santa Barbara, California
KL = Hemingway Collection, John F. Kennedy Library, Colombia Point, Boston, Mass.
Baker = Carlos Baker. *Ernest Hemingway: Selected Letters, 1917–1961.* New York: Charles Scribner's Sons, 1981.

Date	Letter	Location
June 9, 1937	Cowley to Hemingway	KL
_____, 1940	Hemingway to Cowley	N
Sept. 3, 1945	Hemingway to Cowley	N
Oct. 17, 1945	Hemingway to Cowley	KL, Baker
Oct. 28, 1947	Cowley to Hemingway	N
Nov. 14, 1947	Hemingway to Cowley	N
Jan. 15, 1948	Hemingway to Cowley	N
April 9, 1948	Hemingway to Cowley	N
April 13, 1948	Hemingway to Cowley	N
May 25, 1948	Cowley to Hemingway	N

Date	Letter	Location
June 9, 1948	Hemingway to Cowley	N
June 22, 1948	Cowley to Hemingway	N
June 25, 1948	Hemingway to Cowley	N
June 28, 1948	Hemingway to Cowley	N
July 5, 1948	Hemingway to Cowley	N
July 11, 1948	Cowley to Hemingway	N, KL
July 15, 1948	Hemingway to Cowley	N
Aug. 5, 1948	Cowley to Hemingway	N
Aug. 19, 1948	Hemingway to Cowley	N
Aug. 25, 1948	Hemingway to Cowley	N
Aug. 28, 1948	Cowley to Hemingway	not preserved
Sept. 5, 1948	Hemingway to Cowley	N
Nov. 8, 1948	Cowley to Hemingway	N
Nov. 16, 1948	Hemingway to Cowley	N
Nov. 29, 1948	Hemingway to Cowley	N
Dec. 3, 1948	Hemingway to De Voto	N sent to Cowley
Jan. 1, 1949	Cowley to Hemingway	N
Jan. 24, 1949	Hemingway to Cowley	N
Feb. 6, 1949	Cowley to Hemingway	N
Feb. 9, 1949	Hemingway to Cowley	N
Feb. 9, 1949	Mary to Cowley	N
Feb. 10, 1949	Hemingway to Cowley	N
Feb. 17, 1949	Cowley to Mary	N
March 9, 1949	Hemingway to Cowley	N
May 3, 1949	Cowley to Hemingway	N, KL
June 10, 1949	Hemingway to Cowley	N
Sept. 24, 1949	Cowley to Hemingway	N
Sept. 29, 1949	Hemingway to Cowley	N
Oct. 7, 1949	Cowley to Hemingway	N, KL
Oct. 11, 1949	Hemingway to Cowley	Baker
Dec. 14, 1949	Cowley to Hemingway	N
Jan. 27, 1950	Hemingway to Cowley	N
April 18, 1951	Cowley to Hemingway	N, KL
April 19, 1951	Hemingway to Cowley	N
May 9, 1951	Cowley to Hemingway	N, KL
May 13, 1951	Hemingway to Cowley	N
May 19, 1951	Cowley to Hemingway	N, KL
June 1, 1951	Hemingway to Cowley	N
June 2, 1951	Hemingway to Cowley	N

Date	Letter	Location
June 8, 1951	Cowley to Hemingway	N
June 15, 1951	Hemingway to Cowley	N
July 19, 1951	Cowley to Hemingway	N, KL
July 24, 1951	Hemingway to Cowley	N
Aug. 11, 1951	Cowley to Hemingway	N, KL (Includes copy of Cowley's Intro. to *The Portable Fitzgerald*)
Sept. 16, 1951	Hemingway to Cowley	N
Nov. 3, 1951	Cowley to Hemingway	N, KL (Includes information on copyright law)
Nov. 8, 1951	Hemingway to Cowley	N
Nov. 14, 1951	Cowley to Hemingway	N, KL
Nov. 20, 1951	Hemingway to Cowley	N
Dec. 14, 1951	Hemingway to Cowley	N
Dec. 25, 1951	Cowley to Hemingway	N, KL
Dec. 31, 1951	Hemingway to Cowley	N
Jan. 17, 1952	Hemingway to Cowley	N
Jan. 28, 1952	Cowley to Hemingway	N, KL
_____, 1952	Hemingway to Cowley	N
May 4, 1952	Hemingway to Cowley	N
May 15, 1952	Hemingway to Cowley	N
May 24, 1952	Cowley to Hemingway	N, KL
May 29, 1952	Hemingway to Cowley	N
Aug. 3, 1952	Cowley to Hemingway	N
Aug., 1952	Hemingway to Cowley	N
Dec., 1952	Hemingway to Cowley	N

Notes

1 From *Blue Juniata: Collected Poems* (New York: Viking, 1968), p. 96. This poem is reprinted here with the permission of Malcolm Cowley.

2 Ernest Hemingway to Malcolm Cowley, 16 September 1951. This letter is in the possession of Maurice Neville, Santa Barbara, California.

3 See James D. Brasch and Joseph Sigman, "Reading Habits," *Hemingway's Library: A Composite Record* (New York: Garland, 1981),

p. xviii. Hemingway's library contained considerable material by Cowley: *Exile's Return: A Literary Odyssey of the 1920's* (1951); *The Literary Situation* (1954); *After the Genteel Tradition: American Writers since 1910* (1937) (2 copies); *The Stories of F. Scott Fitzgerald: A Selection of 28 Stories*, Introduction by Malcolm Cowley (1951); *Tender Is the Night*, with the author's final revsions, preface by Malcolm Cowley (1951); André Gide, *Imaginary Interviews*, translated from the French by Malcolm Cowley (1944); *Interviews*, edited with an introduction by Malcolm Cowley (1958); Robert Terrall, ed., *Great Scenes from Great Novels*, Introduction by Malcolm Cowley (1956); *The Portable Faulkner* (1946), *The Portable Hawthorne* (1948), and *The Portable Hemingway* (1944), all selected and edited by Malcolm Cowley.

4 "Nightmare and Ritual in Hemingway," Introduction to *The Portablé Hemingway*, ed. Malcolm Cowley (New York: Viking, 1945). Malcolm Cowley's introduction is reprinted in Robert P.Weeks, ed., *Hemingway: A Collection of Critical Essays* (Englewood Cliffs: Prentice-Hall, 1962). See also Malcolm Cowley to Ernest Hemingway, 24 September 1949, in the possession of Maurice Neville.

5 Malcolm Cowley, "A Portrait of Mr. Papa," *Life*, 10 January 1949, pp. 86–101. This essay is reprinted in John K. M. McCaffery, ed., *Ernest Hemingway: The Man and His Work* (Cleveland: World, 1950).

6 Only two of Hemingway's letters to Cowley were included in Carlos Baker's *Ernest Hemingway: Selected Letters, 1917–1961* (New York: Scribner's, 1981). The entire correspondence between Hemingway and Cowley is currently in the hands of Maurice Neville (Santa Barbara, Calif.) whose longstanding interest in Hemingway's works and generosity enabled me to study these letters. Peter Buckley, a longtime friend of Hemingway's, generously brought the letters to my attention. I am also endebted to Alfred Rice of the Hemingway Foundation for permission to quote excerpts from Hemingway's letters to Cowley. Mr. Cowley has encouraged me and graciously assisted in this assessment of the correspondence. He also deposited copies of thirteen letters which he sent to Hemingway in the Hemingway Collection of the John F. Kennedy Library, Boston, Mass. Jo August Hills, Curator of the Hemingway Collection, generously facilitated my examination of these copies.

7 For a useful discussion of "invention" (Latin: *inventio*) as defined and applied by Aristotle and Cicero with an indication of more recent implications, see Edward P. J. Corbett, *Classical Rhetoric for the*

Modern Student (New York: Oxford University Press, 1971), pp. 33–39, *et passim. Inventio* was concerned with a system or method for finding arguments (subject matter to illustrate or support a speaker's point of view).

8 Ernest Hemingway to Malcolm Cowley, 19 August 1948, in the possession of Maurice Neville.

9 Ernest Hemingway to Malcolm Cowley, 16 September 1951, in the possession of Maurice Neville.

10 Hemingway also found it necessary to explain his position to John Atkins (*The Art of Ernest Hemingway* [London: P. Nevill, 1952]): "I have refused to cooperate with anyone writing any sort of biography as there are too many people involved in my life to write about it truly. Also it makes me sick to read about it, true or false. My work is all I give a damn about and so many people have tried to pull my life (good, bad or worse) into all criticism of it that now a book of mine is judged by some people on whether I hit some man in a place like the Stork Club (after being goaded into it), than on the merits or demerits of the book."

"Cowley came down here to write something about me for *Life*. . . . I found that after the first night I talked with him that it made me feel truly nauseated to talk about myself, and I compromised by giving him a list of people I had served under or with or who had known me at different times in my life. It was from this material and from others who claimed to know me that he wrote the article which appeared in *Life* and McCaffery [*Ernest Hemingway: The Man and His Work*]. It would take many letters to tell you how accurate or inaccurate it is and then I might be wrong. Any man is liable to be prejudiced about his life, since he knows things about it that as kind and good a critic as Cowley would never understand." Ernest Hemingway to John Atkins, 24 October 1951, in the possession of Maurice Neville.

11 Ernest Hemingway to Malcolm Cowley, 10 February 1949, in the possession of Maurice Neville.

12 Ernest Hemingway to Malcolm Cowley, 9 March 1949, in the possession of Maurice Neville. *Vogue* played a particularly dirty trick on him, and his work was not only disturbed, but other vibrations resulted as well:

For instance, an editor of *Vogue* called up and got through on the phone by saying she was the wife of one of my best friends. This was the entering wedge. Was untrue, of course; then she asked to bring a model out to make some fashion pictures using the Finca for background shots. I said sure to be accommodating and because I hadn't seen a really pretty girl since Mary went north to settle her parents in Gulfport. So they took some pictures of the model and me just after they had finished their work. They said these were just personal for ourselves and not to be published. In two months, they were in *Vogue*. The one they published was in *Vogue* with me lying on a couch with only shorts on with a very beautiful and nice girl who is in *Vogue* every month and on the covers half the time and looking down at me. This thing does you a lot of good around the house. (Ernest Hemingway to Malcolm Cowley, 13 May 1951, in the possession of Maurice Neville.)

13 Hemingway wrote to Fenton: "Are you sure that you are quite all right in the head? The sudden rages and general truculence are disquieting in a scholar. I do not believe your university would approve of them nor of the tone of some of your letters" (Ernest Hemingway to Charles Fenton, 13 July 1952, in the possession of Maurice Neville). Fenton was a particularly annoying problem for Hemingway. Hemingway wrote him again: "Many months ago I warned you to cease and desist on your project for writing a book on my literary and journalistic apprenticeship, which has degenerated or enlarged into a full-scale invasion of privacy" (Ernest Hemingway to Charles Fenton, 10 February 1953, in the possession of Maurice Neville). See also Ernest Hemingway to Charles Fenton, 29 July 1952, 9 October 1952 (Hemingway, *Selected Letters*, pp. 774, 786); and Ernest Hemingway to Dorothy Connable, 17 February 1953: "Fenton is one of those who think that literary history, or the secret of creative writing, lies in old laundry lists" (Hemingway, *Selected Letters*, p. 805). In April 1953, Hemingway instructed his lawyer, Alfred Rice, to intervene (Ernest Hemingway to Alfred Rice, 26 and 27 April 1953 [*Letters*, p. 818]). Fenton's book, *The Apprenticeship of Ernest Hemingway: The Early Years*, was published in 1954 by Farrar, Straus & Young, New York.

14 Max Eastman and Edmund Wilson were constantly attacked by Hemingway because, in his opinion, they refused to admit to mistakes and, therefore, were "the death of honest criticism." Ernest Hemingway to Malcolm Cowley, 3 September 1945, in the possession of Maurice Neville.

15 Ernest Hemingway to Malcolm Cowley, 30 October 1947, in the possession of Maurice Neville.

16 See Carlos Baker, *Ernest Hemingway: A Life Story* (New York: Scribner's, 1969), p. 464.

17 Malcolm Cowley to James D. Brasch, 23 December 1980, in the possession of James D. Brasch, McMaster University, Hamilton, Canada.

18 Ernest Hemingway to Malcolm Cowley, 19 August 1948, in the possession of Maurice Neville.

19 See Baker, *Life Story*, pp. 408–10, *et passim*.

20 Malcolm Cowley to Ernest Hemingway, 18 April 1951, 9 May 1951, and 19 May 1951, in the possession of Maurice Neville. Carbon copies of these letters are in the Hemingway Collection, John F. Kennedy Library.

21 Ernest Hemingway to Malcolm Cowley, 9 March 1949 in the possession of Maurice Neville. Cowley's misinterpretation of the Oak Park years evidently upset Hemingway so much that Mary felt called upon to step in. Her letter to Cowley is included in the Neville collection. She pointed out a number of his errors and insisted that Cowley had heard reports which confused Hemingway with his brother Leicester (Mary Welsh Hemingway to Malcolm Cowley, 9 February 1949, in the possession of Maurice Neville).

22 Ernest Hemingway to Malcolm Cowley, 10 June 1949, in the possession of Maurice Neville.

23 Malcolm Cowley to Ernest Hemingway, 28 January 1952, in the possession of Maurice Neville. A copy is in the Hemingway Collection, John F. Kennedy Library. Hemingway summarized his exasperation in two letters written directly to Bledsoe, 9 December 1951 (Hemingway, *Selected Letters*, pp. 743–46); and 17 and 31 January 1952 (Hemingway, *Selected Letters*, pp. 747–48).

24 Ernest Hemingway to Arthur Mizener, 4 January 1951, in Hemingway, *Selected Letters*, p. 717.

25 Arthur Mizener, "F. Scott Fitzgerald's Tormented Paradise: The rediscovered novelist of the '20's was beset by drink, debt, a mad wife." *Life*, 15 January 1951, pp. 82–88.

26 Ernest Hemingway to Malcolm Cowley, 1 June 1951, in the possession of Maurice Neville.

27 Ernest Hemingway to Malcolm Cowley, 19 April 1951, in the possession of Maurice Neville.

28 Mizener had written in *Life:* "To the telling of this story [*The Great Gatsby*] Fitzgerald brought what Malcolm Cowley has called his 'double vision,' that special view in which he saw his own life: 'It was as if all his novels described a big dance to which he had taken . . . the prettiest girl . . . and as if at the same time he stood outside the ballroom, a little Midwestern boy with his nose to the glass, wondering

how much the tickets cost and who paid for the music.'" "F. Scott Fitzgerald's Tormented Paradise," p. 101.

29 Ernest Hemingway to Malcolm Cowley, 8 November 1951, in the possession of Maurice Neville.

30 Ernest Hemingway to Malcolm Cowley, 8 November 1951, in the possession of Maurice Neville.

31 F. Scott Fitzgerald, *Tender Is the Night*, republished "With the Author's Final Revisions," ed. Malcolm Cowley (New York: Scribner's, 1951).

32 Ernest Hemingway to Malcolm Cowley, 20 November 1951, in the possession of Maurice Neville.

33 Ernest Hemingway, *A Moveable Feast* (New York: Scribner's, 1964).

34 Ernest Hemingway, *A Moveable Feast* Manuscript. Kennedy Library Roll 19, Target 171, Hemingway Collection, John F. Kennedy Library.

35 Ernest Hemingway to Malcolm Cowley, 16 September 1951, in the possession of Maurice Neville.

36 Hemingway's view of Cowley as an editor must be taken in the context of a projected three-volume edition of *A Farewell to Arms*, *The Sun Also Rises*, and *For Whom the Bell Tolls* concocted by Perkins, Cowley, and Hemingway, to be edited by Cowley. See Ernest Hemingway to Charles Scribner, 28 June 1947, in Hemingway, *Selected Letters*, pp. 621–23.

37 Hemingway wrote to Arthur Mizener: "Fitzgerald was romantic, ambitious, and Christ, Jesus, God knows how talented. . . . He was uneducated and refused to educate himself in any way. He would make great studies about football, say, and war but it was all bullshit. . . . Above all he was completely undisciplined." Ernest Hemingway to Arthur Mizener, 22 April 1950, in Hemingway, *Selected Letters*, p. 690.

38 Ernest Hemingway to Malcolm Cowley, 16 September 1951, in the possession of Maurice Neville.

39 Ernest Hemingway to Malcolm Cowley, 16 September 1951, in the possession of Maurice Neville.

40 Ernest Hemingway to Malcolm Cowley, 20 November 1951, in the possession of Maurice Neville.

41 Ernest Hemingway to Malcolm Cowley, 16 November 1948, in the possession of Maurice Neville.

42 Ernest Hemingway to Malcolm Cowley, 24 July 1951, in the possession of Maurice Neville.

43 Ernest Hemingway to Malcolm Cowley, 16 September 1951, in the possession of Maurice Neville.

44 *Life*, 1 September 1952, pp. 35–54.

45 Jay Leyda, *The Melville Log*, 2 vols. (New York: Harcourt, Brace, 1951).

46 Malcolm Cowley to Ernest Hemingway, 3 November 1951, in the possession of Maurice Neville. A carbon copy is in the Hemingway Collection, John F. Kennedy Library.

47 Malcolm Cowley to Ernest Hemingway, 3 November 1951, in the possession of Maurice Neville. A carbon copy is in the Hemingway Collection, John F. Kennedy Library.

48 Malcolm Cowley to Ernest Hemingway, 3 November 1951, in the possession of Maurice Neville. A carbon copy is in the Hemingway Collection, John F. Kennedy Library.

49 Ernest Hemingway to Malcolm Cowley, 8 November 1951, in the possession of Maurice Neville.

50 Ernest Hemingway to Malcolm Cowley, 20 November 1951, in the possession of Maurice Neville.

51 About the same time, Hemingway was trying to explain to John Atkins how he had invented the character of Col. Cantwell in *Across the River and into the Trees* (1950):

> Col. Buck Lanham was my best friend and we went through many strange things together. He was also a poet, a lover of pictures, and literature and a man of violent opinions. I used some of his characteristics and some of four other colonels or generals I knew (two of them) and of them since the First War in inventing that Colonel Cantwell everyone hated so much. . . . If anything I knew too much, rather than too little about war from platoons through company battalion, regimental and divisional level. (Ernest Hemingway to John Atkins, 28 December 1952, in the possession of Maurice Neville)

52 This essay is readily available in *The Portable Henry James*, ed. Morton Zabel (New York: Viking, 1956), pp. 391–418.

53 Ernest Hemingway to Malcolm Cowley, 29 May 1952, in the possession of Maurice Neville.

54 See note 3 and Michael S. Reynolds, *Hemingway's Reading, 1910–1940: An Inventory* (Princeton: Princeton University Press, 1981).

55 Ernest Hemingway to Malcolm Cowley, 10 February 1949, in the possession of Maurice Neville.

56 See Norman Mailer, *The Naked and the Dead* (New York: New American Library, 1951), p. 99.

57 Ernest Hemingway to Malcolm Cowley, 10 February 1949, in the possession of Maurice Neville.

58 Malcolm Cowley to Ernest Hemingway, 3 August 1952, in the possession of Maurice Neville.

59 Ernest Hemingway to Malcolm Cowley, August 1952, in the possession of Maurice Neville.

60 Malcolm Cowley to Ernest Hemingway, 3 August 1952, in the possession of Maurice Neville.

61 Ernest Hemingway to Malcolm Cowley, August 1952, in the possession of Maurice Neville.

62 Ernest Hemingway to Malcolm Cowley, August 1952, in the possession of Maurice Neville.

63 Ernest Hemingway to Malcolm Cowley, August 1952, in the possession of Maurice Neville.

64 Malcolm Cowley to Ernest Hemingway, 3 August 1952, in the possession of Maurice Neville.

65 Ernest Hemingway to Malcolm Cowley, August 1952, in the possession of Maurice Neville.

66 Ernest Hemingway to Malcolm Cowley, August 1952, in the possession of Maurice Neville.

67 Hemingway's library contained about 225 books on fishing, including three on marlin classification (see note 3).

68 Ernest Hemingway to Malcolm Cowley, August 1952, in the possession of Maurice Neville.

69 See Emily Stipes Watts, *Ernest Hemingway and the Arts* (Urbana: University of Illinois Press, 1971); and Meyle Chin Hagemann, "Hemingway's Secret: Visual to Verbal Art," *Journal of Modern Literature*, 7 (1979), 87–112.

70 Malcolm Cowley, "Hemingway's Novel Has the Rich Simplicity of a Classic," *Sunday*, 7 September 1952, pp. 1, 17. Cowley explained the cessation this way: "Memory tells me, beyond a shadowy doubt, that the correspondence ended quite explicably. There had been a fight about the Oak Park section of my *LIFE* article, which was based on material dug up for me by old Otto McFeeley, who had edited *The Oak Leaf* when Ernest delivered it as a boy. What I said was absolutely accurate, except that I had softened the statements made by McFeeley so that they wouldn't hurt Ernest. He was hurt all the same, and angry, but we smoothed things over. The final breaking-off came as an indirect result of Philip Young's biography, about which Ernest

was greatly exercised. . . . After that we exchanged nothing but Christmas cards, and not every year" (Malcolm Cowley to James D. Brasch, 11 May 1982, in the possession of James D. Brasch).

71 Cowley, "Hemingway's Novel," p. 1.
72 Cowley, "Hemingway's Novel," p. 17.
73 Cowley, "Hemingway's Novel," p. 17.
74 Cowley, "Hemingway's Novel," p. 17.
75 Ernest Hemingway to Malcolm Cowley, 4 May 1952; letter sent 15 May 1952. This letter is in the possession of Maurice Neville.
76 Ernest Hemingway to Charles Poore, 23 January 1953, in Hemingway, *Selected Letters*, p. 800.
77 Malcolm Cowley to Conrad Aiken, 7 July 1961, in the Huntington Library, Pasadena, Calif. Cowley's admiration for Hemingway's knowledge was a recurring theme of his two chapters, "Hemingway in Paris" and "Hemingway the Old Lion," in *A Second Flowering: Works and Days of the Lost Generation* (New York: Viking, 1973).

Contributors

Millicent Bell is a Professor of English at Boston University. She has also taught at Brown University and at a number of universities in Europe, including the Sorbonne. She has published scores of articles in learned journals and three books: *Hawthorne's View of the Artist* (1962), *Edith Wharton and Henry James: The Story of Their Friendship* (1965), and *Marquand: An American Life* (1979), which received the Winship Prize and was also nominated for the National Book Award in biography. She is currently at work on a biography of Henry James.

James D. Brasch is an Associate Professor of American literature at McMaster University in Hamilton, Ontario. He has published on Ernest Hemingway in the *Fitzgerald/Hemingway Annual, College Literature, Modernist Studies,* and the *Canadian Review of American Studies* but is perhaps best known for *Hemingway's Library: A Composite Record* (1981), a book done in collaboration with Joseph Sigman. In their research for that book Professors Brasch and Sigman were granted access to the library in the Finca Vigia in Cuba. Professor Brasch is now at work on a book entitled *Hemingway and Art* and on another that will publish the entire correspondence between Hemingway and Malcolm Cowley.

Peter L. Hays is a Professor of English at the University of California, Davis, where he served for a time as chairman of the department. He has published over forty articles on American literature, including several on Ernest Hemingway, perhaps the best known of which is "Hemingway and the Fisher King," which appeared in *University Review* in 1966. Others of his essays have explored Hemingway's relationship with Ford Madox Ford, F. Scott Fitzgerald, Joseph Conrad, and William Faulkner.

Patrick Hemingway is the son of Ernest Hemingway and his second wife, Pauline Pfeiffer. He was born in Kansas City, Missouri, and spent his childhood in Key West, Florida, and Havana, Cuba. He attended Stanford University for two years and then got his B.A. from Harvard, where he studied the history and literature of fifteenth- and sixteenth-century Europe. With the exception of relatively brief periods in Europe,

India, Australia, Chile, and the United States, Mr. Hemingway has lived most of his adult life in East Africa, where he was first a professional hunter and safari outfitter and later worked for the Food and Agricultural Organization of the United Nations as an instructor at the College of African Wildlife Management in Tanzania. Since his retirement in 1975 he has lived in Bozeman, Montana.

Robert W. Lewis is a Professor of English at the University of North Dakota and editor of the *North Dakota Quarterly*. He has taught at the University of Nebraska, the University of Illinois, the University of Texas, and at several universities in Italy and Egypt. His publications on Ernest Hemingway include a well-known book, *Hemingway on Love* (1965), and over a dozen articles in scholarly journals.

James Nagel is a Professor of English at Northeastern University and editor of the scholarly journal *Studies in American Fiction*. He has published over a score of articles on American literature as well as eight books, including *American Fiction: Historical and Critical Essays* (1977), *Stephen Crane and Literary Impressionism* (1980), and *American Literature: The New England Heritage* (1981), edited with Richard Astro.

Charles Scribner, Jr., is chairman of Charles Scribner's Sons Publishing Company, the firm his great-grandfather founded in the nineteenth century. He was a classics major at Princeton and later served five years of active duty with the United States Naval Reserve. In 1966 he was given an honorary Master of Arts degree from Princeton, and in 1976 he received the Curtis Benjamin Award for Creative Publishing from the Association of American Publishers for the *Dictionary of the History of Ideas*. From 1966 to 1968 he served as president of the American Book Publishers Council. He is the author of a children's book, *The Devil's Bridge* (1978), and the editor of *The Enduring Hemingway* (1974).

Carol H. Smith is a Professor of English at Rugers University and a specialist in modern British and American writers. In 1978–79 she was president of the Association of Departments of English. Her book, *T. S. Eliot's Dramatic Theory and Practice*, was published in the United States by Princeton University Press and in England by Oxford. Her articles are devoted to Eliot's drama, to contemporary poets, and to various issues in women's studies. Beyond her current interest in Hemingway, she is also at work on a book examining the late verse of six modernist poets.

Paul Smith, Professor of English at Trinity College in Hartford, is President of the Hemingway Society. He has published on Herman Melville, Percy Bysshe Shelley, critical theory, and the English curriculum; his textbook, *An Anatomy of Literature*, edited with Robert D. Faulke, appeared in 1972. His more recent work has been devoted to Hemingway studies, and it includes an essay on the early manuscripts in the *Journal of Modern Literature* and another on "Out of Season" included in *Critical Essays on "In Our Time,"* edited by Michael Reynolds.

Tom Stoppard was born in Czechoslovakia in 1937 and was educated on the Continent and in England. One of the foremost living playwrights in English, he has been, at various points in his career, a novelist, a writer for radio and television, and a director. Among his many awards are the *Evening Standard* drama award for the best play of the year in 1972 for *Jumpers*, and in 1974 the best comedy of the year award for *Travesties*. Mr. Stoppard received a Tony for the best play of the year in 1968 for *Rosencrantz and Guildenstern Are Dead*. He has twice received the New York Drama Critics Circle Award for best play: in 1968 for *Rosencrantz and Guildenstern* and in 1976 for *Travesties*.

Jacqueline Tavernier-Courbin is an Associate Professor of English at the University of Ottawa, where she is also the editor of *Thalia: Studies in Literary Humor*. She has published numerous articles on modern American literature; "The Mystery of the Ritz Hotel Papers," a paper delivered at the Hemingway conference in 1980, appeared in *College Literature*. Her book, *Ernest Hemingway: L'Éducation européenne de Nick Adams*, was published in Paris by Didier in 1978.

Adeline R. Tintner is an independent scholar living in New York who is widely recognized as a leading authority on Henry James. Trained in both English and art history, she has published over a hundred papers, primarily on the iconography of James's fiction, work that has resulted in a forthcoming book entitled *The Museum World of Henry James*. Also in preparation is a volume entitled *Henry James Redoes the Classics*, to be published by the Clarendon Press.

Max Westbrook, Professor of English at the University of Texas at Austin, is well known to students of American literature. He has long been interested in realism and naturalism and has published some thirty articles as well as three books, the best known of which is, perhaps, *The Modern American Novel: Essays in Criticism* (1966). His work on Hemingway has produced several articles and a monograph, written in collaboration with Robert W. Lewis, "'The Snows of Kilimanjaro': Collated and Annotated," published in the *Texas Quarterly*. He is currently working on the Hemingway manuscripts at the University of Texas.

Index